T0320022

The New Economy and Beyond

Volume V in the Bush School Series in
the Economics of Public Policy

Edited by Dennis W. Jansen

The New Economy and Beyond

Past, Present and Future

Edited by

Dennis W. Jansen

Texas A&M University, USA

BUSH SERIES IN THE ECONOMICS OF PUBLIC POLICY

Edward Elgar

Cheltenham, UK • Northampton, MA, USA

Published by
Edward Elgar Publishing Limited
Glensanda House
Montpellier Parade
Cheltenham
Glos GL50 1UA
UK

Edward Elgar Publishing, Inc.
136 West Street
Suite 202
Northampton
Massachusetts 01060
USA

A catalogue record for this book
is available from the British Library

Library of Congress Cataloguing in Publication Data
The new economy and beyond: past, present, and future / [edited by]
  Dennis W. Jansen.
        p. cm. – (Bush series in the economics of public policy)
    Papers from a conference held at Texas A&M University in April 2002, and
hosted by the George Bush School of Government and Public Service with the
support of the Department of Economics.
    1. United States–Economic conditions–2001–Congresses. 2. Production
(Economic theory)–Congresses. 3. Information technology–United States–
Congresses. 4. United States–Economic policy–2001–Congresses.
    5. Economic forecasting–United States–Congresses. I. Jansen, Dennis W.
II. Bush School series in the economics of public policy.

HC106.83.N48 2006
338′.06′097309051–dc22   2005049476
ISBN-13: 978 1 84542 544 9
ISBN-10: 1 84542 544 8

Printed and bound in Great Britain by MPG Books Ltd, Bodmin, Cornwall

Contents

List of figures	vi
List of tables	vii
List of contributors	viii

1. Introduction: what is the New Economy?   1
   Dennis W. Jansen

2. Projecting productivity growth: lessons from the US growth resurgence   12
   Dale W. Jorgenson, Mun S. Ho and Kevin J. Stiroh

3. 'Baumol's disease' has been cured: IT and multifactor productivity in US services industries   34
   Jack E. Triplett and Barry P. Bosworth

4. The New Economy and the challenges for macroeconomic policy   72
   Stephen G. Cecchetti

5. Competition policy in network industries: an introduction   96
   Nicholas Economides

6. Persistent price dispersion in online markets   122
   Michael R. Baye, John Morgan, and Patrick Scholten

7. Network meltdown: the legacy of bad economics   144
   Stan Liebowitz

8. Should we teach an old economy dog New Economy tricks? The role of a postal service in the New Economy   174
   Michael D. Bradley and Dennis W. Jansen

Index   197

Figures

3.1	Nonfarm labor productivity	35
4.1	Real GDP growth	76
4.2	Growth in US real output per hour, nonfarm business sector	76
4.3	Inventory-to-sales ratio: goods sector	77
4.4	Temporary help supply services employment	78
4.5	Asset-backed securities as a percentage of total liabilities	78
4.6	US consumer prices, headline and core measures	83
4.7	US consumer prices: medical care	84
4.8	Domestic US spot oil prices: West Texas Intermediate crude oil	84
4.9	Blue chip forecasts of real GDP relative to actual	88
4.10	Blue chip forecasts of the CPI relative to actual	89
5.1	A star network	99
5.2	A virtual network of complementary goods	99
5.3	Willingness to pay as a function of expected quantity	102
5.4	Diffusion in the presence of network effects	105
5.5	A one-sided bottleneck	110
6.1	Raw measures of price dispersion over time	131
6.2	Measures of price dispersion controlling for differences in shipping	133
6.3	Measures of price dispersion controlling for inventory differences	134
8.1	The effect of electronic diversion on rates	184
8.2	The effect of electronic diversion on volumes	184
8.3	Household mail rates by scenario	191
8.4	Business mail rates by scenario	191
8.5	Effects of diversion on volume	192
8.6	Postal share of electronic mail revenues	192
8.7	Revenues from physical and electronic products	193

Tables

2.1	Growth in private domestic output, the sources of growth 1959–2000	18
2.2	Sources of growth in average labor productivity 1959–2000	20
2.3	Output and labor productivity projections	27
3.1	Alternative estimates of the acceleration of productivity growth, post-1995	36
3.2	The ten most IT intensive industries, economy wide	41
3.3	Labor productivity growth, service industries	43
3.4	Average service industry labor productivity	45
3.5	Average service industry labor productivity, excluding brokers	46
3.6	The top 10 labor productivity growth service industries, 1995–2000	49
3.7	The bottom 10 labor productivity growth service industries, 1995–2000	51
3.8	Contributions to labor productivity acceleration	53
3.9	Contributions to labor productivity acceleration	54
3.10	Average service industry multifactor productivity	55
3.11	Comparison of authors' calculations and BLS industry labor productivity data	56
3A.1	The decomposition of labor productivity	66
4.1	Contributions to growth of real nonfarm business output, 1974 to 1999	80
4.2	The change in the 1990s	81
5.1	Quantities, market coverage, and prices under incompatibility	106
5.2	Profits, consumers' and total surplus under incompatibility	106
6.1	Sample prices posted by four firms on 5 November 1999	129
6.2	Summary statistics for dispersion measures	130
6.3	Product life cycle and range of prices	136
6.4	Product life cycle, range of prices, and number of firms	137
6.5	Percentage of price dispersion explained by observable and unobservable firm heterogeneities	139
8.1	Calibrating the baseline model	183
8.2	Calibrating the electronic penetration model	190

Contributors

Michael R. Baye is the Bert Elwert Professor of Business Economics and Public Policy in the Kelley School of Business at Indiana University, Bloomington.

Michael D. Bradley is Professor of Economics at The George Washington University.

Barry P. Bosworth is Senior Fellow in the Economic Studies Program and the Robert V. Roosa Chair in International Economics at the Brookings Institution.

Stephen G. Cecchetti is currently Professor of Economics at Ohio State University. He is a Research Associate of the National Bureau of Economic Research.

Nicholas Economides is Professor of Economics in the Stern School of Business at New York University.

Dennis W. Jansen is Professor of Economics at Texas A&M University.

Dale W. Jorgenson is the Frederic Eaton Abbe Professor of Economics at Harvard University. Jorgenson has been President of the American Economic Society and the Econometric Society. He is a member of the American Philosophical Society, the Royal Swedish Academy of Sciences, the U.S. National Academy of Sciences, and the American Academy of Arts and Sciences. He is a Fellow of the American Association for the Advancement of Science, the American Statistical Association, and the Econometric Society. He is a recipient of the John Bates Clark Medal of the American Economic Association.

Mun S. Ho is Visiting Scholar at Resources for the Future in Washington, D.C.

Stan Liebowitz is Professor of Economics in the School of Management at the University of Texas, Dallas.

John Morgan is Professor of Economics in the Haas School of Business and in the Department of Economics at the University of California, Berkeley.

Patrick Scholten is Assistant Professor of Economics at Bentley College.

Kevin J. Stiroh is Assistant Vice President in the Banking Studies Function of the Research and Statistics Group at the Federal Reserve Bank of New York.

Jack E. Triplett is Visiting Scholar in the Economics Studies Program at the Brookings Institution.

1. Introduction: what is the New Economy?

Dennis W. Jansen

INTRODUCTION

What is the New Economy? Is it new? What makes it new? What are the implications of the New Economy for antitrust and regulation policy, and for macroeconomic policy? These are some of the questions that were examined by a gathering of eminent scholars at a conference at Texas A&M University in April 2002. This conference, hosted by the George Bush School of Government and Public Service with the support of the Department of Economics, is part of an annual conference series on economics and public policy.

The phrase 'the New Economy' means different things to different people. In the popular press it is often used to refer to the information economy, to the high-tech economy, to the technology revolution, or to the many-faceted impact of the explosive growth of the World Wide Web. The New Economy has been used to signify the increased productivity brought forth by various technological innovations, or to refer to the long-lasting expansion from 1991 through 2000, or even to the long-lasting stock market boom from 1987 through 2000.

In addition to sometimes confusing or confused definitions, there are clear excesses in the hype that has sometimes accompanied the phrase 'New Economy'. When popular prognosticators were saying that the New Economy would be immune to business cycles and recessions, economists would cringe, wondering when the recession would hit to prove such claims false. When stock market oracles were predicting DOW 30 000 and the like, economists concerned with the already-high PE ratios would wonder when the bear market would begin, and how bad it would be for stockholders.

However, despite these excesses, it is the opinion of many respected researchers and academics that there *is* something new about the New Economy. It is not quite so new or revolutionary as journalists wanted us to believe, or needed to hype in order to generate interest from their readers.

But it is safe to say that the economy has changed in the last decade or so, and that these changes are of sufficient importance to deserve the title 'New Economy'.

In organizing this conference I wanted to provide an overview of various aspects of the New Economy. The conference began with a look at what I regard as the defining feature of the New Economy, the productivity growth brought on by the information technology revolution. Academic economists have debated how to measure this increase in productivity, its causes, and even its existence. Two papers addressed this issue, the first presented by Dale Jorgenson of Harvard University, and the second by Jack Triplett of the Brookings Institution.

PRODUCTIVITY AND THE NEW ECONOMY

Dale Jorgenson, with coauthors Mun S. Ho and Kevin J. Stiroh, led off the conference with their paper titled 'Projecting productivity growth: Lessons from the US growth resurgence'. Economists have long known that the growth rate of average labor productivity declined in the mid-1970s, and considerable research effort has been devoted to explaining this decline. Jorgenson et al. measure productivity growth as 2.97 per cent per year over 1959–73, declining by over one-half, to 1.44 per cent per year, for 1974–95. This decline has long been a concern, as a decline in the growth rate of labor productivity leads to concerns regarding the future growth rate of living standards. Jorgenson et al. find that this decline in productivity growth is due to a decline in the growth of capital services per worker (capital deepening), a decline in the growth of labor quality, and a decline in growth of what economists call total factor productivity. The increase in average labor productivity growth since 1995, a growth rate of 2.36 per cent per year over 1995–2000, is thus regarded as a welcome reversal of the decline in the mid-1970s. The source of this increased productivity growth is capital deepening and increased total factor productivity growth. Jorgenson et al. estimate that growth due to IT capital deepening has doubled from 1959–73 to 1974–94, and doubled again from 1995–2000. They estimate that TFP growth due to IT-related factors has also experienced two doubles from the 1959–73 period to the 1995–2000 period. These IT-related factors account for an additional 0.71 per cent annual productivity growth from 1974–94 to 1995–2000. For comparison, the total additional annual productivity growth over these periods is estimated as 0.92 per cent. Thus Jorgenson et al. estimate that the IT 'revolution' is responsible for the lion's share of the additional labor productivity growth experienced by the US economy over the last half of the 1990s.

Jorgenson then turns to providing an estimate of future US productivity growth. This is an important issue for long-term economic projections including debt and deficit projections as well as Social Security and Medicare projections. It is also a difficult task, fraught with uncertainty.

Difficulties in estimating productivity growth and the related concept of potential GDP growth have been with us since the concept of potential GDP was first introduced, so the recent change in productivity growth is not unprecedented. In fact, the decline in labor productivity by roughly half in the mid-1970s not only led to research seeking an explanation but also caused consternation among policy-makers. The failure of monetary policy in the later half of the 1970s has been blamed in some quarters on the Federal Reserve System's slow realization and slow response to the decline in productivity growth. Thus the experience of rising labor productivity growth rates in the mid-1990s is just the flip side of the experience two decades earlier.

In Jorgenson et al.'s base-case projections of trend labor productivity growth for the decade 2000–10 is 2.21 per cent per year, with corresponding output growth of 3.31 per cent per year. Estimates of labor productivity growth range from the pessimistic projection of 1.33 per cent per year – basically the growth rate over 1973–94 – to the optimistic projection of 2.92 per cent per year. The output growth rate projection ranges from the pessimistic 2.43 per cent per year to the optimistic 4.02 per cent per year. For comparison, this is below the 1995–2000 average of 4.60 per cent annual growth in output, due to slower projected growth in hours worked.

The productivity and output growth rate projections have large ranges of values due to uncertainties regarding future technical change in the production of information technology equipment and related investment patterns.

Following the presentation by Jorgenson, Jack E. Triplett presented his joint paper with Barry P. Bosworth, ' "Baumol's disease" has been cured: IT and multifactor productivity in US services industries'. This paper addressed two issues from the productivity literature. First, what are the contributions of information technology (IT) and multifactor productivity (MFP) to the extraordinary performance of the US economy in the last half of the 1990s. That extraordinary performance included historically low unemployment rates without accompanying inflation, and labor productivity growth doubling after 1995 from its lackluster performance over the prior two decades. These developments are often taken as evidence of the New Economy, especially if they can be related to increased IT use.

The second research issue concerns what is called 'Baumol's disease', the idea that the very nature of service industries make them less likely to exhibit productivity growth. The argument is that service industries are labor-intensive, and that it is inherently difficult to substitute capital for labor in service industries. The evidence seems to support this conclusion, as service industries have long exhibited low growth rates of labor productivity compared to, say, manufacturing industries.

Triplett and Bosworth examined whether IT impacts on productivity by looking at those parts of the economy that are heavy IT users. They identify service industries as the most intensive IT industries, and find a substantial contribution of IT to growth of productivity in service industries. They do not, however, find a greater impact of IT on the service industries after 1995. Instead, they find that MFP in the service industries grew more rapidly after 1995.

Triplett and Bosworth then look at the various service industries to estimate labor productivity growth over recent years. They estimate productivity growth for 27 two-digit services industries and find that in recent years labor productivity in these industries has grown as fast as in the rest of the economy. Further, they find that the major contributor to labor productivity growth in the service industries was an acceleration in multifactor productivity. Thus the authors conclude that, in the New Economy, Baumol's disease has been cured.

MACROECONOMIC IMPLICATIONS OF AND FOR THE NEW ECONOMY

An important question is what if anything will be the effect of the New Economy on macroeconomic policy, and the implications of the New Economy for macroeconomics in general. Stephen Cecchetti presented 'The New Economy and the challenges for macroeconomic policy', an overview of the relation between advances in information and communication technology and macroeconomic policy-making. Cecchetti argues that certain features of the New Economy make fiscal policy less attractive for stabilization purposes while at the same time increasing the difficulties facing monetary policy-makers. He points out both short-term and longer-term difficulties. Short-run difficulties include the problems of estimating potential output, especially when the productivity trend is shifting. Part of the reason for the great interest in measuring labor productivity growth rates and predicting future labor productivity growth rates is the importance of distinguishing permanent from transitory changes in growth rates when making macroeconomic policy. Many debates over monetary policy at the Federal Reserve System in the past decade turned on issues of deciding if the observed productivity growth rates were signaling a permanent or a transitory shift in growth rates.

Cecchetti points to three changes to the structural underpinnings of the economy that are likely to have lasting effects. These are (1) a reduction in the level of inventories, as production is tied more closely to demand and responds more quickly to changes in demand; (2) the rising proportion of temporary workers, a phenomenon that gives companies the ability to respond more quickly to business conditions by adjusting the size of their workforce; and (3) innovations in finance that provide companies and consumers better access to resources even when times are tough. The first two features, which increase the speed at which output adjusts to changing demand conditions, have the potential for making it more important for policy-makers to themselves respond more quickly to business cycle conditions. That, combined with the difficulty of distinguishing permanent from transitory shocks, has the potential to make macroeconomic policy-making more difficult in the New Economy.

The evolution of the financial system poses a particularly difficult challenge for central bankers. Since monetary policy acts initially through its impact on the balance sheets of financial firms, the explosion of asset-backed securities has likely changed the mechanism by which interest rate changes affect the real economy. As more borrowers have access to primary capital markets, and fewer need banks, it may become more difficult for the actions of central bankers to alter the future path of output and inflation.

The first three papers presented a general overview of The New Economy, including an overview of the productivity increase and how it can be linked to information technology, and an overview of the implications of The New Economy for macroeconomic policy making. The next four papers dealt with more specific issues of the New Economy. Nicholas Economides of New York University addressed the special features of network industries and the implications for antitrust policy. John Morgan, then of Princeton, presented evidence on pricing on the Internet, evidence that casts doubt on the law of one price. Stanley Leibowitz of the University of North Texas argued that the New Economy is not so new after all, and took issue with some of the claims regarding the importance of network effects in the New Economy. Finally, Michael Bradley of the George Washington University presented an analysis of a large old-economy industry that appears to exhibit network effects, the postal service, and examines how the New Economy is impacting its future role and even its future survival.

NETWORK INDUSTRIES AND ANTITRUST POLICY

Nicholas Economides, in 'Competition policy in network industries: An introduction', discusses the importance of network economics in the New Economy, as well as the application of antitrust law and regulatory rules to network industries. Some of the relevant features of network industries include network effects, market structure, market share and profits inequality, choice of technical standards, relationship between the number of active firms and social benefits, existence of market power, leveraging of market power in complementary markets, and innovation races. He analyses the application of antitrust laws and antitrust policy in network industries, and finds there are significant differences in the effects of antitrust laws and policies on network and non-network industries.

Economides emphasizes that network industries make up a large part of the economy. His primary examples are telecommunications, including voice and data services, and computer software and hardware. Telecommunications includes the Internet and World Wide Web. These two sectors have been engines of growth for the national and world economy. Other networks that precede the New Economy include airlines, railroads, roads, and shipping, and the delivery services that 'live' on these networks, including the postal service and its competitors.

Economides also discusses *virtual networks*, collections of compatible goods that share a common technical platform. All computers running Windows 95 can be thought of as a virtual network. Compatible computer software and hardware make up a network, and so do computer operating systems and compatible applications. More generally, networks are comprised of complementary components, so they also encompass wholesale and retail networks, as well as information networks and servers such as telephone Yellow Pages, Yahoo, Google, etc.

Adding to the importance of networks from a public policy point of view is the fact that network industries often provide necessities. Monopolization in such a setting can have significant social and political implications.

There may be a number of anti-competitive concerns in a network industry. The focus of his chapter is the question: Since network industries have special common features, are there special competition policy issues arising out of key features of network industries? If yes, what is the framework of the public policies that can be pursued to address these issues?

Economides reaches the following series of conclusions regarding antitrust intervention in network industries. First, the benchmark case against which to judge the firm is not the perfectly competitive equilibrium but is instead a network industries equilibrium that involves substantial inequality. Second, harming a competitor is not sufficient reason for antitrust action. The important issue should be harm caused to consumers. Third, appropriate caution should be exercised due to uncertainty regarding the evolution of a network industry in the absence of any anti-competitive action. Fourth, it should be recognized that in a network industry monopoly may maximize total surplus. Fifth, and related to the first point, it is not possible for the long-term equilibrium to involve equal market shares, and even in the short run such an equilibrium may have low total surplus. Sixth, competition limits the importance of path dependence and the value of the installed base, so that upheavals do occur in network industries. Lock-in can be and is overcome. Economides recommends that antitrust policy adopt these guidelines and recognize that antitrust policy for network industries has different requirements from antitrust policy for other industries.

PRICE DISPERSION

John Morgan, presented 'Persistent price dispersion in online markets', a paper coauthored with Michael R. Baye and Patrick Scholten. This examined the failure of the 'law of one price' by looking at Internet markets. In response to the observed failure of the law of one price, economists such as George Stigler and Hal Varian have proposed explanations for how dispersed prices can comprise an equilibrium. One approach generates price dispersion because of heterogeneities in costs or service levels, which lead to an equilibrium in which different firms charge different prices for otherwise homogeneous products. An alternative approach generates price dispersion through randomized pricing strategies by firms.

Internet markets provide an ideal setting for examining price dispersion for homogeneous products. Information on pricing by alternative suppliers is easily obtained, including information on shipping costs and taxes. Thus Internet markets provide an almost-ideal environment for testing the law of one price as well as theories explaining equilibrium price dispersion for homogeneous products.

Morgan et al. find that price dispersion is large and persistent even in well-established online retail markets. They collect data on leading price comparison sites on the Internet and find price dispersion for identical consumer electronics products listed by multiple retailers. On average, they find that the highest price for a consumer electronics product is 57 per cent above the lowest available price. They also find that a consumer who simply consults the comparison site to find the lowest price would save about $31 relative to a randomly selected supplier.

Morgan et al. report that this price dispersion persists across products and across time. They find no convergence to the 'law of one price', even controlling for differences in shipping charges and inventories. They find various ways to control for advertising, disclosures about shipping costs, consumer service, and a variety of other features and still find that 28 per cent of price dispersion remains unexplained.

NETWORK ECONOMICS – A DISSENTER

Stan Liebowitz presented 'Network meltdown: the legacy of bad economics'. This questions whether the New Economy is all that new, and also questions claims that a new economics is needed for study of the New Economy. Liebowitz argues that the Internet, an important component of the New Economy, creates value by reducing the costs of transmitting information, similar to the contribution of the automobile and airplane in reducing the cost of transportation. The reduction in information transmission costs is an important achievement. But, Liebowitz argues, it does not change the laws of economics.

What distinguishes the Internet from prior telecommunication technologies is its ability to quickly retrieve information. Users can quickly find information and retrieve it for current or future uses. But this characteristic of the Internet is not revolutionary in its implications for economics.

Liebowitz points out several changes the Internet may bring to business. It may well reduce the market power conveyed to firms based on geographic location. It may also have an impact on brand name loyalty, although here Liebowitz is uncertain as to the direction of the effect.

Liebowitz specifically addresses some of the features of the Internet that are often touted as being especially important. These include network effects, economies of scale, and the first mover advantage and its related symptom, lock-in. Liebowitz acknowledges that the Internet and companies either existing on the Internet or companies supplying infrastructure for the Internet are in part characterized by some of these features. But, he argues, other firms and other industries that long preceded the New Economy also had these features. Liebowitz presents case studies to support his claims. In the end, he believes that too much is made of the Internet as requiring a new or special economics.

THE POSTAL SERVICE: WHERE THE NEW ECONOMY MEETS THE OLD

The final paper, presented by Michael Bradley, was 'Should we teach an old economy dog New Economy tricks? The role of a postal service in the New Economy', coauthored with Dennis Jansen. Michael Bradley argues that the US Postal Service provides an excellent case study of an 'old economy' institution that is being affected by the New Economy and by competition from firms and products that are part of the New Economy.

Bradley argues that the postal services industry remains large and critical for the smooth functioning of the economy. The timely, secure and reliable delivery of mail communications remains a vital element of the economy's infrastructure. Households and businesses depend on physical mail for delivery of bills, documents, payments, and merchandise. The important public policy issue is how to deal with the effect of the New Economy on postal services. Historically the US government has taken a special interest in guaranteeing the existence of universal postal services, regarding this as a fundamental infrastructure issue. Thus there is a continuing public policy interest in the US Postal Service and the impact of the New Economy on it.

The impact of the New Economy on the US Postal Service has been mixed. While email dominates many interpersonal and business communications, this has come at the expense of telecommunications more than postal services. In fact, Internet shopping has increased demand for package delivery. Further, advances in computing power have dramatically increased the sophistication of direct mailing in targeting selected audiences while at the same time reducing the cost of preparing such mailings, leading to growth in advertising mail. Finally, computerization of mail processing has dramatically increased productivity.

Despite these positives, the major anticipated effect of the New Economy on postal services is negative. This follows from the assumed diversion of volume from the postal mail stream to the electronic message stream. The main concern is bill presentment and bill payment, bulk mail reply mail, and bulk mail documents. About one-third of the US Postal Service's First Class mail stream is made up of bills and statements, and both seem particularly vulnerable to electronic diversion. While the speed with which this diversion takes place is uncertain, most analysts agree that it will happen.

The key question is what impact this diversion will have on the future of postal services, what role they will play in the economy and what response, if any, should be put in place to ensure the best social outcome in light of this change. Bradley begins by constructing a model of a postal service that embodies some of the key aspects that relate to the impact of the New Economy on postal service performance. Solving this model gives a baseline scenario for estimating the effects of electronic diversion from the physical mail stream. This diversion has a number of effects, as the postal service must raise rates to offset lost revenue associated with lost volume. Because demand is inelastic at current prices, this works, at least initially. But marginal costs rise as economies of scale are reversed, and markups increase. Eventually elasticity increases and, at some point, no increase in price generates additional revenue. The postal service is no longer a viable private entity and some policy action would be required.

Various policy actions have been suggested to deal with this situation, including allowing or encouraging the postal service to enter the electronic messaging market. This has been prevalent in Canada and in various European countries including Denmark, the UK, and France. Bradley uses his model to study the effect of adopting such a policy, and finds that the postal service can avoid increasing its rate on physical mail to unsustainable levels by entering the electronic messaging market. Even modest revenues earned in the electronic arena could defer the onset of public subsidies to the postal service.

This analysis raises substantial additional policy issues, including issues of cross-subsidization, the advisability of government competing with private firms, and concerns for efficiency of the postal service. However, postal services are likely to continue to be important in the New Economy, so that these issues will require policy-makers to decide on the appropriate reaction to the impact of the New Economy on the postal service.

CONCLUSION

These eight chapters provide a good overview of the New Economy, including the right amount of skepticism regarding just how new or unique it is. In retrospect, I wish I had included a piece on the stock market in the New Economy, but I think this collection provides an introduction and background that will prove useful to anyone interested in the New Economy, especially policy-makers, analysts, and academics wanting a general overview of it.

The issues raised here are mostly unsettled, and researchers continue to focus on various aspects of the New Economy. In particular, research continues on the productivity increase that marks it, including deeper explanations for the increase in the mid-1990s, and, ideally, better explanations for the decrease in the mid-1970s that persisted for two decades. The debate continues over just how unique is this productivity increase, how it fits into economic history, and how it compares to past experiences with innovation and adoption of new technologies.

Research on the impact of globalization and its effects on the New Economy, and the effects of the New Economy on globalization, also continues. I expect that an important area for future research will be the role of network effects in international economics and in the diffusion of innovations across countries.

The impact of the New Economy on monetary policy-making is perhaps a bit more esoteric, although the declining role of the monetary base and the very real problem of monetary policy-making in the absence of government debt instruments, while not necessarily New Economy topics, may become very important issues in the next decade.

The role of network effects and the appropriate antitrust policy for network industries is a research area just beginning to flower, encouraged by the Microsoft antitrust case and the efforts of many economists as expert witnesses or interested observers on both sides of the issue. The arguments over just how important are these network effects, and how unique their role is in the New Economy, will continue.

Pricing on the Internet is a fascinating topic for economists, and the results presented in this volume suggest that the law of one price may need to be mentioned with caveats in the future. The idea of equilibrium price dispersion for homogenous products in a market is a theoretical idea that has more empirical support than many might have predicted, and the availability of data from prices posted on the Internet makes for an almost-ideal testing environment.

Finally, the impact of the technological innovations of the New Economy on various old-economy industries such as the postal service will be an area that continues to be of interest to both academics and policymakers. Whether the postal service will survive as currently constituted, with universal service requirements and other restrictions, remains an open question. Indeed, some of the network features that characterize the postal service may make it especially vulnerable to the effects of competition made possible by the new technologies characterizing the New Economy. Policymakers will ultimately face the question of how to handle the problem of the potential demise of the postal service, at least as we know it.

2. Projecting productivity growth: lessons from the US growth resurgence

Dale W. Jorgenson, Mun S. Ho, and Kevin J. Stiroh

INTRODUCTION

The unusual combination of more rapid output growth and lower inflation from 1995 to 2000 has touched off a strenuous debate among economists about whether improvements in US economic performance can be sustained. This debate has intensified with the recession of March to November 2001 and subsequent recovery, and the economic impacts of the events of September 11 are still imperfectly understood. Both add to the considerable uncertainties about future growth that currently face decision makers in both the public and private sectors.

The range of informed opinion can be illustrated by projections of labor productivity growth reported at the 'Symposium on Economic Policy for the Information Economy' in August 2001, organized by the Federal Reserve Bank of Kansas City and held at Jackson Hole, Wyoming. J. Bradford Delong and Lawrence H. Summers (2001), Professor of Economics at UC-Berkeley, and President of Harvard University and former Secretary of the Treasury respectively, offered the most optimistic perspective with a projection of labor productivity growth of 3.0 per cent per year.[1] A more pessimistic tone was set by Martin N. Baily (2001), former Chairman of the Council of Economic Advisers, who speculated that labor productivity would average near the low end of the 2.0 to 2.5 per cent per year range.

This uncertainty is only magnified by the observation that recent productivity estimates remain surprisingly strong for an economy in recession. The Bureau of Labor Statistics (BLS 2002) estimates that business sector productivity grew 1.9 per cent per year during 2001, while business sector output grew only 0.9 per cent per year as the US economy slowed during the 2001 recession. Growth of both labor productivity and output, however, appear considerably below trend rates, partially reflecting the collapse of investment spending that began toward the end of 2000 and has continued through 2001.

In this chapter we review the most recent evidence and quantify the proximate sources of growth using an augmented growth accounting framework that allows us to focus on information technology (IT). Despite the downward revision to the GDP and investment in some IT assets in the annual GDP revisions by the Bureau of Economic Analysis (BEA) in July 2001, we conclude that the US productivity revival remains largely intact and that IT has played a central role. For example, the capital deepening contribution from computer hardware, software, and telecommunications equipment to labor productivity growth for 1995–2000 exceeded the contribution from all other capital assets. We also find increases in total factor productivity (TFP) in both the IT-producing sectors and elsewhere in the economy, although the non-IT component is smaller than in earlier estimates.

We then turn to the future of US productivity growth. Our overall conclusion is that the projections of Jorgenson and Stiroh (2000), prepared more than eighteen months ago, are largely on target. Our new base-case projection of trend labor productivity growth for the next decade is 2.21 per cent per year, only slightly below the average of the period 1995–2000 of 2.36 per cent per year. Our projection of output growth for the next decade, however, is only 3.31 per cent per year, compared with the 1995–2000 average of 4.60 per cent, due to slower projected growth in hours worked.

We emphasize that projecting growth for periods as long as a decade is fraught with uncertainty. Our pessimistic projection of labor productivity growth is only 1.33 per cent per year, while our optimistic projection is 2.92 per cent. For output growth, the range is from 2.43 per cent in the pessimistic case to 4.02 per cent in the optimistic. These ranges result from fundamental uncertainties about future technological changes in the production of information technology equipment and related investment patterns, which Jorgenson (2001) traced to changes in the product cycle for semiconductors, the most important IT component.

The starting point for projecting US output growth is the projection of future growth of the labor force. The growth of hours worked of 2.24 per cent per year from 1995–2000 is not likely to be sustainable because labor force growth for the next decade will average only 1.10 per cent. An abrupt slowdown in growth of hours worked would have reduced output growth by 1.14 per cent, even if labor productivity growth had continued unabated. We estimate that labor productivity growth from 1995–2000 also exceeded its sustainable rate, however, leading to an additional decline of 0.15 per cent in the trend rate of output growth, so that our base-case scenario projects output growth of 3.31 per cent for the next decade.

The next section reviews the historical record, extending the estimates of Jorgenson and Stiroh (2000) to incorporate data for 1999 and 2000 and revised estimates of economic growth for earlier years. We employ the same methodology and summarize it briefly. The following section presents our projections of the trend growth of output and labor productivity for the next decade. We then compare these with projections based on alternative methodologies. The last section concludes the chapter.

REVIEWING THE HISTORICAL RECORD

Our methodology for analysing the sources of growth is based on the production possibility frontier introduced by Jorgenson (1996, pp. 27–8). This framework captures substitution between investment and consumption goods on the output side and between capital and labor inputs on the input side. Jorgenson and Stiroh (2000) and Jorgenson (2001) have used the production possibility frontier to measure the contributions of information technology (IT) to US economic growth and the growth of labor productivity.

THE PRODUCTION POSSIBILITY FRONTIER

In the production possibility frontier output (Y) consist of consumption goods (C) and investment goods (I), while inputs consist of capital services (K) and labor input (L). Output can be further decomposed into IT investment goods – computer hardware (I_c), computer software (I_s), communications equipment (I_m) – and all other non-IT output (Y_n). Capital services can be similarly decomposed into the capital service flows from hardware (K_c), software (K_s), communications equipment (K_m), and all other capital services (K_n).[2] The input function (X) is augmented by total factor productivity (A). The production possibility frontier can be represented as:

$$Y(Y_n, I_c, I_s, I_m) = A \cdot X(K_n, K_c, K_s, K_m, L) \qquad (2.1)$$

Under the standard assumptions of competitive product and factor markets, and constant returns to scale, Equation (2.1) can be transformed into an equation that accounts for the sources of economic growth:

$$\bar{w}_{Y_n} \Delta \ln Y_n + \bar{w}_{I_c} \Delta \ln I_c + \bar{w}_{I_s} \Delta \ln I_s + \bar{w}_{I_m} \Delta \ln I_m = \bar{v}_{K_n} \Delta \ln K_n$$
$$+ \bar{v}_{K_c} \Delta \ln K_c + \bar{v}_{K_s} \Delta \ln K_s + \bar{v}_{K_m} \Delta \ln K_m + \bar{v}_L \Delta \ln L + \Delta \ln A \qquad (2.2)$$

where $\Delta x \equiv x_t - x_{t-1}$. The average output shares are denoted by $\bar{w}$ and $\bar{v}$ the average input shares of the subscripted variables, and $\bar{w}_{Y_n} + \bar{w}_{I_c} + \bar{w}_{I_s} + \bar{w}_{I_m} = \bar{v}_{K_n} + \bar{v}_{K_c} + \bar{v}_{K_s} + \bar{v}_{K_m} + \bar{v}_L = 1$. The shares are averaged over period t and $t-1$. We refer to the share-weighted growth rates in equation (2.2) as the contributions of the inputs and outputs.

Average labor productivity (ALP) is defined as the ratio of output to hours worked, so that $ALP = y = Y/H$, where the lower-case variable (y) denotes output (Y) per hour (H). Equation (2.2) can be rewritten in per hour terms as:

$$\Delta \ln y = \bar{v}_{K_n} \Delta \ln k_n + \bar{v}_{K_{IT}} \Delta \ln k_{IT} + \bar{v}_L (\Delta \ln L - \Delta \ln H) + \Delta \ln A \quad (2.3)$$

where $\bar{v}_{K_{IT}} = \bar{v}_{K_c} + \bar{v}_{K_s} + \bar{v}_{K_m}$ and $\Delta \ln k_{IT}$ is the growth of all IT capital services per hour.

Equation (2.3) decomposes ALP growth into three sources. The first is capital deepening, defined as the contribution of capital services per hour, which is decomposed into non-IT and IT components. The interpretation of capital deepening is that additional capital makes workers more productive in proportion to the capital share. The second factor is labor quality improvement, defined as the contribution of labor input per hour worked. This reflects changes in the composition of the workforce and raises labor productivity in proportion to the labor share. The third source is total factor productivity (TFP) growth, which raises ALP growth point-for-point.

In a fully developed sectoral production model, like that of Jorgenson et al. (2002), growth of TFP reflects the productivity contributions of individual sectors. It is difficult, however, to create the detailed industry data needed to measure industry-level productivity in a timely and accurate manner. The Council of Economic Advisors (CEA 2001), Jorgenson and Stiroh (2000) and Oliner and Sichel (2000, 2002) have employed the price dual of industry-level productivity to generate estimates of TFP growth in the production of IT assets.

Intuitively, the idea underlying the dual approach is that declines in relative prices for IT investment goods reflect fundamental technological change and productivity growth in the IT-producing industries. We weight these relative price declines by the shares in output of each of the IT investment goods in order to estimate the contribution of IT production to economy-wide TFP growth. This enables us to decompose aggregate TFP growth as:

$$\Delta \ln A = \bar{u}_{IT} \Delta \ln A_{IT} + \Delta \ln A_n \quad (2.4)$$

where $\bar{u}_{IT}$ represents IT's average share of output; $\Delta \ln A_{IT}$ is IT-related productivity growth; $\bar{u}_{IT}\Delta \ln A_{IT}$ is the contribution to aggregate TFP from IT-production; $\Delta\ln A_n$ reflects the contribution to aggregate TFP growth from the rest of the economy, which includes TFP gains in other industries as well as reallocation effects as inputs and outputs are shifted among sectors.

We estimate the contribution to aggregate TFP growth from IT production, $\bar{u}_{IT}\Delta A_{IT}$, by estimating output shares and growth rates of productivity for computer hardware, software, and communications equipment. Productivity growth for each investment good is measured as the negative of the rate of price decline, relative to the price change of capital and labor inputs. The output shares are the final expenditures on these investment goods, divided by total output.[3] This likely understates IT output because we ignore the production of intermediate goods, but this omission is relatively small. Finally, the non-IT contribution to aggregate TFP growth, ΔA_n, is estimated as a residual from equation (2.4).

Data

We briefly summarize the data required to implement equations (2.1) to (2.4) here; more detailed descriptions are available in Ho and Jorgenson (1999) and the appendices of Jorgenson and Stiroh (2000). Our output measure is somewhat broader than the one used in the official labor productivity statistics, published by BLS (2001a, 2001b) and employed by Gordon (2000) and Oliner and Sichel (2000, 2002). Our definition of the private US economy includes the nonprofit sector and imputed capital service flows from residential housing and consumer durables. The imputations raise our measure of private output by $778 billion in current dollars in 2000 or 9 per cent of nominal private GDP in 2000.

Our output estimates reflect the most recent revisions to the US National Income and Product Accounts (NIPA), released in July 2001. These revisions included a downward adjustment to software investment, as well as a new quality-adjusted price index for local area networks (LAN). Both of these are incorporated into our estimates of IT investment.

Our capital service estimates are based on the Tangible Wealth Survey, published by the BEA and described in Herman (2001). This includes data on business investment and consumer durable purchases for the US economy through 2000. We construct capital stocks from the investment data by the perpetual inventory method. We assume that the effective capital stock for each asset is the average of the current and lagged estimates. The data on tangible assets from BEA are augmented with inventory data to form our measure of the reproducible capital stock. The total capital stock also includes land and inventories.

Finally, we estimate capital service flows by multiplying rental prices and effective capital stocks, as originally proposed by Jorgenson and Griliches (1996). Our estimates incorporate asset-specific differences in taxes, asset prices, service lives, and depreciation rates. This is essential for understanding the productive impact of IT investment, because IT assets differ dramatically from other assets in rates of decline of asset prices and depreciation rates.

We refer to the difference between the growth in aggregate capital service flows and effective capital stocks as the growth in capital quality. That is:

$$\Delta \ln KQ = \Delta \ln K - \Delta \ln Z \qquad (2.5)$$

where KQ is capital quality, K is capital service flow, and Z is the effective capital stock. The aggregate capital stock Z is a quantity index over 70 different effective capital stocks plus land and inventories, using investment goods prices as weights, while the aggregate flow of capital services K is a quantity index of the same stocks using rental (or service) prices as weights. The difference in growth rates is the growth rate of capital quality, KQ. As firms substitute among assets by investing relatively more in assets with relatively high marginal products, capital quality increases.

Labor input is a quantity index of hours worked that takes into account the heterogeneity of the workforce among sex, employment class, age, and education levels. The weights used to construct the index are the compensation of the various types of workers. In the same way as for capital, we define growth in labor quality as the difference between the growth rate of aggregate labor input and hours worked:

$$\Delta \ln LQ = \Delta \ln L - \Delta \ln H \qquad (2.6)$$

where LQ is labor quality, L is the labor input index, and H is hours worked. As firms substitute among hours worked by hiring relatively more highly skilled and highly compensated workers, labor quality rises.

Our labor data incorporate the Censuses of Population for 1970, 1980, and 1990, the annual Current Population Surveys (CPS), and the NIPA. We take total hours worked for private domestic employees directly from the NIPA (Table 6.9c), self-employed hours worked for the non-farm business sector from the BLS, and self-employed hours worked in the farm sector from the Department of Agriculture.

Results

Table 2.1 reports our estimates of the components of equation (2.2), the sources of economic growth. For the period as a whole, output grew 3.6

Table 2.1 Growth in private domestic output, the sources of growth 1959–2000

	1959–2000	1959–73	1973–95	1995–2000	1995–2000 Less 1973–95
Growth in private domestic output (Y)	3.61	4.24	2.99	4.60	1.61
Contribution of selected output components					
Other output (Y_n)	3.30	4.10	2.68	3.79	1.12
Computer investment (I_c)	0.16	0.07	0.17	0.37	0.20
Software investment (I_s)	0.09	0.03	0.09	0.26	0.18
Communications investment (I_m)	0.07	0.05	0.06	0.17	0.11
Contribution of capital and CD services (K)	1.80	1.99	1.54	2.38	0.84
Other (K_n)	1.44	1.81	1.18	1.52	0.34
Computers (K_c)	0.19	0.09	0.20	0.47	0.28
Software (K_s)	0.09	0.03	0.09	0.25	0.16
Communications (K_m)	0.08	0.06	0.07	0.13	0.06
Contribution of labor (L)	1.16	1.12	1.12	1.42	0.30
Aggregate total factor productivity (TFP)	0.66	1.13	0.33	0.80	0.47
Contribution of capital and CD quality	0.47	0.34	0.41	1.09	0.69
Contribution of capital and CD stock	1.33	1.65	1.14	1.28	0.15
Contribution of labor quality	0.28	0.39	0.23	0.17	−0.06
Contribution of labor hours	0.88	0.73	0.89	1.26	0.37

Note: A contribution of an output or input is defined as the share-weighted, real growth rate.

Source: Author's calculations based on BEA, BLS, Census Bureau, and other data.

per cent per year. Capital input made the largest contribution to growth of 1.8 percentage points, followed by 1.2 percentage points from labor input. Less than 20 per cent of output growth, 0.7 percentage points, directly reflects TFP. These results are consistent with the other recent growth accounting decompositions like CEA (2001), Jorgenson and Stiroh (2000), and Oliner and Sichel (2000, 2002).

The data also show the substantial acceleration in output growth after 1995. Output growth increased from 3.0 per cent per year for 1973–95 to 4.6 per cent for 1995–2000, reflecting large increases in IT and non-IT investment goods. On the input side, more rapid capital accumulation contributed 0.84 percentage points to the post-1995 acceleration, while faster growth of labor input contributed 0.30 percentage points and accelerated TFP growth the remaining 0.47 percentage points. The contribution of capital input from IT increased from 0.36 percentage points per year for 1973–95 to 0.85 for 1995–2000, exceeding the increased contributions of all other forms of capital.

The last panel in Table 2.1 presents an alternative decomposition of the contribution of capital and labor inputs using equations (2.5) and (2.6). Here, the contribution of capital and labor reflect the contributions from capital quality and capital stock, and labor quality and hours worked, respectively, as:

$$\Delta \ln Y = \bar{v}_K \Delta \ln Z + \bar{v}_K \Delta \ln KQ + \bar{v}_L \Delta \ln H + \bar{v}_L \Delta \ln LQ + \Delta \ln A \quad (2.7)$$

Table 2.1 shows that the revival of output growth after 1995 can be attributed to two forces. First, a massive substitution toward IT assets in response to accelerating IT price declines is reflected in the rising contribution of capital quality, while the growth of capital stock lagged considerably behind the growth of output. Second, the growth of hours worked surged, as the growth of labor quality declined. A fall in the unemployment rate and an increase in labor force participation drew more workers with relatively low marginal products into the workforce. We employ equation (2.7) in projecting sustainable growth of output and labor productivity in the next section.

Table 2.2 presents estimates of the sources of ALP growth, as in equations (2.3) and (2.4). For the period as a whole, growth in ALP accounted for nearly 60 per cent of output growth, due to annual capital deepening of 1.13 percentage points, improvement of labor quality of 0.28 percentage points, and TFP growth of 0.66 percentage points. Growth in hours worked of 1.54 percentage points per year accounted for the remaining 40 per cent of output growth.

Looking more closely at the post-1995 period, we see that labor productivity increased by 0.92 percentage points per year from 1.44 for 1973–95

Table 2.2   Sources of growth in average labor productivity 1959–2000

	1959–2000	1959–73	1973–95	1995–2000	1995–2000 less 1973–95
Output growth (Y)	3.61	4.24	2.99	4.60	1.61
Hours growth (H)	1.54	1.27	1.55	2.24	0.68
Average labor productivity growth (ALP)	2.07	2.97	1.44	2.36	0.92
Capital deepening	1.13	1.44	0.88	1.40	0.52
IT capital deepening	0.32	0.16	0.32	0.76	0.44
Other capital deepening	0.82	1.28	0.56	0.64	0.08
Labor quality	0.28	0.39	0.23	0.17	−0.06
TFP growth	0.66	1.13	0.33	0.80	0.47
IT-related contribution	0.23	0.10	0.24	0.51	0.27
Other contribution	0.43	1.03	0.08	0.29	0.20

Note: A contribution of an output or input is defined as the share-weighted, real growth rate.

Source: Author's calculations based on BEA, BLS, Census Bureau, and other data.

to 2.36 for 1995–2000, while hours worked increased by 0.68 percentage points from an annual rate of 1.55 for 1973–95 to 2.24 for 1995–2000. The labor productivity growth revival reflects more rapid capital deepening of 0.52 percentage points and accelerated TFP growth of 0.47 percentage points per year; the contribution of labor quality declined. Nearly all the increase in capital deepening was from IT assets with only a small increase from other assets. Finally, we estimate that improved productivity in the production of IT-related assets contributed 0.27 percentage points to aggregate TFP growth, while improved productivity growth in the rest of the economy contributed the remaining 0.20 percentage points. These results suggest that IT had a substantial role in the revival of labor productivity growth through both capital deepening and TFP channels.

Our estimate of the magnitude of the productivity revival is somewhat lower than that reported in earlier studies by BLS (2001a), Jorgenson and Stiroh (2000), Oliner and Sichel (2000). These studies were based on data reported prior to the July 2001 revision of the NIPA, which substantially lowered GDP growth in 1999 and 2000. Our estimates of the productivity revival are also lower than the estimates in BLS (2001b), however, which does include the July 2001 revisions in GDP.

BLS (2001b) reports business sector ALP growth of 2.68 percentage points for 1995–2000 and 1.45 for 1973–95, an increase of 1.23

percentage points, compared to our estimated acceleration of 0.92 percentage points. This divergence is a combination of a slower acceleration of our broader concept of output and our estimates of more rapid growth in hours worked. BLS (2001b), for example, reports that hours grew 1.95 per cent per year for 1995–2000 in the business sector, while our estimate is 2.24.

Our estimate of private domestic employee hours are taken directly from the NIPA and includes workers in the non-profit sector, while the BLS estimate does not. In addition, BLS (2001b) has revised the growth in business sector hours in 2000 downward by 0.4 percentage points, based on new data from the *2000 Hours at Work Survey*. Our estimate of labor quality change is also slightly different from BLS (2001a) due to the different methods of estimating the wage–demographic relationships, and our use of only the March CPS data as opposed to the monthly CPS data used by BLS. These differences ultimately appear in our estimated contribution to TFP from non-IT sources, because this cannot be observed directly without detailed industry data and we therefore estimate it as a residual.

PROJECTING PRODUCTIVITY GROWTH

While there is little disagreement about the resurgence of ALP growth after 1995, there has been considerable debate about whether this is permanent or temporary. Changes in the underlying trend growth rate of productivity are likely to be permanent, while cyclical factors such as strong output growth or extraordinarily rapid investment are more likely to be temporary. This distinction is crucial for understanding the sources of the recent productivity revival and projecting future productivity growth.

This section presents our projections of trend rates of growth for output and labor productivity over the next decade, abstracting from business cycle fluctuations. Our key assumptions are that output and the reproducible capital stock will grow at the same rate, and that labor hours will grow at the same rate as the labor force.[4] These are characteristic features of the US and most industrialized economies over periods of time longer than a typical business cycle. For example, US output growth averaged 3.6 per cent per year for 1959–2000, while our measure of the reproducible capital stock grew 3.9 per year.[5]

We begin by decomposing the aggregate capital stock into the reproducible component, Z_R, and business sector land, $LAND$, which we assume to be fixed. This implies:

$$\Delta \ln Z = \overline{\mu}_R \Delta \ln Z_R + (1 - \overline{\mu}_R)\Delta \ln LAND = \overline{\mu}_R \Delta \ln Z_R \qquad (2.8)$$

where $\overline{\mu}_R$ is the value share of reproducible capital stock in total capital stock.

We then employ our projection assumptions to construct estimates of trend output and productivity growth, conditional on the projected growth of the remaining sources of economic growth. More formally, if $\Delta \ln Y = \Delta \ln Z_R$, then combining equations (2.3), (2.4), (2.7), and (2.8) imply that trend labor productivity and output growth are given by:

$$\Delta \ln y = \frac{\overline{v}_K \Delta \ln KQ - \overline{v}_K(1 - \overline{\mu}_R)\Delta \ln H + \overline{v}_L \Delta \ln LQ + \overline{u}_{IT}\Delta \ln A_{IT} + \ln A_n}{1 - \overline{v}_K \overline{\mu}_R}$$

$$\Delta \ln Y = \Delta \ln y + \Delta \ln H \tag{2.9}$$

Equation (2.9) is a long-run relationship that averages over cyclical and stochastic elements and removes the transitional dynamics relating to capital accumulation. The second part of a definition of trend growth is that the unemployment rate remains constant and hours growth matches labor force growth. Growth in hours worked was exceptionally rapid in the 1995–2000 period, as the unemployment rate fell from 5.6 per cent in 1995 to 4.0 in 2000, so output growth was considerably above its trend rate.[6] To estimate hours growth over the next decade, we employ detailed demographic projections based on Census Bureau data.

In order to complete intermediate-term growth projections based on equation (2.9), we require estimates of capital and labor shares, IT output shares, reproducible capital stock shares, capital quality growth, labor quality growth, and TFP growth. Labor quality growth and the various shares are relatively easy to project, while extrapolations of the other variables involve much greater uncertainty. Accordingly, we present three sets of projections – a base-case scenario, a pessimistic scenario, and an optimistic scenario.

We hold labor quality growth, hours growth, the capital share, the reproducible capital stock share, and the IT output share constant across the three scenarios. We refer to these as the 'common assumptions'. We vary IT-related TFP growth, the contribution to TFP growth from non-IT sources, and capital quality growth across these scenarios and label them 'alternative assumptions'. Generally speaking for these variables, the base-case scenario incorporates data from the business cycle of 1990–2000, the optimistic scenario assumes the patterns of 1995–2000 will persist, and the pessimistic case assumes that the economy reverts back to 1973–95 averages.

Common Assumptions

Hours growth ($\Delta \ln H$) and labor quality growth ($\Delta \ln LQ$) are relatively easy to project. The Congressional Budget Office (CBO 2001a), for example, projects growth in the economy-wide labor force of 1.1 per cent per year, based on Social Security Administration (SSA) projections of population growth. Potential hours growth is projected at 1.2 per cent per year for the non-farm business sector for 2001–11, based on CBO projections of hours worked for different demographic categories of workers. The CBO estimate of potential hours growth is a slight increase from earlier projections due to incorporation of recent data from the 2000 Census and changes in the tax laws that will modestly increase the supply of labor. CBO (2001a) does not employ the concept of labor quality.

We construct our own projections of demographic trends. Ho and Jorgenson (1999) have shown that the dominant trends in labor quality growth are due to rapid improvements in educational attainment in the 1960s and 1970s, and the rise in female participation rates in the 1970s. The improvement in educational attainment of new entrants into the labor force largely ceased in the 1990s, although the average educational level continued to rise as younger and better educated workers entered the labor force and older workers retired.

We project growth in the population from the demographic model of the Bureau of Census, which breaks the population down by individual year of age, race and sex.[7] For each group the population in period t is equal to the population in period $t - 1$, less deaths plus net immigration. Death rates are group-specific and are projected by assuming a steady rate of improvement in health. The population of newborns in each period reflects the number of females in each age group and the age- and race-specific fertility rates. These fertility rates are projected to fall steadily.

We observe labor force participation rates in the last year of our sample period. We then project the work force by assuming constant participation rates for each sex-age group. The educational attainment of workers aged a in period t is projected by assuming that it is equal to the attainment of the workers of age $a - 1$ in period $t - 1$ for all those who are over 35 years of age in the last year of the sample. For those who are younger than 35 we assume that the educational attainment of workers aged a in forecast period t is equal to the attainment of workers aged a in the base year.

Our index of labor quality is constructed from hours worked and compensation rates. We project hours worked by multiplying the projected population in each sex–age–education group by the annual hours per person in the last year of the sample. The relative compensation rates for each group are assumed to be equal to the observed compensation in the sample period. With these projected hours and compensation we forecast the quality index over the next 20 years.

Our estimates suggest that hours growth ($\Delta \ln H$) will be about 1.1 per cent per year over the next ten years, which is quite close to the CBO (2001a) estimates, and 0.8 per cent per year over a twenty-year period. We estimate that growth in labor quality ($\Delta \ln LQ$) will be 0.27 per cent per year over the next decade and 0.17 per cent per year over the next two decades. This is considerably lower than the 0.49 per cent growth rates for the period 1959–2000, which was driven by rising average educational attainment and stabilizing female participation.

The capital share ($\bar{v}_K$) has not shown any obvious trend over the last 40 years. We assume it holds constant at 42.8 per cent, the average for 1959–2000. Similarly, the fixed reproducible capital share ($\bar{\mu}_R$) has shown little trend and we assume it remains constant at 80.4 per cent, the average for 1959–2000.

We assume the IT output share ($\bar{u}_{IT}$) stays at 5.1 per cent, the average for 1995–2000. This is likely a conservative estimate, because IT has steadily increased in importance in the US economy, rising from 2.1 per cent of output in 1970 to 2.7 per cent in 1980 to 3.9 per cent in 1990 to 5.7 per cent in 2000. On the other hand, there has been speculation that IT expenditures in the late 1990s were not sustainable due to Y2K investment, the NASDAQ bubble, and abnormally rapid price declines.[8]

Alternative Assumptions

IT-related productivity growth ($\Delta \ln A_{IT}$) has been extremely rapid in recent years with a substantial acceleration after 1995. For 1990–95 productivity growth for production of the three IT assets averaged 7.4 per cent per year, while the 1995–2000 average growth rate was 10.3 per cent. These growth rates are high, but quite consistent with industry-level productivity estimates for high-tech sectors. For example, BLS (2001a) reports productivity growth of 6.9 per cent per year for 1995–99 in industrial and commercial machinery, which includes production of computer hardware, and 8.1 per cent in electronic and other electric equipment, which includes semiconductors and telecommunications equipment.

Jorgenson (2001) argues the large increase in IT productivity growth was triggered by a much sharper acceleration in the decline of semiconductor prices. This can be traced to a shift in the product cycle for semiconductors in 1995 from three years to two years, a consequence of intensifying competition in the semiconductor market. It would be premature to extrapolate the recent acceleration in productivity growth into the indefinite future, however, because this depends on the persistence of a two-year product cycle for semiconductors.

To better gauge the future prospects of technological progress in the semiconductor industry, we turn to *The International Technology Roadmap for Semiconductors.*[9] This projection, performed annually by a consortium of industry associations, forecast a two-year product cycle through 2003 and a three-year product cycle thereafter. This is a reasonable basis for projecting the productivity growth related to IT for the US economy. Moreover, continuation of a two-year cycle provides an upper bound for growth projections, while reversion to a three-year cycle gives a lower bound.

Our base-case scenario follows the *International Technology Roadmap for Semiconductors* and averages the two-year and three-year cycle projections with IT-related growth of 8.8 per cent per year, which equals the average for 1990–2000. The optimistic projections assume that the two-year product cycle for semiconductors remains in place over the intermediate future so that productivity growth in the production of IT assets averages 10.3 per cent per year, as it did for 1995–2000. Our pessimistic projection assumes the semiconductor product cycle reverts to the three-year cycle in place during 1973–95 when IT-related productivity growth was 7.4 per cent per year. In all cases, the contribution of IT to aggregate TFP growth reflects the 1995–2000 average share of about 5.1 per cent.

The TFP contribution from non-IT sources (ΔA_n) is more difficult to project because the post-1995 acceleration is outside standard growth models, so we present a range of alternative estimates that are consistent with the historical record. Our base-case uses the average contribution from the full business cycle of the 1990s and assumes a contribution 0.20 percentage points for the intermediate future. This assumes that the myriad of factors that drove TFP growth in the 1990s – like technological progress, innovation, resource reallocations, and increased competitive pressures – will continue into the future. Our optimistic case assumes that the contribution for 1995–2000 of 0.29 percentage points per year will continue for the intermediate future, while our pessimistic case assumes that the US economy will revert back to the slow-growth period from 1973–95 when this contribution averaged only 0.08 per cent per year.

The final step in our projections is to estimate the growth in capital quality ($\Delta \ln KQ$). The workhorse aggregate growth model with one capital good has capital stock and output growing at the same rate in a balanced growth equilibrium, and even complex models typically have only two capital goods. The US data, however, distinguish between several dozen types of capital and the historical record shows that substitution between these types of capital is an important source of output and productivity growth. For the period 1959–2000, for example, capital quality growth contributed 0.47 percentage points to output growth as firms substituted toward short-lived assets with higher marginal products. This corresponds to a growth in capital quality of about 1.0 per cent per year.

An important difficulty in projecting capital quality growth from recent data, however, is that investment patterns in the 1990s may partially reflect an unsustainable investment boom in response to temporary factors like Y2K investment and the NASDAQ stock market bubble, which skewed investment toward IT assets. Capital quality for 1995–2000 grew at 2.5 per cent per year as firms invested heavily in IT, for example, but there has been a sizable slowdown in IT investment in the second half of 2000 and 2001. Therefore, we are cautious about relying too heavily on the recent investment experience.

Our base-case again uses the average rate for 1990–2000, which was 1.75 percentage points for capital quality; this effectively averages the high rates of substitution in the late 1990s with the more moderate rates of the early 1990s and uses evidence from the complete business cycle of the 1990s. Our optimistic projection ignores the belief that capital substitution was unsustainably high in the late 1990s and assume that capital quality growth will continue at the 2.45 per cent annual rate of the period 1995–2000. Our pessimistic scenario assumes that the growth of capital quality reverts back to the 0.84 annual growth rate seen for 1973–95.

Output and Productivity Projections

Table 2.3 assembles the components of our projections and presents the three scenarios. The top panel shows the projected growth of output, labor productivity, and the effective capital stock. The second panel reports the five factors that are held constant across scenarios – hours growth, labor quality growth, the capital share, the IT output share, and the reproducible capital stock share. The bottom panel includes the three components that vary across scenarios – TFP growth in IT, the TFP contribution from other sources, and capital quality growth. Table 2.3 also compares the projections with our actual data for the same series for 1995–2000.

Our base-case scenario puts trend labor productivity growth at 2.21 per cent per year, and trend output growth at 3.31 per cent per year. Projected productivity growth falls just short of our estimates for 1995–2000, but output growth is considerably slower due to the large slowdown in projected hours growth; hours grew 2.24 per cent per year for 1995–2000 compared to our projection of only 1.1 per cent per year for the next decade. Capital stock growth is projected to fall in the base-case to 2.66 per cent per year, from 2.94 for 1995–2000.

Table 2.3   Output and labor productivity projections

	1995–2000	Projections		
		Pessimistic	Base-case	Optimistic
Projections				
Output growth	4.60	2.43	3.31	4.02
ALP growth	2.36	1.33	2.21	2.92
Effective capital stock	2.94	1.96	2.66	3.23
Common assumptions				
Hours growth	2.24	1.10	1.10	1.10
Labor quality growth	0.299	0.265	0.265	0.265
Capital share	0.438	0.428	0.428	0.428
IT output share	0.051	0.051	0.051	0.051
Reproducible capital stock share	0.798	0.804	0.804	0.804
Alternative assumptions				
TFP growth in IT	10.33	7.39	8.78	10.28
Implied IT-related TFP contribution	0.52	0.37	0.44	0.52
Other TFP contribution	0.29	0.08	0.20	0.29
Capital quality growth	2.45	0.84	1.75	2.45

Notes:
In all projections, hours growth and labor quality growth are from internal projections, capital share and reproducible capital stock shares are 1959–2000 averages, and IT output shares are for 1995–2000.
Pessimistic cases uses 1973–95 average growth of capital quality, IT-related TFP growth, and non-IT TFP contribution.
Base case uses 1990–2000 averages and optimistic cases uses 1995–2000 averages.

Our base-case scenario incorporates the underlying pace of technological progress in semiconductors embedded in the *International Technology Roadmap* forecast and puts the contribution of IT-related TFP below that of 1995–2000 as the semiconductor industry eventually returns to a three-year product cycle. The slower growth is partially balanced by larger IT output shares. Other TFP growth also makes a smaller contribution. Finally, the slower pace of capital input growth is offset by slower hours growth, so that strong capital deepening brings the projected growth rate near the observed rates of growth for 1995–2000.

Our optimistic scenario puts labor productivity growth just below 3.0 per cent per year and reflects the assumption of continuing rapid technological progress. In particular, the two-year product cycle in semiconductors is assumed to persist for the intermediate future, which drives rapid TFP in production of IT assets as well as continued substitution toward IT assets and rapid growth in capital quality. In addition, other TFP growth continues the relatively rapid contribution seen after 1995.

Finally, the pessimistic projection of 1.33 per cent annual growth in labor productivity assumes that many trends revert back to the sluggish growth rates of the 1973–95 period and the three-year product cycle for semiconductors begins immediately. The larger share of IT, however, means that even with the return to the three-year technology cycle and slower TFP growth, labor productivity growth will equal the rates seen in the 1970s and 1980s.

ALTERNATIVE METHODOLOGIES AND ESTIMATES

This section briefly reviews alternative approaches to estimating productivity growth trends from the historical record and projecting productivity growth going forward. We begin with the econometric methods for separating trend and cyclical components of productivity growth employed by Gordon (2000), French (2001), and Roberts (2001). A second approach is to control for factors that are most likely to be cyclical, such as factor utilization, in the augmented growth accounting framework of Basu et al. (2001). A third approach, the CBO (2001a, 2001b) calibrates a growth model to the historical record and uses the model to project growth of output and productivity. Finally, Oliner and Sichel (2002) present a projection methodology based on a growth accounting framework.

1. Econometric Estimates

We begin with the studies that employ econometric methods for decomposing a single time series between cyclical and trend components. Gordon (2000) estimates that of the 2.75 per cent annual labor productivity growth rate during 1995–99, 0.50 per cent can be attributed to cyclical effects and 2.25 per cent to trend. The post-1995 trend growth rate is 0.83 per cent higher than the growth rate from 1972–95. Capital and labor input growth and price measurement changes account for 0.52 per cent, TFP growth in the computer sector for 0.29 per cent, leaving a mere 0.02 per cent to be explained by acceleration in TFP growth in the other sectors of the private economy. In this view the productivity revival is concentrated in the computer-producing sector.

Other studies have employed state–space models to distinguish between trend and cycles for output. Roberts (2001) uses time-varying parameter methods to model the growth of labor and total factor productivity. He represents trend productivity as a random walk with drift, and allows the drift term to be a time-varying parameter. These estimates suggest that trend labor productivity growth has increased from 1.6 per cent per year during 1973–94 to 2.7 per cent by 2000, while trend TFP growth rose from 0.5 per cent during 1985–95 to 1.1 per cent during 1998–2000. This estimate of trend labor productivity falls between our base-case and optimistic projection.

French (2001) uses a Cobb–Douglas production function to model trends and cycles in total factor productivity growth. He considers filtering methods and concludes that they are all unsatisfactory due to the assumption that innovations are normally distributed.[10] He applies a discrete innovations model with two high–low TFP growth regimes, and finds that the trend TFP growth after 1995 increases from 1.01 per cent to 1.11 per cent.

Finally, Hansen (2001) provides a good primer of recent advances in the alternatives to random walk models – testing for infrequent structural breaks in parameters. Applying these methods on the manufacturing sector of the US, he finds strong evidence of a break in labor productivity in the mid-1990s, the breakdate depending on the sector being analysed. We do not compare his specific estimates because they are only for manufacturing.

2. Augmented Growth Accounting

Basu et al. (2001) present an alternative approach to estimating trend growth in total factor productivity by separately accounting for factor utilization and factor accumulation. They extend the growth accounting framework to incorporate adjustment costs, scale economies, imperfect competition, and changes in utilization. Industry-level data for the 1990s suggests that the post-1995 rise in productivity appears to be largely a change in trend rather than a cyclical phenomenon, since there was little change in utilization in the late 1990s. While Basu et al. are clear that they do not make predictions about the sustainability of these changes, their results suggest that any slowdown in investment growth is likely to be associated with a temporary increase in output growth as resources are reallocated away from adjustment and toward production.

3. Calibration and Projection

CBO (2001a) presents medium term projections for economic growth and productivity for 2003–11 for both the overall economy and the non-farm business sector. CBO's most fully developed model is for the non-farm business sector. Medium-term projections are based on historical trends in the labor force, savings and investment, and TFP growth. These projections allow for possible business cycle fluctuations, but CBO does not explicitly forecast fluctuations beyond two years (CBO 2001a, p. 38).

For the non-farm part of the economy, CBO (2001a) projects potential output growth of 3.7 per cent per year and potential labor productivity of 2.5 per cent per year. For the economy as a whole, CBO projects potential labor productivity growth of 2.1 per cent per year, which is quite close to our estimates.

For the non-farm business economy, CBO (2001a) utilizes a Cobb–Douglas production function without labor quality improvement. CBO's relatively high projection of labor productivity growth for the non-farm business sector reflects projections of capital input growth of 4.8 per cent per year and TFP growth of 1.4 per cent per year.[11] CBO's relatively rapid rate of capital input growth going forward is somewhat slower than their estimate of 5.2 per cent for 1996–2000, but considerably faster than their estimate of 3.9 per cent annual growth for 1990–2000. This reflects the model of savings and investment used by CBO, as well as the expectation of continued substitution toward short-lived IT assets. Potential TFP growth of 1.4 per cent per year reflects an estimated trend growth of 1.1 per cent per year, augmented by the specific effects of computer quality improvement and changes in price measurement.

CONCLUSION

Our primary conclusion is that a consensus has emerged about trend rates of growth for output and labor productivity. Our central estimates of 2.21 per cent for labor productivity and 3.31 per cent for output are very similar to Gordon (2000) and CBO (2001a), and only slightly more optimistic than Baily (2001).[12] Our methodology assumes that trend growth rates in output and reproducible capital are the same, and that hours growth is constrained by the growth of the labor force to form a balanced growth path. While productivity is projected to fall slightly from the pace seen in the late 1990s, we conclude that the US productivity revival is likely to remain intact for the intermediate future.

Our second conclusion is that trend growth rates are subject to considerable uncertainty. For the US economy this can be identified with the future product cycle for semiconductors and the impact on other high-tech gear. The switch from a three-year to a two-year product cycle in 1995 produced a dramatic increase in the rate of decline of IT prices. This is reflected in the investment boom of 1995–2000 and the massive substitution of IT capital for other types of capital that took place in response to price changes. The issue that must be confronted by policy-makers is whether this two-year product cycle can continue, and whether firms will continue to respond to the dramatic improvements in the performance/price ratio of IT investment goods.

As a final point, we have not tried to quantify another important source of uncertainty, namely, the economic impacts of the events of September 11. These impacts are already apparent in the slowdown of economic activity in areas related to travel and increased security, as well as higher government expenditures for the war in Afghanistan and enhanced homeland security. The cyclical effects will likely produce only a temporary reduction in productivity as civilian plants operate at lower utilization rates. Even a long-term reallocation of resources from civilian to public goods or to security operations, however, should only produce a one-time reduction in productivity levels, rather than a change in the trend rate of growth of output and productivity.

NOTES

1. DeLong and Summers (2001) do not actually provide a point estimate, but state 'It is certainly possible – if not probable – that when US growth resumes trend productivity will grow as fast or faster than it did in the late 1990s (p. 17).' The 3.0 per cent estimate is attributed to Mr Summers in a review of the Jackson Hole Symposium in *The Economist*, 8 September 2001.
2. Note that our output and capital service flow concepts include the service flows from residential structures and consumer durables. See Jorgenson and Stiroh (2000) for details.
3. Output shares include expenditures on consumption, investment, government, and net exports for each IT asset. Note that the use of the price dual to measure technological change assumes competitive markets in IT production. As pointed out by Aizcorbe (2002) and Hobijn (2001), the market for many IT components, notably semiconductors and software, is not perferctly competitive and part of the drop in prices may reflect oligopolistic behavior rather than technological progress. Aizcorbe (2002), however, concludes that declining markup accounts for only about one-tenth of the measure declines in the price of microprocessors in the 1990s, so the use of prices to measure technological progress seems a reasonable approximation.
4. The assumption that output and the capital stock grow at the same rate is similar to a balanced growth path in a standard growth model, but our actual data with many heterogeneous types of capital and labor inputs make this interpretation only an approximation.
5. Reproducible assets include equipment, structures, consumer durable assets, and inventories, but exclude land.
6. These unemployment rates are annual averages for the civilian labor force, 16 years and older from BLS.
7. The details of the population model are given in Bureau of the Census (2000).
8. See McCarthy (2001) for determinants of investment in the late 1990s.
9. The International Technology Roadmap for Semiconductors (ITRS) is 'an assessment of the semiconductor technology requirements'. The ITRS assesses challenges and needs of the industry over the forthcoming 15 years. See International Technology Roadmap for Semiconductors (2000), http://public. itrs.net.

10. Both Roberts (2001) and French (2001) employ the Stock and Watson (1998) method of dealing with the zero bias.
11. See CBO (2001b) for details. Note also that CBO assumes a capital share of 0.3, which is substantially smaller than our estimate of 0.43.
12. Note that our output concept is slightly different, so the estimates are not directly comparable. Nonetheless, the broad predictions are similar.

REFERENCES

Aizcorbe, Ana (2002), 'Why are semiconductor prices falling so fast? Industry estimates and implications for productivity measurement', mimeo, Federal Reserve Board.

Baily, Martin Neal (2001), 'Macroeconomic implications of the New Economy', paper presented at the Federal Reserve Bank of Kansas City's Symposium on Economic Policy for the Information Economy, Jackson Hole, Wyoming, August 30.

Basu, Susanto, John G. Fernald, and Matthew D. Shapiro (2001), 'Productivity growth in the 1990s: technology, utilization, or adjustment'. Carnegie-Rochester Conference Series on Public Policy, **55** (1), 117–65.

Bureau of the Census (2000), 'Methodology and assumptions for the population projections of the United States: 1999 to 2100', www.census.gov/population/www/documentation/twps 0038.html.

Bureau of Labor Statistics (2001), '2000 hours at work survey', http://stat.bls.gov/mfp/mprhwst1.pdf.

Bureau of Labor Statistics (2001a), 'Multifactor productivity trends, 1999', http://stats.bls.gov/pub/news.release/History/prod3.04102001.news.

Bureau of Labor Statistics (2001b), 'Productivity and costs, third quarter 2001', USDL 01-452.

Bureau of Labor Statistics (2002), 'Productivity and costs, fourth quarter and annual averages, 2001', USDL 02-123.

Congressional Budget Office (2001a), *The Budget and Economic Outlook: An Update*, http://www.cbo.gov/ftpdocs/30xx/doc3019/EntireReport.pdf.

Congressional Budget Office (2001b), 'CBO's method for estimating potential output: an update', http://www.cbo.gov/ftpdocs/30xx/doc3020/PotentialOutput.pdf.

Council of Economic Advisors (CEA) (2001), 'Annual report of the Council of Economic Advisors', in the Economic Report of the President, http://a257.g.akamaitech.net/7/257/2422/17Feb2005/700/www.gpoaccess.gov/usbudget/fy02/pdf/2001.erp.pdf.

DeLong, J. Bradford, and Lawrence M. Summers (2001), 'The New Economy: background, questions, speculations', paper presented at the Federal Reserve Bank of Kansas City's Symposium on Economic Policy for the Information Economy, Jackson Hole, Wyoming, August 30.

French, Mark W. (2001), 'Estimating change in trend growth of total factor productivity: Kalman and HP filters versus a Markov-Switching framework', Finance and Economics Discussion Series, Federal Reserve Board, 2001–44.

Gordon, Robert J. (2000), 'Does the "New Economy" measure up to the great inventions of the past?' *Journal of Economic Perspectives*, **14** (4), 49–74.

Hansen, Bruce E. (2001), 'The new econometrics of structural change: dating breaks in US labor productivity', *Journal of Economic Perspectives*, **15** (4), 117–28.

Herman, Shelby W. (2001), 'Fixed assets and consumer durables for 1925–2000', *Survey of Current Business*, **83** (9), pp. 27–38.

Ho, Mun and Dale W. Jorgenson (1999), 'The quality of the US workforce 1948–95', working paper, Department of Economics, Harvard University.

Hobijn, Bart (2001), 'Is equipment price deflation a statistical artifact?', Federal Reserve Bank of New York, staff report #139.

International Technology Roadmap for Semiconductors. *2000 Update,* Austin TX, Sematech Corporation, December 2000.

Jorgenson, Dale W. (1996), 'The embodiment hypothesis', in Dale W. Jorgenson (ed.), *Productivity Volume 1: Postwar US Economic Growth*, Cambridge, MA: MIT Press, pp. 25–50.

Jorgenson, Dale W. (2001), 'Information technology and the US economy', *American Economic Review*, **91** (1), 1–32.

Jorgenson, Dale W. and Zvi Griliches (1996), 'The explanation of productivity change', in Dale W. Jorgenson (ed.), *Productivity Volume 1: Postwar US Economic Growth*, Cambridge, MA: MIT Press, pp. 51–98.

Jorgenson, Dale W. and Kevin J. Stiroh (2000), 'Raising the speed limit: US economic growth in the information age', *Brookings Papers on Economic Activity, 2000* (1), 125–211.

Jorgenson, Dale W., Mun S. Ho and Kevin J. Stiroh (2002), 'Productivity and labor quality in US industries', paper prepared for NBER/CRIW Conference on Measurement of Capital in the New Economy, April.

McCarthy, Jonathan (2001), 'Equipment expenditures since 1995: the boom and the bust', *Current Issues in Economics and Finance*, **7** (9), 1–6.

Oliner, Stephen D. and Daniel E. Sichel (2000), 'The resurgence of growth in the late 1990s: is information technology the story?', *Journal of Economic Perspectives*, **14** (4), 3–22.

Oliner, Stephen D. and Daniel E. Sichel (2002), 'Information technology and productivity: where are we now and where are we going?', *Economic Review*, Federal Reserve Bank of Atlanta.

Roberts, John M. (2001), 'Estimates of the productivity trend using time-varying parameter techniques', *Finance and Economics Discussion Series*, Federal Reserve Board, 2001–8.

Stock, James H. and Mark W. Watson (1998), 'Median unbiased estimation of coefficient variation in a time-varying parameter model', *Journal of the American Statistical Association*, **93** (441), 349–58.

3. 'Baumol's disease' has been cured: IT and multifactor productivity in US services industries

Jack E. Triplett and Barry P. Bosworth

INTRODUCTION

This chapter addresses two major issues from the recent productivity literature. The first question concerns the contributions of information technology (IT) and of multifactor productivity (MFP) to the extraordinary performance of the US economy in the last half of the 1990s. Unemployment fell to historically low levels, without generating the inflationary consequences many economists predicted. Labor productivity (output per hour) emerged from its twenty-year period of stagnation, doubling after 1995 its anemic 1.3 per cent average annual growth between 1973 and 1995 (Figure 3.1). These developments have been characterized as the emergence of a 'new economy,' which economists and others have often associated in some manner with the increased use of IT.

We look for the impact of IT in the portions of the economy where the IT is. The most IT-intensive industries are services industries. We find a substantial contribution of IT to services industries' labor productivity growth, but the impact of IT is not notably greater after 1995 than before. On the other hand, MFP in the services industries grew much more rapidly after 1995.

A second set of research issues concern what is sometimes called 'Baumol's Disease', the belief that the inherent nature of services makes productivity improvements less likely than in the goods-producing sectors of the economy (Baumol 1967). Service industries have long been the sick industries in terms of productivity growth.

We estimate services industry productivity growth for 27 'two-digit' services industries. We find that labor productivity in services industries has grown as fast recently as it has in the rest of the economy, and that the major contributor was an unprecedented acceleration in multifactor productivity. Baumol's Disease has been cured.

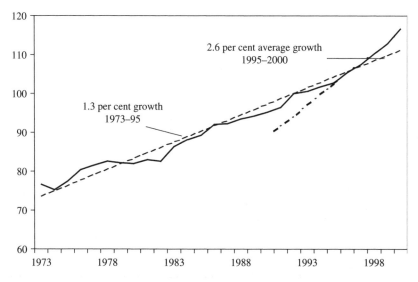

Figure 3.1   Nonfarm labor productivity

PREVIOUS RESEARCH AND COMPARISON WITH OUR STUDY

Labor productivity (LP), as calculated by the US Bureau of Labor Statistics (BLS), equals output growth divided by an index of hours. Figure 3.1 shows the acceleration in labor productivity in the US non-farm business sector after 1995. Non-farm labor productivity in the US grew about 1.3 per cent per year between 1973 and 1995. After 1995, the productivity growth rate rose to 2.6 per cent.[1]

In the now standard productivity–growth accounting framework that originates in the work of Solow (1957), as implemented empirically by Jorgenson and Griliches (1967) and extended by these authors and others, labor productivity can be analysed in terms of contributions of collaborating factors, including capital and intermediate inputs, and of multifactor productivity (MFP). To analyse the effects of IT within this model, capital services, K, are disaggregated into IT capital (K_{IT}) and non-IT capital (K_N), and the two kinds of capital are treated as separate inputs to production. Thus, designating intermediate inputs – combined energy, materials, and purchased services – as M:

$$\Delta \ln LP = w_{K_{IT}} \Delta \ln(K_{IT}/L) + w_{K_N} \Delta \ln(K_N/L)$$
$$+ w_M \Delta \ln(M/L) + \Delta \ln MFP \tag{3.1}$$

Table 3.1   *Alternative estimates of the acceleration of productivity growth,*
post-1995 (Annual rates of change)

Category	Jorgenson and Stiroh	Oliner and Sichel	Council of Economic Advisers	Gordon
Labor productivity	0.9	1.2	1.5	1.4
Cycle	n.a.	n.a.	n.a.	0.4
Trend	0.9	1.2	1.5	1.0
Contribution of:				
Capital per worker	0.3	0.3	0.5	0.4
IT capital	0.3	0.5	n.a.	n.a.
Other capital	0.0	−0.2	n.a.	n.a.
Labor quality	0.0	0.0	0.1	0.0
Multi-factor productivity	0.7	0.8	0.9	0.5
Production of IT	0.3	0.3	0.2	0.3
Other sectors (IT using)	0.4	0.5	0.7	0.2

Note: The post-1995 acceleration is measured relative to a base of 1973–95. The estimates
of Jorgenson–Stiroh extend only through 1998.

Sources: see text.

A number of researchers have calculated the contributions of IT and
MFP to the post-1995 acceleration of labor productivity growth at the
aggregate, economy-wide level (at the aggregate level, of course, the inter-
mediate inputs net out, except for imports, which are normally ignored).
The most prominent examples are Jorgenson and Stiroh (2000, hereafter,
JS), Oliner and Sichel (2000, hereafter, OS), the Council of Economic
Advisers (2000) and Gordon (2000) Results of these studies are summa-
rized in Table 3.1.

Although methodologies and definitions of output differ to an extent
among the four studies, they show broadly similar findings.[2] A major
portion of the acceleration in LP came from increased growth in capital
services per worker (capital deepening). Those studies that separated the
contribution of IT capital from that of non-IT capital (OS and JS) found
that IT capital (K_{IT}) is responsible for all of the acceleration in the capital
contribution to LP. Although non-IT capital (K_N) contributed to growth
after 1995, its contribution to LP growth did not accelerate, it was similar
before and after 1995.

All studies agree that accelerating MFP in the IT-producing industries
also accounts for a substantial amount of the total acceleration. Perhaps
more controversy should have surrounded this finding than has actually

emerged. What the authors term the 'IT-producing' industries are actually the two-digit machinery producing industries in the old US SIC system. Semiconductors are located in the SIC electrical machinery industry, but so are Christmas tree lights. Computers in this old classification system are grouped with drill bits. It is probably true that the electronics portions of the machinery industries account for a major portion of their MFP growth, but the available data do not actually permit us to say that.[3]

In contrast, estimates of trend MFP in IT-using sectors (properly, in these studies all sectors other than the two machinery producing industries) vary substantially. As Table 3.1 shows, those 'IT-using' sectors accounted for 0.2 (the estimate of Gordon) to 0.7 per cent per year (CEA), with JS and OS in the middle, roughly in agreement at about 0.5 per cent. The controversy about the contribution of IT and of MFP in IT-using industries provides part of the motivation for the research reported in this chapter.

Several industry-level studies have focused on the post-1995 productivity acceleration in the US Stiroh (2001) examined 61 industries, using data from the Bureau of Economic Analysis (BEA). An industry is a group of establishments that have similar production functions; approximately, each industry has a different production function from some other industry. Accordingly, one can ask: is there evidence that a large number of production functions shifted after 1995?

Stiroh reported that two-thirds of the 61 industries showed a positive shift in labor productivity after 1995. Moreover, he found that the industries that had positive productivity shifts were more intensive users of IT capital than those industries that did not have upward productivity shifts – that is, the capital deepening effects of *past* IT investments on labor productivity showed up strongly in the industry data. Thus, looking across the range of industries, something changed in the US economy that affected a large number of different production processes, and IT investment had a substantial role in that labor productivity change.

The McKinsey Global Institute (2001, hereafter, MGI) study asked a different question: which industries accounted for the net, economy-wide, US acceleration in labor productivity after 1995? Although a large number of industries showed productivity improvement (the MGI study agreed with Stiroh's findings in this respect), many of those industries have small shares of GDP, so their contribution to the aggregate post-1995 US productivity acceleration is also small. MGI found that six large industries accounted for nearly all of the net, economy-wide labor productivity acceleration, and indeed a large portion of the gross acceleration.[4]

If one is interested in the causes of the *aggregate* productivity acceleration, looking at contributions is the appropriate metric (as it is in the MGI study). On the other hand, if one is asking whether IT makes a widespread impact, then the number of industries is the appropriate metric (as it is in the Stiroh study). These two studies are complementary, not conflicting.

MGI (2001) emphasized the importance of managerial innovations, where IT might be a facilitating tool, as well as competitive pressures that forced widespread imitation of managerial innovations that occurred. The MGI study usefully reminds us that no new capital good is simply inserted into the production environment without a great amount of managerial initiative. This is as true of IT investment as it was of the steam engine two centuries ago. Just because the US now has a large stock of IT does not assure that productivity will continue in the future to grow at its post-1995 rate, contrary to views of some New Economy partisans.

Nordhaus (2002) estimated labor productivity for 67 industries, using the BEA industry database, as did Stiroh. Nordhaus computes value added labor productivity, where the other studies (and ours) compute labor and multifactor productivity per unit of output (in national accounts jargon, 'gross output').

None of the existing studies reports separate information on services industries. We concentrate on services for two reasons. First, we have been leading a Brookings Institution project on the measurement of output and productivity in the services industries, and services industry productivity remains a challenging issue with many unresolved puzzles. An earlier report on this was Triplett and Bosworth (2001).

Second, as we noted in an earlier paper, a very large proportion of US IT investment goes into services industries, and indeed, into the services industries whose output poses the most difficult measurement problems. This association between IT and difficult-to-measure industries was first pointed out by Griliches (1994). As noted earlier, much of the controversy over the sources and interpretation of the post-1995 spurt in productivity growth in the US concerns IT-using industries. Examining services industries provides information on the role of IT-using industries in the US economy.

We explore the impact of IT and of MFP on services industries by estimating equation (3.1) separately for each of 27 two-digit services industries. Although our study uses the same level of two-digit detail employed in the Stiroh and Nordhaus studies (and begins as well from the BEA database they used), our research approach is most nearly similar to that of Jorgenson et al. (2002) who estimated labor productivity, MFP and IT contributions for 39 sectors. Their services sectors are much more aggregated than ours, and their data differ in a number of respects.

THE SERVICES INDUSTRIES PRODUCTIVITY DATABASE

As in our earlier paper, we rely primarily on data from the Bureau of Economic Analysis (BEA) industry output and input program (often referred to as 'GDP by industry'). This program contains industry data at the two-digit level SIC detail for: output (in national accounts language often called 'gross output'), with output price deflators, labor compensation, and purchased intermediate inputs, with intermediate input deflators. Of the industries in the BEA database, we excluded the membership organizations and social services industries because of difficulties surrounding the treatment of capital in nonprofit organizations, in response to a discussion with Michael Harper of BLS, and the 'other services' industry because its data are sometimes combined with the other two. We excluded the holding company industry because it has no natural definition of output under national accounts conventions (interest in national accounts cannot be a payment for a service, nor interest received an income for a producing unit). We combined depository (banks) and nondepository financial institutions because after examining the data it appeared to us that a shift of savings and loan institutions to the depository institutions industry in the 1987 SIC revision was not handled consistently in all the data items; aggregating these two financial industries increases consistency.

The BEA industry data have been improved substantially recently, and the improvements make them more suitable for industry productivity analysis. New at the industry level are measures of industry output and purchased intermediate inputs. Formerly, this BEA database contained only value added, which is conceptually less appropriate for estimating productivity. The improvements are documented in Yuskavage (1996), and in Lum et al. (2000). Certain problems that are apparent only in the improved data are discussed in Yuskavage (2001); we consider these below.

For labor input, we take the BEA series on persons engaged in production, because it is consistent with the other BEA data. BEA makes an adjustment for part-time workers and adds an estimate for self-employed labor.[5] The BEA database contains an estimate of compensation for employees, and an estimate of proprietors' income, but no estimate for the labor earnings of the self-employed.

For capital, the BEA database contains property income. However, we estimate the capital share by industry from the BLS estimate of capital income, which is adjusted to yield consistent estimates of the capital income of the self-employed, as described in the Appendix. Labor compensation is then estimated as a residual in order to get a consistent allocation of capital and labor income for the self-employed.[6] The share of intermediate inputs is based on BEA data.

In our earlier paper, we used BEA data on capital stock at the industry level as a measure of capital input. It is of course well established that the BEA 'wealth' capital stock that is appropriate for national accounts purposes is not the appropriate capital input measure for productivity analysis. Productivity analysis depends on the concept of the 'productive' capital stock, from which one can derive a measure of the capital services the stock renders to production.[7] At the time we did our earlier paper, the theoretically appropriate capital services measures were not available for the services industries we wished to explore.

Now, however, BLS has computed capital service flows by industry that are consistent with the revised BEA capital stock data reported in Hermann and Katz (1997). BLS capital service flow estimates for services industries are presently unpublished and have been provided by Michael Harper. Thus we meld the BLS series on capital services with the BEA data on output and other inputs.

We split our capital share weight to separate IT and non-IT capital shares using BLS capital income proportions. The BLS capital services data also disaggregate IT capital to a lower level than has been available previously. Many studies have investigated the effect of IT, narrowly defined, which means computers and related (peripheral) equipment. Others have broadened the definition of IT to include software. In the US, software investment has in recent years been larger than investment in computer hardware. Yet other studies have further broadened the definition of IT to include communication equipment, leading to the term information and communication technology equipment (or ICT).

An additional category of IT equipment exists in the BLS capital service flows data: 'other IT equipment'. Other IT equipment includes copy machines and so forth, whose use is integral with the management of information. The electronic-driven technological change that characterizes much computer and communications equipment is also evident in such equipment. For this reason, we also work with an IT category that we call ICOT (information, communication and other information technology) equipment.

Capital services for all these definitions of IT (that is, narrow IT, ITC and ICOT) are available in the BLS data for our 27 services industries. We separate capital services (and capital shares) alternatively into IT, ICT and ICOT, and into other (nonIT) capital. We settle, however, on the ICOT definition of IT.

Table 3.2 ranks the ten most IT-intensive US industries, defined here as IT capital's share of value added, according to our three alternative IT

Table 3.2   The ten most IT intensive industries, economy-wide (Alternative definitions of IT capital services as a per cent of value added: 1995–2000 average)

	IT/ VA[a]	Rank	ICT/ VA[b]	Rank	ICOT/ VA[c]	Rank
Depository and nondepository institutions	10.8	1	12.0	3	13.5	3
Wholesale trade	9.4	2	10.6	4	11.5	4
Business services	6.5	3	7.3	7	8.3	10
Insurance carriers	6.0	4	6.7	8	8.3	9
Printing and publishing	5.4	5	6.5	9	8.0	
Industrial machinery and equipment	5.0	6	5.6		6.2	
Transportation services	4.8	7	9.5	5	10.4	7
Pipelines, except natural gas	4.7	8	8.5	6	10.7	5
Electronic and other electric equipment	4.5	9	5.6		6.9	
Telephone and telegraph	4.2	10	32.8	1	33.6	1
Chemicals and allied products	2.9		3.6		10.5	6
Electric, gas, and sanitary services	2.8		5.9	10	9.4	8
Radio and television broadcasting	2.6		24.2	2	25.6	2

Notes:
(a) IT = computer equipment and software
(b) ICT = computer equipment, software, and communications equipment
(c) ICOT = computer equipment, software, communications equipment, and other information technology equipment

Ratios of capital income from the BLS to value added minus indirect business taxes from the BEA GDP by industry file.

definitions. There are some variations in these rankings, and also some surprises. One does not usually think of pipelines, for example, as an IT-intensive industry, nor utilities (electric, gas and sanitation services). But the table makes clear that the most intensive IT industries in the US economy are overwhelmingly services industries. Indeed, for our broadest measures of IT, the chemicals industry is the only non-services industry in the top ten. We also calculated IT intensity as a proportion of total capital services and as a proportion of total cost.[8] Again, the rankings do not remain entirely unchanged, but the overall picture is the one shown in Table 3.2: Most of the highly intensive IT-using industries are in the services sector.

Actually, these IT-intensive industries are in the portions of the services sectors where measurement problems are severe. Of the nine services industries that appear in some column of Table 3.2, five of them have been subjects of Brookings economic measurement workshops.[9]

SERVICES INDUSTRIES: LABOR PRODUCTIVITY GROWTH

We begin by addressing labor productivity, which in our measure is output per person engaged in production. The services industries for which we calculate productivity are given in Table 3.3, where they are ranked according to their rate of labor productivity growth over the 1995–99 interval, and in the Appendix, where they are arranged by SIC code.

First, how did labor productivity in these 27 services industries compare with the performance of the aggregate economy after 1995? We summarize the industry labor productivity changes in Table 3.4.

The unweighted average of the 27 industries exhibits an average labor productivity growth rate, post-1995, of 2.5 per cent per year, nearly identical to the economy-wide average of 2.6 per cent. In the lower panels of Table 3.4, we weight these 27 industries using output, value added, and employment weights.[10] Whatever the weights, the average labor productivity growth rate for the 27 services industries is a bit higher than the unweighted average, and accordingly equal to or a bit higher than the economy-wide average. Labor productivity growth in services is considerably greater after 1995 than before, which means that the services industries are consistent with the economy-wide story (Figure 3.1).

We have reservations about the measure of output in the brokerage industry, which shows a huge labor productivity increase, post-1995 (Table 3.3). BEA measures brokerage output essentially by the number of shares traded. MGI (2001) weighted trades with brokerage fees. Because the greatest growth has been in low-fee trades, this gives a lower rate of output growth than the unweighted trades that make up the national accounts measure of output for this industry.

Accordingly, we excluded brokerage and its 20 per cent per year labor productivity growth and recalculated Table 3.4 – see Table 3.5. The result, predictably, lowers all the average rates of services industry labor productivity, to an unweighted average of 1.9 per cent per year, and an output weighted average of 2.4 per cent per year. Even without brokerage, services industries have weighted average labor productivity growth that is about at the national rate, post-1995.[11]

The right-most columns of Tables 3.4 and 3.5 show that services industries labor productivity, on average, accelerated after 1995, in step with the economy-wide acceleration in labor productivity (Table 3.1). Using the longer 1977–95 interval as the base, labor productivity growth in the 22 industries for which output data extend to 1977 accelerated by 1.4 percentage points (unweighted), post-1995, which about equals the aggregate acceleration reported in Table 3.1. On a weighted basis, acceleration is

Table 3.3 *Labor productivity growth, service industries*

| | 1977–95 | 1987–95 | 1995–2000 | 1995–2000 change | | Output share |
				Relative to 1977–95	Relative to 1987–95	1995–2000 Average
Security, commodity brokers and services	5.4	7.2	20.2	14.8 *	13.0 *	3.1
Telephone and telegraph	6.3	5.8	6.7	0.5 *	0.9 *	4.0
Wholesale trade	2.1	3.3	4.4	2.2 *	1.1 *	9.7
Transportation services		2.3	3.8		1.6 *	0.6
Retail trade	0.7	1.2	3.5	2.8 *	2.3 *	13.8
Pipelines, except natural gas	0.4	0.7	3.5	3.1 *	2.9 *	0.1
Insurance agents, brokers, and services	−2.6	−3.3	3.5	6.1 *	6.8 *	1.2
Business services		3.0	3.5		0.5 *	8.4
Depository and nondepository institutions		3.3	3.1		−0.1	6.8
Miscellaneous repair services	0.9	2.6	2.7	1.8 *	0.1	0.7
Railroad transportation	7.5	6.5	2.6	−4.9	−4.0	0.5
Legal services	−1.2	0.1	2.2	3.0*	2.1 *	2.0
Water transportation		2.3	2.2		−0.1	0.5
Real estate		2.4	2.0		−0.4	16.3
Electric, gas, and sanitary services	−0.3	2.5	1.9	2.2*	−0.5	4.1
Personal services	−0.1	1.7	1.8	1.9*	0.1	1.2
Transportation by air	0.4	−3.4	1.3	0.8 *	4.7 *	1.7
Radio and television broadcasting	0.6	0.2	1.2	0.6 *	1.0 *	1.2
Trucking and warehousing	3.1	4.9	1.0	−2.1	−3.9	3.2
Auto repair, services, and garages	−0.3	1.4	0.9	1.2 *	−0.5	1.7

Table 3.3 (continued)

| | 1977–95 | 1987–95 | 1995–2000 | 1995–2000 change | | Output share 1995–2000 Average |
				Relative to 1977–95	Relative to 1987–95	
Health services	−0.2	−0.5	0.7	1.0 *	1.2 *	9.9
Hotels and other lodging places	0.9	0.7	0.3	−0.6	−0.4	1.5
Local and interurban passenger transit	−2.8	−1.6	−0.2	2.7 *	1.4 *	0.3
Motion pictures	1.3	−0.3	−0.5	−1.7	−0.1	0.8
Amusement and recreation services	0.6	1.9	−0.8	−1.4	−2.7	1.6
Educational services	0.3	0.5	−1.2	−1.5	−1.7	1.5
Insurance carriers	0.2	0.0	−1.4	−1.6	−1.4	3.6

Notes: * Post-1995 accelerating industries.

Labor productivity is output (excluding indirect business taxes) per person engaged in production.

The output share is the sum of industry output (excluding indirect business taxes) from 1995–2000 divided by the sum of all services outputs (excluding IBT) over the same period.

44

Table 3.4   Average service industry labor productivity

	1977–95	1987–95	1995–2000	Acceleration 1995–2000, relative to:	
				1977–95	1987–95
A. Unweighted average					
27 Industries		1.6	2.5	n.a.	0.8
22 Industries	1.0	1.4	2.4	1.4	1.0
B. Weighted by output					
27 Industries		1.9	2.9	n.a.	1.0
22 Industries	1.0	1.6	3.0	2.0	1.4
C. Weighted by value added					
27 Industries		2.0	2.9	n.a.	0.9
22 Industries	1.1	1.6	3.0	1.9	1.4
D. Weighted by employment					
27 Industries		1.5	2.6	n.a.	1.1
22 Industries	0.8	1.3	2.5	1.7	1.2

Notes:
The 27 industries group includes all industries listed in the appendix table and described in the data appendix. The 22 industries group is the subset of the 27 industries group with gross output data available before 1987.

For each paired years t and $t + 1$, the output weight for industry i is the average share for industry i in the two years, where the share in t equals the output (excluding IBT) of industry i in year t over the sum of all services outputs (minus IBT) in year t.

For each paired years t and $t + 1$, the value added weight for industry i is the average share for industry i in the two years, where the share in t equals the value added (excluding IBT) of industry i in year t over total services industries value added (minus IBT) in year t.

For each paired years t and $t + 1$, the employment weight for industry i is the average share for industry i in the two years, where the share in t equals persons engaged in production in industry i in year t over persons engaged in production in all services industries in year t.

The weighted average annual growth rate of labor productivity is

$$100 * \left[\left\{ \prod_t \exp\left(\sum w_{it} * [\ln(Q_{it}/Q_{i,t-1}) - \ln(L_{it}/L_{i,t-1})] \right) \right\}^{1/T-1} \right]$$

where w_{it} is the weight of industry i in year t, Q_{it} is industry i's output in year t, and L_{it} is the number of persons engaged in production in industry i in year t.

greater: 1.7 to 2.0 points. Without brokerage (Table 3.5), the weighted post-1995 acceleration is still around 1.4 points compared with 1977–95, again nearly equal to the aggregate acceleration reported in Table 3.1 (though the unweighted acceleration is lower).[12]

Table 3.4 also implies that some productivity acceleration in services indus-

Table 3.5   Average service industry labor productivity, excluding brokers

	1977–95	1987–95	1995–2000	Acceleration 1995–2000, relative to:	
				1977–95	1987–95
A. Unweighted average					
26 Industries		1.4	1.9		0.4
21 Industries	0.8	1.2	1.6	0.8	0.5
B. Weighted by output					
26 Industries		1.8	2.4		0.6
21 Industries	0.9	1.4	2.3	1.3	0.8
C. Weighted by value added					
26 Industries		1.9	2.4		0.6
21 Industries	1.0	1.5	2.3	1.3	0.9
D. Weighted by employment					
26 Industries		1.5	2.4		1.0
21 Industries	0.8	1.2	2.3	1.5	1.1

Notes:
Excluding security and commodity brokers
Weights constructed as in Table 3.4

tries took place before 1995 (because labor productivity growth is greater for 1987–95 than for 1978–95, for the industries for which a comparison can be made). We do not explore here whether 1995 is the appropriate break point for analysing the recent productivity acceleration in services industries.[13]

Although our results have been anticipated by Sharpe (2000), strong services industry labor productivity growth is nevertheless news, because services sector productivity has long been regarded as the laggard in industry productivity measures. Our earlier paper (Triplett and Bosworth 2001) was consistent with the slow growth in services productivity idea: we calculated implied non-manufacturing productivity numbers and showed that the post-1973 productivity slowdown was greater in the non-goods producing parts of the economy than in manufacturing. Slow growth in the earlier period is also indicated by the entries in Tables 3.4 and 3.5 that show, for example, labor productivity growth rates of 1 per cent or less for the interval extending from 1995 back to 1977.

In the most recent period, services industries, on average, have done about as well as the rest of the economy, both in their average rate of labor productivity improvement and in their post-1995 acceleration. This finding is likely to change a great amount of thinking about productivity and about productivity measurement. The remainder of this chapter provides an initial exploration of the new developments in services industry labor productivity.

LABOR PRODUCTIVITY ACCELERATION: THE DETAILED INDUSTRY RESULTS

Averages always conceal. Not all services industries performed at the sector-wide average. On the other hand, the sector averages are not caused by the performance of one or two large industries, the improvement in labor productivity is broadly based.

For the 22 industries for which output data extend to 1977, 15 (marked with asterisks in the 1977–95 column of Table 3.3) experienced productivity accelerations after 1995, compared with their 1977–95 experiences. Large accelerations (more than 3 percentage points) occurred in security and commodity brokers, in insurance agents (from a negative labor productivity number in the earlier period to 3½ per cent in the latter), in pipelines and in legal services. One industry (local and inter-urban transit) had negative productivity throughout, but its performance improved greatly after 1995 (that is, its productivity growth became less negative), so we put it in the accelerating group. Indeed, local transit has the sixth largest acceleration (2.7 points) in services industries.

In contrast, seven industries experienced decelerations of labor productivity after 1995. Of these, the largest declines were rail transportation (−4.9 percentage points), trucking (−2.1 points), and a group at the bottom of Table 3.3, consisting of insurance carriers, education, amusement and recreation, and motion pictures, whose labor productivity deteriorated by −1.4 to −1.7 percentage points.

For another five of our 27 industries, output data are available only after 1987. Using 1987–95 as the comparison period, the picture is again mixed. Brokerage and insurance agents experienced very large accelerations after 1995. Trucking, railroads, and amusement and recreation show big declines in productivity. Overall, using the 1987–95 period for the comparison, 13 industries experienced accelerations after 1995, five industries recorded changes of only 0.1, positive or negative, so are better recorded as unchanged, and nine were marked by decelerations. Local transit again showed negative productivity in both periods, but its productivity improved greatly after 1995.

These results are similar to those of Stiroh (2001). He reports that in 38 out of 61 industries, labor productivity accelerated post-1995, so it did not accelerate in 23 industries. Stiroh does not separately report goods producing and services producing industries.[14]

CONTRIBUTIONS TO LABOR PRODUCTIVITY GROWTH IN THE SERVICES INDUSTRIES

We next analyse accelerations and decelerations of labor productivity using the growth-accounting model. That is: each industry's change in labor productivity is explained by capital deepening, both from IT capital and from non-IT capital, by increased use of purchased materials and purchased services (intermediate input deepening), and by MFP – see equation (3.1). We perform the contributions to growth exercise for each of the 27 industries.

The full results are displayed in the Appendix. An extract for the ten highest-performing services industries appears in Table 3.6, where they are arrayed by the size of their labor productivity growth, post-1995. The ten industries in Table 3.6 are the services industries that have labor productivity growth that exceeds (more than marginally) the economy-wide labor productivity growth since 1995.

As one might expect, each of those ten top performers experienced productivity acceleration, compared with either of the previous two periods (1987–95 or 1977–95). The sole exception is the financial institutions industry, which has slightly lower productivity growth after 1995.

In these ten industries, labor productivity growth arises from many sources. ICOT capital deepening was a big contributor to labor productivity growth in wholesale trade, transportation services, and banks, and to a lesser extent, in pipelines and business services.

Non-IT capital services were as important as ICOT services in raising labor productivity in pipelines. In other industries, however, non-IT capital was usually less important a contributor to acceleration than was IT capital.

MFP accounted for half or more than half of labor productivity growth in the following industries: brokerage, wholesale trade, retail trade, and pipelines. But MFP was inconsequential in transportation services (which includes travel agents) and business services, even though labor productivity growth was high in those industries. MFP was negative in miscellaneous repair.

The really striking information in Table 3.6 concerns the contribution to labor productivity of increasing use of intermediate inputs. In two industries – brokerage and telephones – purchased materials and services contributed more than 4 per cent annually to labor productivity growth. In transportation services, miscellaneous repair, and business services, purchased intermediate inputs contributed half or more of the growth in labor productivity, and a little bit under half in the insurance agents industry. On the other hand, intermediate inputs made negative contributions in pipelines.

Table 3.6   The top 10 labor productivity growth service industries, 1995–2000

	Contribution to labor productivity (percentage points)					Per cent of contributions			
	LP	MFP	ICOT	Non-ICOT	Intermediate inputs	MFP	ICOT	Non-ICOT	Intermediate inputs
Security, commodity brokers and services	20.2	11.2	0.2	0.1	7.8	58	1	0	41
Telephone and telegraph	6.7	1.6	0.5	0.0	4.5	24	8	0	68
Wholesale trade	4.4	2.4	1.4	0.3	0.2	56	32	7	4
Transportation services	3.8	0.3	1.4	0.0	2.0	9	37	1	53
Retail trade	3.5	3.0	0.3	0.0	0.3	84	8	1	7
Pipelines, except natural gas	3.5	2.9	1.3	1.8	-2.5	83	37	52	-72
Insurance agents, brokers, and services	3.5	1.3	0.2	0.2	1.7	37	6	7	50
Business services	3.5	0.0	1.0	0.0	2.4	0	30	1	69
Depository and nondepository institutions	3.1	0.5	1.5	0.3	0.8	16	49	11	25
Miscellaneous repair services	2.7	-1.2	0.4	0.3	3.3	-45	14	10	121

Notes:

All contributions are average annual growth rates of inputs multiplied by value shares. The contributions do not sum to labor productivity because they are growth rates, which are multiplicative and not additive (e.g. $1.202 = 1.112*1.002*1.001*1.078$). The percentage distribution of the contributions to labor productivity is calculated from the aggregation of log differences over the time period. If i is the input, α is the share, L is the labor input, and Q is output, then the percentage of the contribution of input i to labor productivity growth over time t is:

$$\frac{100*\sum_t \alpha_t [\ln(i_t/i_{t-1}) - \ln(L_t/L_{t-1})]}{\sum_t (\ln Q_t/Q_{t-1}) - \ln(L_t/L_{t-1}))}$$

Increasing purchased intermediate inputs suggests 'contracting out'. These activities contributed mightily to labor productivity growth in some of these services industries, though inconsequentially in others. The result suggests that productivity in the services industries has advanced because of the reallocation of economic activity towards more specialized, and hence more productive, producers. Jorgenson et al. (2002) examine the effects of reallocation among industries on aggregate economic performance.

As we noted earlier, an active research literature on the US labor productivity acceleration (see Table 3.1) has focused mostly on the roles of IT capital and of MFP as contributors to high labor productivity growth. In the services industries, is it MFP or IT capital that accounts for labor productivity growth?

The answer from Table 3.6 is: Sometimes one, sometimes the other, sometimes both (brokers, wholesale trade, pipelines), but seldom neither. Sometimes, however, the *major* factor was neither – the cases where purchased intermediates deepening was a major factor in labor productivity growth include telephone, insurance agents, transportation services, and business services.

Additional insight comes from examining the services industries that had low productivity growth. Table 3.7 arrays the lowest-performing services industries, ranked on their post-1995 labor productivity change.

What accounts for poor industry labor productivity performance? Again, no single factor emerges. The range of causes in Table 3.7 is perhaps best illustrated by two industries near the middle of the list – local transit and hotels. Local transit has excellent MFP performance (at 2.2 per cent annually, it is the best of this low-performing group and among the leaders in the group of 27 industries). But this industry has reduced its use of cooperating factors so much that its labor productivity has turned negative. Hotels, on the other hand, have increased their use of cooperating inputs, including ICOT; but that has done them little good, because their MFP has declined greatly. The performance of the hotel industry, including the failure of its investment in IT to raise labor productivity, is analysed in MGI (2001).

In contrast to the high productivity growth services industries, contracting out in the form of intermediate input deepening is not prominent in the group of industries included in Table 3.7, radio and TV excepted. Several industries substituted internal production against intermediate inputs, which predictably lowered labor productivity. The ICOT contributions are also mostly low, again with the exception of radio and TV.

One should also note the substantial break between the group of industries at the top of Table 3.7, all of which have labor productivity growing at positive rates, and the group of negative productivity industries at the

Table 3.7 The bottom 10 labor productivity growth service industries, 1995–2000

	Contributions to labor productivity (percentage points)					Per cent of contributions			
	LP	MFP	ICOT	Non-ICOT	Intermediate inputs	MFP	ICOT	Non-ICOT	Intermediate inputs
Radio and television broadcasting	1.2	−5.5	2.2	0.9	3.9	−467	180	74	313
Trucking and warehousing	1.0	0.3	0.1	0.2	0.5	27	10	17	47
Auto repair, services, and garages	0.9	1.0	0.1	−0.1	−0.1	106	12	−9	−10
Health services	0.7	−0.4	0.2	0.1	0.8	−53	31	11	110
Hotels and other lodging places	0.3	−1.1	0.2	0.1	1.2	−436	60	34	443
Local and interurban passenger transit	−0.2	2.2	0.0	0.0	−2.3	1215	22	−22	−1315
Motion pictures	−0.5	0.3	0.2	0.2	−1.2	60	48	50	−258
Amusement and recreation services	−0.8	0.0	0.1	0.0	−0.9	−3	6	0	−103
Educational services	−1.2	−0.8	0.0	0.0	−0.4	−68	2	0	−34
Insurance carriers	−1.4	−1.0	0.6	0.2	−1.2	−70	40	15	−85

Notes: Definitions are the same as in Table 3.6.

When labor productivity growth is negative, the signs of the percentage contributions are multiplied by −1, so a positive percentage corresponds to a positive contribution labor productivity. Thus, in these cases, the percents sum to −100.

bottom of the table. Although all of these ten industries are below the national average labor productivity growth of 2.6 per cent for the post-1995 period, growth rates for some industries at the upper end of Table 3.7 would have looked quite respectable in the recent past. Negative productivity industries in the US and Canada are analysed in Sharpe et al. (2002).

OVERALL: CONTRIBUTIONS OF ICOT, INTERMEDIATE INPUTS, AND MFP

We noted at the beginning of this section that much recent research on the US productivity acceleration has examined contributions of IT and of MFP. We have emphasized the diversity in performance in services industries, and especially how diverse are these industries with respect to the factors that have raised their productivity growth. We provide some summary measures in Tables 3.8 and 3.9.

Table 3.8 shows average contributions to labor productivity acceleration across the 22 industries for which data exist since 1977. To economize on space and calculations, we show contributions to the unweighted average labor productivity acceleration. Note that, as shown in Tables 3.4 and 3.5, weighted averages uniformly give higher post-1995 labor productivity accelerations than the unweighted averages we present in Table 3.8. We also calculate contributions excluding the brokerage industry, for the reasons given above.

MFP is the major contributor to acceleration – well over half, whether or not brokerage is excluded. Naturally, both the acceleration itself and the MFP contribution to the acceleration are lower when brokerage is excluded, as already indicated earlier in the chapter.

Increased use of IT capital services also plays a major role in boosting labor productivity, and IT provides a larger relative portion of the acceleration when brokerage is excluded. The reason that IT does not play a larger role in the analysis of post-1995 labor productivity acceleration is that its contribution to labor productivity in these services industries was already prominent before 1995. Investment in IT is not new, and it has long been known that much IT investment took place in services (Griliches 1992; Triplett and Bosworth 2001). MGI (2001) contains a compatible result in its detailed examinations of a small number of services industries: It was often not new IT, or new IT investment, that was associated with rapid productivity change, but instead IT capital technology that had been around for a decade or two. Our analysis supports this part of the MGI conclusion: IT capital was a major contributor to LP growth post-1995, but its effects are visible well before.

Table 3.8   *Contributions to labor productivity acceleration (1995–2000 relative to 1977–95)*

	Labor productivity acceleration	Contribution to labor productivity acceleration			
		MFP	IT capital	Non-IT capital	Intermediate inputs
Unweighted average, 22 service industries	1.4	0.9	0.2	0.1	0.2
Unweighted average, 21 service industries (excluding brokers)	0.8	0.5	0.2	0.1	0.0
Unweighted average, 15 accelerating industries	3.0	1.7	0.3	0.1	0.9
Unweighted average, (excluding brokers) 14 accelerating industries	2.2	1.1	0.3	0.2	0.7

Notes:
For each industry, i, acceleration is calculated as: accel $i = \text{AAGR}_{i,\,95\text{-}00} - \text{AAGR}_{i,\,77\text{-}95}$
Group accelerations are the average of each industry's acceleration in the group, that is: Σ_i accel i/n, i.e. the labor productivity acceleration is the difference in the average annual labor productivity growth rates in the two time periods, or

$$\frac{100}{n} * \sum_i \left\{ \left[\prod_t \exp\left[\ln(Q_{it}/Q_{i,t-1}) - \ln(L_{it}/L_{i,t-1}) \right] \right]^{1/T-1} \right\}$$

where for the 1995–2000 time period, $t = 1996, 97, \ldots 2000$ and $T = 5$. Likewise, for the 1977–95 period, t $=1978, 1979, \ldots 1995$ and $T = 18$.

We also display in Table 3.9 contributions to labor productivity acceleration for those 13 industries that actually experienced acceleration. For those industries, the average labor productivity acceleration is of course considerably larger than for the whole group of 22. Again, MFP is the main contributor to acceleration, accounting for well over half. All the other factors also play a role, but IT actually follows intermediate deepening in the size of its contribution. As before, this is not because IT does not contribute to growth, but because its contribution to growth was already evident in the services industry data before 1995.

In Table 3.9, we perform the same calculations for the full set of 27 industries, but we are constrained by data availability to analysing the post-1995 acceleration relative to the shorter 1987–95 base. Though the unweighted average acceleration is lower for the shorter period, the results of the contributions exercise are very similar: Accelerating MFP is the major engine

Table 3.9   *Contributions to labor productivity acceleration (1995–2000 relative to 1987–95)*

	Labor productivity acceleration	Contribution to labor productivity acceleration			
		MFP	IT capital	Non-IT capital	Intermediate inputs
Unweighted average, 27 service industries	0.9	0.6	0.2	0.1	−0.1
Unweighted average, all 26 service industries (excluding brokers)	0.4	0.3	0.2	0.1	−0.2
Unweighted average, 13 accelerating industries	3.0	1.6	0.4	0.2	0.8
Unweighted average, 12 accelerating industries (excluding brokers)	2.2	1.0	0.4	0.3	0.5

Note: Accelerations calculated as in Table 3.8, except for substituting 1987 for 1977 where relevant

of labor productivity acceleration, with increased use of IT capital services trailing increased use of intermediates as a tool for accelerating labor productivity growth. Excluding the brokerage industry has the same effects as for the previous analysis that used the longer 1977–95 base.

Average MFP growth for services industries is shown in Table 3.10. MFP shows a marked acceleration after 1995 in services industries, whether judged by unweighted or weighted averages. On a weighted basis (all weighting systems give similar results), MFP was close to zero in the earliest period (1977–95), picked up a bit for the 1987–95 interval (0.4 per cent per year for the broadest group of industries), and exceeds 1 per cent per year after 1995 (on a weighted basis). Excluding brokerage (not shown) gives similar results.

MFP growth is thus a major contributor to services industry labor productivity growth and to post-1995 acceleration. MFP is also the major source of the post-1995 acceleration of LP in services industries.

CAVEATS AND QUESTIONS

In the analysis for this chapter, we have 'pushed' the industry data very far. Even though the production function paradigm applies best to industry

Table 3.10   *Average service industry multifactor productivity*

	1977–95	1987–95	1995–2000
A. Unweighted MFP average			
27 Industries		0.1	0.7
22 Industries	−0.1	0.0	0.8
B. MFP weighted by output			
27 Industries		0.4	1.2
22 Industries	0.1	0.2	1.4
C. MFP weighted by value added			
27 Industries		0.4	1.2
22 Industries	0.1	0.2	1.4
D. MFP weighted by employment			
27 Industries		0.1	1.2
22 Industries	−0.1	0.1	1.4

Note: Industry groups and weights constructed as in Table 3.4

data, concern has long been expressed that the consistency of US industry-level data creates formidable problems for carrying out productivity analysis at the detailed level – see Baily and Gordon (1988), and Gordon (2001). Our data are at the 'subsector' level (two-digits of the old SIC system), rather than at the 'industry' level (four-digit SIC). Nevertheless, the concern has validity.

We should first note, however, that the concern applies to any use of the industry data, it does not apply solely to our estimation of contributions to labor productivity. It also applies, for example, to attempts to group industries into 'IT-intensive' and 'non-intensive' industries, a popular approach to analysing the impact of IT. If the industry data do not prove consistent, then analysing the industry data grouped in some way or other suffers from the same data deficiencies.

Earlier, we noted that the BLS industry labor productivity program prepares estimates that differ from ours in some aspects of methodology. BLS output measures are different from those of BEA, they compute output per labor hour instead of output per worker (as we do), and other differences occur in certain industries. We use the BEA database mainly because it provides comprehensive coverage of industries. The BLS data are available only for selected industries, so it is impossible to get from them an understanding of economy-wide or sectoral labor productivity trends.

Table 3.11 compares our labor productivity estimates with an alternative published BLS industry labor productivity series that presents output per

Table 3.11 *Comparison of authors' calculations and BLS industry labor productivity data*

SIC number	Industry name	Average annual growth rates, 1995–2000	
		Authors' calculations	BLS
40	Railroad transportation	2.6	
4011	Railroad transportation		3.8
42	Trucking and warehousing	1.0	
4213	Trucking, except local		0.9
45	Transportation by air	1.3	
4512,13,22(PTS)	Air transportation		0.4
481, 482, 489	Telephone and telegraph	6.7	
481	Telephone communications		6.3
483–484	Radio and television broadcasting (a)	1.2	1.0
49	Electric, gas, and sanitary services	1.9	
491–493	Electric and gas utilities (a)		9.2
52–59	Retail trade (a)	3.5	4.0
60–61	Depository and nondepository institutions	3.1	
602	Commercial banks		2.6
70	Hotels and other lodging places	0.3	
701	Hotels and motels		0.8
72	Personal services	1.8	1.7
75	Auto repair, services, and garages	0.9	
753	Automotive repair shops		0.9
78	Motion pictures	−0.5	
783	Motion picture theaters		1.6

Notes:
BLS labor productivity is output per employee

(a) BLS average annual labor productivity growth is the unweighted average of more detailed industry components. The BLS retail trade labor productivity growth is the average growth rate of all two-digit SIC retail trade industries.

worker, so it is conceptually closer to our Table 3.3. As Table 3.11 suggests, in many cases the BLS data are published only for selected three- or four-digit industries that account for only a fraction of the two-digit industries to which they belong. After allowing for the differences in coverage, the correspondence is reasonably close in some cases (trucking, telephone, radio-TV, and personal services), less so in others. Many of these differences in productivity growth rates are no doubt due to coverage differences. However, methodological and date inconsistencies do exist between BEA and BLS databases, and in some cases affect the conclusions. Gordon (2001) emphasizes these inconsistencies. Bosworth (2001) contains a detailed discussion of inconsistencies in the data for transportation industries.

Some of the major inconsistencies of industry data have been discussed quite openly by the statistical agencies themselves. Yuskavage (2001) has provided an important analysis. One can estimate industry value-added two ways. Industry purchases of intermediate inputs can be subtracted from industry gross output, leaving value-added as residual. Then, industry labor compensation (usually considered the most accurately estimated input) can be subtracted from value-added, leaving capital income as a residual. Alternatively, value-added can be estimated directly from labor compensation and information on capital income; then intermediate input purchases are obtained residually by subtracting value-added from gross output. These two methods do not yield consistent results. Inaccuracy in the first arises because intermediate input purchases collected in the economic censuses and other Census Bureau surveys are less accurate than the output information collected from the same surveys. The limitation in the second approach is the potential inaccuracy of measuring the capital input. As noted in the Appendix, self-employed income creates another inconsistency, and our use of BLS capital shares (in order to use the BLS adjustment for self-employment income) creates an inconsistency with BEA capital and labor shares.

If labor input and gross output are measured well (and this includes the deflators for output), then labor productivity would be measured accurately, regardless of inaccuracy in the other inputs. This is the reason why many analyses at the industry level have considered only LP. If any of the other inputs were measured inaccurately, this creates mismeasurement in MFP. To the extent that purchased services are inaccurately measured in Census Bureau collections, for example, the result is mismeasured MFP, so input measurement problems inherently limit the accuracy of our industry MFP measures.

In addition, the productivity growth model imposes by assumption the condition that capital earns its marginal product. If that assumption is incorrect, then capital's contribution to production is misstated and MFP is mismeasured. These errors would also bias our estimates of capital's contribution to labor productivity growth.

Moreover, the allocations of capital services across industries may be problematic. As described earlier, we use detailed IT capital services data for our 27 industries, which are available for each year of our study. However, the basic information for allocating IT capital by industry is the

BEA capital flow table; the latest year for which this is available is 1992 (Bonds and Aylor 1998). If IT capital flowed to different industries in the last half of the 1990s, our IT intensity and IT capital services variables would be mismeasured. Even for 1992, the basis for allocating high-tech capital across using industries is weak: Triplett and Gunter (2001), for example, point to the puzzling presence of medical scanners in agriculture and business services industries in the BEA capital flow table (apparently an artifact of balancing input–output tables), and similar anomalies may be present for IT capital. If so, IT capital is inaccurately allocated to using industries in our data, which creates consequent errors in the contribution of IT capital services and of MFP.

Michael Harper of BLS has suggested to us that the allocation of capital across non-profit organizations may create inconsistencies in some of the industries. We have excluded the membership organizations industry from our analysis for this reason, but some other industries may also be affected by this data problem.

Then, there is the age-old problem of deflators, not only for output but also for purchased inputs. How does one measure the price, and therefore the output, of a service industry? Or of the purchased services that are a growing part of intermediate inputs? These are not idle questions. The difficulties, both conceptual and practical, are many, and have long been considered thorny problems (see the volumes on these topics edited by Griliches (1992) and Fuchs (1969)). Indeed, McGuckin and Stiroh (2001) contend that increasing mismeasurement of output in the US economy amounts to half a percentage point in economic growth.[15] An assessment of output measurement in some of the services industries that are IT-intensive is Triplett and Bosworth (2001). See also the various papers and workshop agendas on the website for the Brookings Program on Economic Measurement (http://www.brook.edu/es/research/projects/productivity/productivity.htm), as well as the discussions of services measurement issues in the Eurostat handbook on price and output measures in national accounts (Eurostat 2001).

Against all this, we feel that the US statistical system has recently made substantial improvements to industry-level data. These improvements have not widely been noticed. No doubt measurement problems remain, but the situation today is far better than it was when Baily and Gordon (1988) reviewed consistency of the industry data for productivity analysis.

First, the BEA GDP by industry accounts now include a full accounting for inputs and outputs. That full accounting imposes the discipline of a check that was not present when the accounts focused only on value-added. Put another way, when only an estimate of value-added was available at the industry level, the problems discussed by Yuskavage (2001) were simply unknown to researchers, unless they dug deeply beneath the veneer of the published statistics.

Second, the Census Bureau, in the 1997 economic censuses, collected more penetrating information on purchased services than had been the case in earlier economic statistics for the United States. Information on purchased inputs at the industry level is still a problem for productivity analysis, but the state of the statistics is much improved over earlier years.

Third, the Bureau of Labor Statistics, in its Producer Price Index (PPI) program, has moved aggressively in the 1990s into constructing output prices for services industries. A number of these initiatives have been discussed in the series of Brookings workshops on economic measurement. All the problems of services sector deflation have not been solved, and for some services industries the difficulty of specifying the concept of output limits the validity of deflators. But the remaining problems should not obscure the progress. Tremendous improvement has occurred since the discussion of measurement problems in the services industries in Griliches (1994).

Does improved measurement account for the acceleration in service industry productivity? That is, is the productivity surge in services in some sense a statistical illusion? Perhaps the cure for Baumol's disease was found years ago, only the statistics didn't record it, or perhaps the services industries were never sick, it was just, as Griliches suggested, that the measuring thermometer was wrong.

A full answer to that question is beyond the scope of this chapter. For one accelerating industry, however, the answer is clearly 'Yes': The acceleration in medical care labor productivity (-0.5 before 1995, $+0.7$ per cent after, with MFP 'accelerating' from -1.5 to -0.4) is undoubtedly the effect of the new BLS medical care PPI industry price indexes that began in 1992 and replaced the old CPI-based medical care deflators in national accounts (see Berndt et al. 2001). The PPI indexes rose more slowly than the CPI indexes they replaced (an overlap period confirms that it was methodology, not health care cost containment, that accounts for the difference).

Medical care productivity was understated by a large amount before 1992. Triplett (1999) calculates an account for one portion of medical care (mental health care services), using a combination of the difference between the new PPI and the old CPI mental health care components, and new price indexes for depression from Berndt et al. (2001). The 'backcasted' result increased the estimated rate of growth of mental health care services, which is -1.4 per cent annually, calculated from available government data, to $+5.0$ per cent for the 1990–95 period. If the results for mental health carried over to the entire medical care sector, they imply a proportionate increase in medical care labor productivity (which we estimate as -0.5 per cent annually for 1987–95, from Table 3.3) and MFP (-1.5 per cent annually for the same 1987–95 period). Accordingly, the improvements in PPI price indexes account for the improved measured productivity in medical care, but medical care productivity is probably still understated substantially. Negative MFP for the health care industry (−0.4, see industry 80 in the Appendix) may be one indication.

CONCLUSION

In their labor productivity and MFP performance, services industries have long appeared unhealthy, especially so since the great productivity slowdown after 1973. With some exceptions, they appear lively and rejuvenated today.

We find that post-1995 services industries labor productivity growth has proceeded at about the economy-wide rate. Moreover, services industries have experienced an acceleration of labor productivity after 1995 that is comparable with the aggregate acceleration that has received so much attention. These changes are broadly based, they are not just the effects on the average of a small number of large industries. For example, of the 22 industries for which data exist for the whole period of our study, 13 experienced accelerating LP after 1995.

With respect to the sources of labor productivity improvement in services industries, growth in MFP, IT capital deepening, and increased use of intermediate inputs (especially in the fastest-growth services industries) all played a role. With respect to the post-1995 acceleration of labor productivity, however, MFP is the dominant factor in the acceleration, because IT capital deepening was as prominent a source of labor productivity growth before 1995 as after.

Finally, Griliches (1992, 1994) suggested that measurement difficulties, particularly conceptual problems in defining and measuring output and price deflators, might have made these industries' productivity performance in the past seem less robust than it actually was. In our assessment, the US industry database has been much improved in the last decade, and the improved database makes us more confident in industry productivity estimates, even though much measurement work remains to be done to improve our understanding of productivity trends in services industries.

NOTES

1. These data do not incorporate the GDP revisions announced in the summer of 2002.
2. Jorgenson and Stiroh use a broad measure of output that includes housing and services of consumer durables. Oliner and Sichel use the output concept that corresponds to GDP and the published BLS productivity measures. The Council of Economic Advisers

(2000) uses an income-side measure of output growth that shows even greater acceleration than the conventional measures of nonfarm business output (from the national accounts) that are used in the other studies. Gordon (2000) bases his estimates on quarterly measures and he obtains a lower estimate of the acceleration in labor productivity and MFP because he attempts to adjust separately for cyclical influences, a factor which is not explicitly dealt with by the other studies. Jorgenson et al. (2002) have updated the findings in Jorgenson and Stiroh (2000). We have not incorporated their updated results into Table 3.1.

3. The new NAICS industry classification system separates out electronics producing industries and groups them together, which is exactly what economic analysis requires.

4. The net acceleration (taking account of positive, accelerating industries and also of industries that experienced decelerating productivity) was 1.4 index points, measured relative to the 1987–95 period. This estimate is comparable with those of Table 3.2, though constructed differently. The gross acceleration (considering only the industries that experienced productivity accelerations) was 1.8 index points.

5. The BLS labor productivity and multi-factor productivity programs estimate worker hours by industry, not just employment, and in principle, hours are a better measure of labor input. BLS also adjusts for labor quality, which is missing from our labor input data. Jorgenson et al. (2002) also estimate quality-adjusted labor hours.

6. Imputing capital returns and labor compensation to the self-employed from data on employed and employers in the same industry results in a total that exceeds proprietors' income. Thus, BLS constrains capital and labor income of the self-employed so that it combines to reported proprietors' income.

7. The development of 'productive stock' concepts for production analysis stems from the work of Jorgenson (1963), and the empirical implementation in Jorgenson and Griliches (1967). Reviews of national accounts and productivity concepts for capital are contained in Hulten (1990), Triplett (1996), Schreyer (2001), and also the OECD manual on capital (2001).

8. There is no natural way to define 'IT intensive'. The ratio of IT to output will be greater, other things equal, in more capital-intensive industries. The ratio of IT to total capital may be misleading for industries that use little capital. Our estimation (below) uses the share of IT in total costs because that is appropriate for estimating productivity contributions. Stiroh (2001) presents data on the ratio of IT to labor, which is another measure of IT intensity that is of interest for some purposes.

9. http://www.brook.edu/dybdocroot/es/research/projects/productivity/productivity.htm.

10. The correct aggregation of industry productivity uses Domar (1961) weights, which are the ratio of industry i's output to final output, in our case aggregate services sector output. We lack a measure of services industries output that excludes intra-industry transactions, and for this reason do not use Domar weights in Table 3.4.

11. We also performed the calculations excluding both brokerage and insurance carriers (the industry with the largest negative productivity growth). The results were not much changed, compared with Table 3.4.

12. For the full set of 27 industries, the labor productivity acceleration can only be computed relative to 1987–95. At 0.9 percentage points, unweighted (i.e., 2.5 − 1.6), it is a little below the economy-wide acceleration of 1.3 percentage points, but the periods over which acceleration is calculated are different. In all cases, excluding brokerage lowers the average acceleration. Note that post-1995 labor productivity growth is not appreciably different for the full set of 27 industries and the smaller set of 22 (Table 3.4).

13. Stiroh (2001) performed statistical tests on data for 61 industries, and concluded that 1995 was the appropriate break point for annual data. Parham (2002), on the other hand, contends that productivity acceleration should be measured with respect to productivity peaks. Productivity peaks analysis gives lower acceleration in the US than does use of 1995 as a break point, and 1973–95 or 1987–95 as a comparison interval.

14. However, he notes that the security and commodity brokers industry has a very high productivity growth rate, and comments that strong productivity growth in this industry may be an artifact of the way that output is measured. We agree with his assessment.

He also included holding and investment companies in this remark, an industry we excluded on the basis that its output is particularly ill-defined. Had we included it, it would have been in the accelerating group. This underscores that errors in measuring output do not always bias downward output growth and productivity. Corrado and Slifman (1999), in a widely noticed paper, adjusted negative industry productivity rates upward on the grounds that negative productivity indicated measurement errors, especially when, as they emphasized, profits were positive. They are likely to be right, at least in some cases. But chopping off one tail of a distribution on the grounds that outliers are signs of measurement errors cannot produce a better estimate of the mean unless one is certain that measurement errors are absent elsewhere in the distribution.

15. However, they introduce the implicit assumption that improving the measurement of output will raise output growth rates. This has sometimes been the case, empirically. But we are not convinced that services sector output was measured better in the US in the 1950s and 1960s, as their assumption must imply if it is applied to the 1973–95 era.

REFERENCES

Baily, Martin N. and Robert Gordon (1988), 'The productivity slowdown, measurement issues, and the explosion of computer power', *Brookings Papers on Economic Activity*, **19** (2), 347–420.

Baumol, William J. (1967), 'Macroeconomics of unbalanced growth: The anatomy of urban crises', *American Economic Review*, **57** (3), 415–26.

Berndt, Ernst, David Cutler, Richard Frank, Zvi Griliches, Joseph Newhouse and Jack Triplett (2000), 'Medical care prices and output', in Anthony J. Cutler and Joseph P. Newhouse (eds), *Handbook of Health Economics* v. 1A, Amsterdam: Elsevier, pp. 119–80.

Berndt, Ernst R., Susan H. Busch and Richard G. Frank (2001), 'Treatment price indexes for acute phase major depression', in David Cutler and Ernst R. Berndt (eds), *Medical Care Output and Productivity*, Chicago: University of Chicago Press, pp. 463–505.

Bonds, Belinda and Tim Aylor (1998), 'Investment in new structures and equipment by type', *Survey of Current Business*, **78** (12), 26–51.

Bosworth, Barry P. (2001), 'Overview: data for studying transportation productivity', paper presented at the Brookings Workshop on Transportation Output and Productivity, 4 May 2001. Available at http://www.brook.edu/dybdocroot/es/research/projects/productivity/workshops/20010504.htm.

Corrado, Carol and Slifman, Lawrence (1999), 'Decomposition of productivity and unit costs', *American Economic Review Papers and Proceedings*, **89** (2), 328–32.

Council of Economic Advisers (2000), *The Annual Report of the Council of Economic Advisers*, Washington, DC: US Government Printing Office.

Domar, Evsey D. (1961), 'On the measurement of technological change', *Economic Journal*, **71**, 709–29.

Eurostat (2001), *Handbook on Price and Volume Measures in National Accounts*, Luxembourg: Office for Official Publications of the European Communities.

Fuchs, Victor R. (ed.) (1969), *Production and Productivity in the Service Industries*, *National Bureau of Economic Research Studies in Income and Wealth*, vol. 34, New York: Columbia University Press.

Gordon, Robert (2000), 'Does the "New Economy" measure up to the great inventions of the past?', *Journal of Economic Perspectives*, **14** (4), 49–74.

Gordon, Robert (2001), 'Did the productivity revival spill over from manufacturing to services? Conflicting evidence from four data sources', paper presented at NBER Summer Institute, July, 2001.

Griliches, Zvi (ed.) (1992), *Output Measurement in the Service Sectors, National Bureau of Economic Research, Studies in Income and Wealth*, vol. 56. Chicago: University of Chicago Press.

Griliches, Zvi (1994), 'Productivity, R&D, and the data constraint', *American Economic Review*, **84** (1), 1–23.

Herman, Shelby W. and Arnold J. Katz (1997), 'Improved estimates of fixed reproducible tangible wealth, 1929–95', *Survey of Current Business*, **77** (5), 69–92.

Hulten, Charles R. (1990), 'The measurement of capital', in Ernst R. Berndt and Jack E. Triplett (eds), *Fifty Years of Economic Measurement: The Jubilee Conference on Research in Income and Wealth*, Studies in Income and Wealth 54, Chicago: University of Chicago Press for the National Bureau of Economic Research, pp. 119–52.

Jorgenson, Dale W. (1963), 'Capital theory and investment behavior', *American Economic Review*, **53** (2), 247–59.

Jorgenson, Dale W. and Zvi Griliches (1967), 'The explanation of productivity change', *Review of Economic Studies*, **34** (3), no. 99, pp. 249–80.

Jorgenson, Dale W. and Kevin J. Stiroh (2000), 'Raising the speed limit: US economic growth in the information age', Brookings Papers on Economic Activity, 1:2000, pp. 125–211.

Jorgenson, Dale W., Mun S. Ho and Kevin J. Stiroh (2002), 'Information technology, education, and the sources of economic growth across US industries', paper presented at the Texas A&M New Economy Conference, April.

Lum, Sherlene K.S., Brian C. Moyer and Robert E. Yuskavage (2000), 'Improved estimates of gross product by industry for 1947–98', in Bureau of Economic Analysis, *Survey of Current Business*, June, pp. 24–54.

McGuckin, Robert and Kevin Stiroh (2001), 'Do computers make output harder to measure?' *Journal of Technology Transfer*, **26**, 295–321.

McKinsey Global Institute (MGI) (2001), 'United States productivity growth 1995–2000', Washington, DC: McKinsey Global Institute, http://www.mckinsey.com/mgi/reports/pdfs/productivity/usprod.pdf.

Nordhaus, William D. (2002), 'Productivity growth and the New Economy', *Brookings Papers on Economic Activity*, 2002(2).

Organisation for Economic Co-operation and Development (OECD) (2001), *Measuring Capital: A Manual on the Measurement of Capital Stocks, the Consumption of Fixed Capital, and Capital Services*. Available at http://www.oecd.org/EN/document/0,EN-document-0-nodirectorate-no-15–6786–0,00.html.

Oliner, Stephen D. and Daniel E. Sichel (2000), 'The resurgence of growth in the late 1990s: Is information technology the story?' *Journal of Economic Perspectives*, **14**, 3–22.

Parham, Dean (2002), 'Productivity growth in Australia: Are we enjoying a miracle?', paper presented at the Melbourne Institute/*The Australian* conference, Towards Opportunity and Prosperity, 4–5 April.

Schreyer, Paul (2001), 'OECD Manual – Measuring Productivity: Measurement of Aggregate and Industry-Level Productivity Growth', manuscript, OECD: Paris, March.

Sharpe, Andrew (2000), 'The productivity renaissance in the US service sector', *International Productivity Monitor*, **1**, Fall, 6–8.

Sharpe, Andrew, Someshwar Rao and Jianmin Tang (2002), 'Perspectives on negative productivity growth in US services industries', paper presented at the Brookings Workshop on Services Industry Productivity: New Estimates and New Problems, 17 May. Available at http://www.brook.edu/dybdocroot/es/research/projects/productivity/ workshops/20020517.htm.

Solow, Robert M. (1957), 'Technical change and the aggregate production function', *Review of Economics and Statistics*, **39** (3), 312–20.

Stiroh, Kevin (2001), 'Information technology and US productivity revival: What does the industry data say?' *American Economic Review*, **92** (5), 1559–76.

Triplett, Jack E. (1996), 'Depreciation in production analysis and in income and wealth accounts: Resolution of an old debate', *Economic Inquiry*, **34** (1), 93–115.

Triplett, Jack E. (1999), 'A real expenditure account for mental health care services, 1972–95', paper presented at the Brooking Workshop on Measuring Health Care. December. Available at http://www.brook.edu/dybdocroot/es/research/projects/productivity/workshops/19991217.htm.

Triplett, Jack E. and Barry P. Bosworth (2001), 'Productivity in the services sector', in Daniel M. Stern (ed.), *Services in the International Economy*, Ann Arbor: University of Michigan Press, pp. 23–52.

Triplett, Jack E. and David Gunter (2001), 'Medical equipment', paper presented at the Brookings Workshop on Economic Measurement: The Adequacy of Data for Analyzing and Forecasting the High-Tech Sector, 12 October. Available at http://www.brook.edu/dybdocroot/es/research/projects/productivity/workshops/20011012.htm.

Yuskavage, Robert E. (1996), 'Improved estimates of gross product by industry, 1959–94', *Survey of Current Business*, **76** (8), pp. 133–55.

Yuskavage, Robert E. (2001), 'Issues in the measure of transportation output: the perspective of the BEA industry accounts', paper presented at the Brooking Workshop on Transportation Output and Productivity, 4 May. Available at http://www.brook.edu/dybdocroot/es/research/projects/productivity/workshops/20010504.htm.

DATA APPENDIX

The data are obtained from two sources; the BEA GDP by industry file and unpublished capital input and capital services data from the BLS. Value added in the GDP by industry file is the sum of the compensation of employees, indirect business taxes, and property-type income. Gross output, which is value-added plus intermediate inputs, is not available before 1977, and for some industries, is not available before 1987.

The real value of gross output is obtained from the BEA industry file. As measures of the growth in the real value of the inputs, we use persons engaged in production for labor, the quantity index for intermediate inputs from BEA for intermediate inputs, and the real capital input index from BLS for capital.

The income shares used in the growth accounting calculations are all expressed as shares of output minus indirect business taxes (GDP at factor cost). Capital share and its distribution among different types of capital is obtained from the BLS data set, and intermediate inputs are from BEA. The labor compensation share of output is calculated as a residual for reasons discussed below.

The BEA compensation data does not include the labor earnings of the self-employed, which are all assigned to capital. The BLS uses an elaborate algorithm to adjust their capital and labor income shares for the self-employed. Thus, we used their estimates of capital income and obtained labor compensation by subtracting the capital income from GDP at factor cost. This does introduce one source of inconsistency in the current data set. Because the BLS methodology includes property and motor vehicle taxes as part of capital income, our measure, which excludes all indirect business taxes, understates the amount of labor income. This problem will be corrected in a future revision.

Our broad definition of service industries includes the SIC groups transportation; communications; trade; fire, insurance and real estate (FIRE); and services. We exclude the following service industries from the analysis: holding and other investment offices, social services, membership organizations, and other services. In those cases we lacked consistent measures of output and all of the inputs.

Table 3A.1 The decomposition of labor productivity

SIC Number		1977–95	1987–95	1995–2000
40	Railroad transportation			
	Labor	7.5	6.5	2.6
	MFP	4.3	3.2	0.9
	Capital deepening	0.8	0.3	0.3
	ICOT capital	0.0	0.0	0.1
	Non-ICOT capital	0.7	0.3	0.2
	Intermediate input deepening	2.3	2.9	1.4
41	Local and interurban passenger transit			
	Labor	-2.8	-1.6	-0.2
	MFP	-1.1	-1.0	2.2
	Capital deepening	-0.5	-0.5	0.0
	ICOT capital	0.0	0.0	0.0
	Non-ICOT capital	-0.5	-0.5	0.0
	Intermediate input deepening	-1.2	-0.1	-2.3
42	Trucking and warehousing			
	Labor	3.1	4.9	1.0
	MFP	0.5	1.1	0.3
	Capital deepening	0.2	0.2	0.3
	ICOT capital	0.1	0.1	0.1
	Non-ICOT capital	0.1	0.1	0.2
	Intermediate input deepening	2.4	3.6	0.5
44	Water transportation			
	Labor		2.3	2.2
	MFP		1.5	-0.2
	Capital deepening		-0.2	-0.1
	ICOT capital		0.0	0.1
	Non-ICOT capital		-0.3	-0.2
	Intermediate input deepening		1.0	2.5
45	Transportation by air			
	Labor	0.4	-3.4	1.3

MFP	1.2	1.4	0.4
Capital deepening	-0.3	-0.6	0.9
ICOT capital	0.1	0.1	0.6
Non-ICOT capital	-0.4	-0.6	0.3
Intermediate input deepening	-0.5	-4.2	0.0
46 Pipelines, except natural gas			
Labor	0.4	0.7	3.5
MFP	-2.0	-3.9	2.9
Capital deepening	1.2	1.5	3.1
ICOT capital	0.3	0.7	1.3
Non-ICOT capital	0.8	0.8	1.8
Intermediate input deepening	1.3	3.2	-2.5
47 Transportation services			
Labor		2.3	3.8
MFP		-0.5	0.3
Capital deepening		0.0	1.4
ICOT capital		0.7	1.4
Non-ICOT capital		-0.7	0.0
Intermediate input deepening		2.8	2.0
481, 482, 489 Telephone and telegraph			
Labor	6.3	5.8	6.7
MFP	1.6	1.5	1.6
Capital deepening	2.1	1.6	0.5
ICOT capital	1.1	0.9	0.5
Non-ICOT capital	1.0	0.7	0.0
Intermediate input deepening	2.5	2.5	4.5
483–484 Radio and television broadcasting			
Labor	0.6	0.2	1.2
MFP	-1.1	2.0	-5.5
Capital deepening	1.4	1.8	3.1
ICOT capital	0.8	1.0	2.2
Non-ICOT capital	0.6	0.8	0.9
Intermediate input deepening	0.4	-3.4	3.9

Table 3A.1 (continued)

SIC Number		1977–95	1987–95	1995–2000
49	Electric, gas, and sanitary services			
	Labor	−0.3	2.5	1.9
	MFP	0.1	0.8	0.4
	Capital deepening	0.7	0.9	1.0
	ICOT capital	0.3	0.3	0.3
	Non-ICOT capital	0.3	0.6	0.7
	Intermediate input deepening	−1.0	0.8	0.5
50–51	Wholesale trade			
	Labor	2.1	3.3	4.4
	MFP	1.0	1.1	2.4
	Capital deepening	0.8	0.6	1.7
	ICOT capital	0.6	0.5	1.4
	Non-ICOT capital	0.2	0.1	0.3
	Intermediate input deepening	0.3	1.5	0.2
52–59	Retail trade			
	Labor	0.7	1.2	3.5
	MFP	0.2	0.4	3.0
	Capital deepening	0.3	0.3	0.3
	ICOT capital	0.1	0.1	0.3
	Non-ICOT capital	0.2	0.2	0.0
	Intermediate input deepening	0.2	0.5	0.3
60–61	Depository and nondepository institutions			
	Labor		3.3	3.1
	MFP		0.0	0.5
	Capital deepening		1.4	1.9
	ICOT capital		1.0	1.5
	Non-ICOT capital		0.4	0.3
	Intermediate input deepening		1.9	0.8

62	Security, commodity brokers and services	Labor	5.4	7.2	20.2
		MFP	1.6	2.9	11.2
		Capital deepening	0.6	0.6	0.2
		ICOT capital	0.3	0.1	0.2
		Non-ICOT capital	0.3	0.5	0.1
		Intermediate input deepening	3.1	3.6	7.8
63	Insurance carriers	Labor	0.2	0.0	−1.4
		MFP	−2.1	−0.2	−1.0
		Capital deepening	0.8	0.7	0.8
		ICOT capital	0.4	0.4	0.6
		Non-ICOT capital	0.4	0.3	0.2
		Intermediate input deepening	1.6	−0.5	−1.2
64	Insurance agents, brokers, and services	Labor	−2.6	−3.3	3.5
		MFP	−1.7	−3.3	1.3
		Capital deepening	−0.1	0.1	0.4
		ICOT capital	0.0	0.1	0.2
		Non-ICOT capital	−0.1	0.0	0.2
		Intermediate input deepening	−0.9	0.0	1.7
65	Real estate	Labor		2.4	2.0
		MFP		1.0	1.4
		Capital deepening		0.1	0.0
		ICOT capital		0.0	0.0
		Non-ICOT capital		0.1	0.0
		Intermediate input deepening		1.2	0.6
70	Hotels and other lodging places	Labor	0.9	0.7	0.3
		MFP	−0.5	0.1	−1.1
		Capital deepening	0.3	0.3	0.2
		ICOT capital	0.1	0.1	0.2
		Non-ICOT capital	0.3	0.3	0.1
		Intermediate input deepening	1.0	0.3	1.2

Table 3A.1 (continued)

SIC Number		1977–95	1987–95	1995–2000
72	Personal services			
	Labor	-0.1	1.7	1.8
	MFP	-0.7	-0.6	0.3
	Capital deepening	0.1	0.3	0.2
	ICOT capital	0.0	0.1	0.1
	Non-ICOT capital	0.0	0.2	0.1
	Intermediate input deepening	0.5	1.9	1.2
73	Business services			
	Labor		3.0	3.5
	MFP		0.8	0.0
	Capital deepening		0.0	1.1
	ICOT capital		0.2	1.0
	Non-ICOT capital		-0.2	0.0
	Intermediate input deepening		2.2	2.4
75	Auto repair, services, and garages			
	Labor	-0.3	1.4	0.9
	MFP	-0.6	-1.0	1.0
	Capital deepening	0.4	1.0	0.0
	ICOT capital	0.1	0.1	0.1
	Non-ICOT capital	0.3	0.9	-0.1
	Intermediate input deepening	-0.1	1.5	-0.1
76	Miscellaneous repair services			
	Labor	0.9	2.6	2.7
	MFP	-0.4	-0.4	-1.2
	Capital deepening	0.1	0.2	0.7
	ICOT capital	0.1	0.2	0.4
	Non-ICOT capital	0.0	0.0	0.3
	Intermediate input deepening	1.2	2.9	3.3
78	Motion pictures			
	Labor	1.3	-0.3	-0.5
	MFP	0.1	-1.2	0.3

	Capital deepening	0.1	0.3	0.4
	ICOT capital	0.1	0.2	0.2
	Non-ICOT capital	0.0	0.1	0.2
	Intermediate input deepening	1.1	0.6	-1.2
79	Amusement and recreation services			
	Labor	0.6	1.9	-0.8
	MFP	0.7	0.1	0.0
	Capital deepening	-0.4	-0.3	0.1
	ICOT capital	0.0	0.0	0.1
	Non-ICOT capital	-0.4	-0.2	0.0
	Intermediate input deepening	0.3	2.1	-0.9
80	Health services			
	Labor	-0.2	-0.5	0.7
	MFP	-1.2	-1.5	-0.4
	Capital deepening	0.2	0.1	0.3
	ICOT capital	0.1	0.1	0.2
	Non-ICOT capital	0.1	0.0	0.1
	Intermediate input deepening	0.8	0.9	0.8
81	Legal services			
	Labor	-1.2	0.1	2.2
	MFP	-1.6	-0.3	0.4
	Capital deepening	0.1	0.1	0.3
	ICOT capital	0.1	0.1	0.3
	Non-ICOT capital	0.0	-0.1	0.0
	Intermediate input deepening	0.3	0.4	1.5
82	Educational services			
	Labor	0.3	0.5	-1.2
	MFP	-0.2	-0.1	-0.8
	Capital deepening	0.0	0.0	0.0
	ICOT capital	0.0	0.0	0.0
	Non-ICOT capital	0.0	0.0	0.0
	Intermediate input deepening	0.5	0.6	-0.4

Note: All numbers are average annual percentages.

4. The New Economy and the challenges for macroeconomic policy

Stephen G. Cecchetti[*]

> In the New Economy, many of the old classical rules of economics no longer apply; over the years, the US has made and learned new rules all its own. (*Time Magazine*, 31 December 1958)

INTRODUCTION

The New Economy poses many old challenges. Computers and the Internet have reduced the cost of providing and obtaining information, as did telephones and televisions in the mid-twentieth century, although perhaps less rapidly. The difficulties of integrating new technology into the production of goods and services may be somewhat less than in the past, but the upheaval caused by it does not seem qualitatively different from what we have seen since the beginning of the Industrial Revolution.[1] There are surely many difficult challenges, but they are not new.

For macroeconomic policy the story is similar. The goal of macroeconomic policy is to assure high and stable growth with low and stable inflation. The details of how to do this remain illusive. The job of fiscal and monetary policy-makers has always been complex, and it is surely not getting any easier. But again, this is not new. Economists continue to argue about the potential for government tax and expenditure policies to stabilize the economy, and the decades-long debate over the exact nature of the monetary transmission mechanism continues. It is as impossible now to give detailed advice to policy-makers about when and by how much to adjust their instruments as it was 30 years ago.

Monetary and fiscal policies share the job of economic management. Unlike most government actions, interest rates can be changed literally overnight. By contrast, changing tax and expenditure policies usually means legislative action, making it very slow. Monetary policy is a much better stabilization tool, while fiscal policy should focus on building solid foundations for long-term growth. The fact that today's economy is more nimble in responding to shocks places these roles into even starker relief than they were a decade ago. Ensuring short-term economic stability in today's world is the job of the central bank, and that is where I will focus my attention.

Ever-faster computers and telecommunications equipment have created new challenges for central bankers. Most important, the economy has become naturally more resilient over the past decade. We have seen important changes in the structure of goods, labor and financial markets. As the economy has become more nimble in adjusting to external shocks, policy-makers must become more agile in their reactions. The central bankers' job has become more difficult, since they need to recognize risks and act more quickly, but at the same time, the costs of inaction may have gone down, as the economy seems to heal itself more rapidly.

Even in the New Economy, the primary challenges facing monetary policy-makers in their daily work are the same as they have ever been. Stabilizing prices means forecasting inflation, which requires estimates of the sustainable, or potential, growth rate of the economy. As if this isn't a sufficiently daunting task, central bankers would be helpless without some idea of how changes in their interest rate instrument will alter the path of future output and inflation.

Difficulties in estimating potential GDP growth have been with us since the concept was first introduced more than 40 years ago. Over the years, trend productivity growth has undergone occasional periods of transition when estimating future potential output has been very difficult. In the US, we entered such a period in the middle 1990s, and things have not stabilized yet. For policy-makers, the problem is that it takes time to realize that the trend rate of growth has shifted. Figures 4.1 and 4.2, which plot real GDP growth and output per hour for the US from 1980 to 2001, make this point abundantly clear. It is nearly impossible to tell even in hindsight that the growth rate in potential GDP rose markedly in the mid-1990s.

The recent change in the productivity growth rate is not unprecedented. The increase in the sustainable growth rate of the American economy is in many ways just the mirror image of the slowdown that came in the mid-1970s. Then, the sustainable growth rate of the American economy fell from roughly 4 per cent to a level closer to 2½ per cent. Coming at a time of substantial domestic and international turbulence, it took several years to realize that the change had occurred.

Beyond the difficulties created by shifts in the sustainable growth rate of the economy, the structural underpinnings of the economy are constantly evolving. Over the 1990s we can point to three very important, and probably lasting, changes. Technology has been used to make production more responsive to changes in product demand, thereby reducing the level of inventories. The growth in the proportion of workers hired on a temporary basis had given companies the ability to adjust the size of their workforce rapidly in response to changing business conditions. And finally, innovations in finance have helped to assure that companies and consumers have access to resources even when times are tough.

The evolution of the financial system poses a particularly difficult challenge for central bankers. Since monetary policy acts initially through its impact on the balance sheets of financial firms, the explosion of asset-backed securities has likely changed the mechanism by which interest rate changes affect the real economy. As more borrowers have access to primary capital markets, and fewer need banks, it may become more difficult for the actions of central bankers to alter the future path of output and inflation.

Reduced demand for cash and reserves, the primary liabilities issued by the central bank, poses a second challenge to central bankers. But again, this problem is not new. The metamorphosis of the financial system has been ongoing for decades, if not centuries. And, as a result, the changes in the monetary transmission mechanism have been continuous. One clear sign of this is the constant attempts to broaden the set of financial instruments that are included in a given monetary aggregate, in the belief that the liquidity of the new instruments are somehow equivalent to that of those that were in the previous definition. But the connection between the elements of the central bank balance sheet and the monetary aggregate has never been that tight anyway, and so it is difficult to mourn the further decline in their usefulness as policy guides.

What is new is the widespread belief that the rate of change in the financial system has somehow increased, and so the end game, where demand for cash and reserves have dropped to zero, may be fast approaching. My own view is that the difficulties this poses for central bankers are still several decades off.[2]

In the remainder of this chapter, I will discuss both short- and long-term challenges that the evolution of the macroeconomic structure poses for fiscal and monetary policy. In the next section, I present evidence of the changes wrought over the past decade or so. I focus first on the reduced cyclical volatility of US growth, then on the increase in the level of average growth, and finally on the sources of the low inflation of the last half of the 1990s. The next section discusses the implications of these changes for fiscal and monetary policy. In the final section, I provide some comments on my views on how information technology will transform policy in the longer run.

ELEMENTS OF THE 'NEW' ECONOMY

The United States economy has evolved significantly from what it was just a few decades ago. Today, information technology is everywhere. Once the preserve of scientific laboratories and the back offices of financial institutions, today semiconductors are buried inside home appliances and automobiles. Computer chips control everything from elevators to airplane traffic.

The Internet, initiated several decades ago by the United States Department of Defense in an effort to link research universities together, has now grown into an important part of domestic and international commerce. I no longer have to leave my desk to shop for and purchase books, clothes, furniture, or virtually anything else. It is even simple to order wine, cheese and chocolate by clicking. Not only that, but I can place my order 24 hours a day, 7 days a week while sitting in my home wearing nothing but my underwear. This is all truly revolutionary.

As computers became both ubiquitous and increasingly powerful, two things happened. First, in the mid-1980s, the *volatility* of US GDP growth declined, and then, in 1995, the *level* of growth rose. Along with this came a marked fall in average inflation. The goal of this section is to describe these changes and speculate about their sources.

A More Stable Economy

Using sophisticated statistical procedures, Margaret Mary McConnell and Gabriel Perez Quiros (2000) establish that what our eyes suggest in Figure 4.1 *is* really there. They show that growth has been markedly less volatile since 1984 than it was in the preceding 25 years. This also shows up in the growth as output per hour, which has been positive since 1993 as seen in Figure 4.2.

McConnell and Perez Quiros attribute the fall in aggregate volatility to a change in the inventory behavior of durable goods manufacturers. In the past, unintended shifts in inventory levels have been blamed for a significant part of business-cycle fluctuations. When demand fell, manufacturers would find themselves with substantial unsold stock and be forced to cut back on production, reducing employment and leading to an overall economic downturn. Beginning in the mid-1980s, the inventory-to-sales ratio of these manufacturers began to decline, and it continued to decline steadily through the 1990s. Figure 4.3 tracks the fall for the goods producing sector from an average of 2.1 prior to 1984 to a level of 1.54 by the end of 2001. (These figures can be interpreted as number of quarters supply on hand.) Technology has enabled companies to keep better track of production and sales, speeding the rate at which they are able to respond to

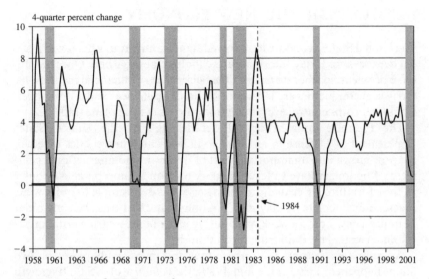

Figure 4.1   Real GDP growth

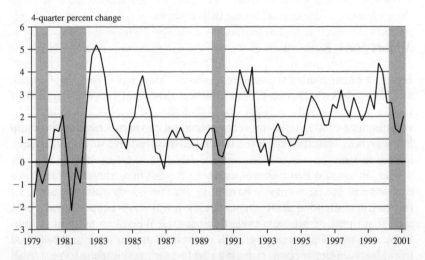

Figure 4.2   Growth in US real output per hour, nonfarm business sector

changes in demand. Techniques like just-in-time inventory control policies
have reduced the amplitude of inventory fluctuations and stabilized overall
economic activity.

The general resilience and stability of the US economy is nowhere more
apparent than in the 2000–01 episode. This mini-recession, with a peak to

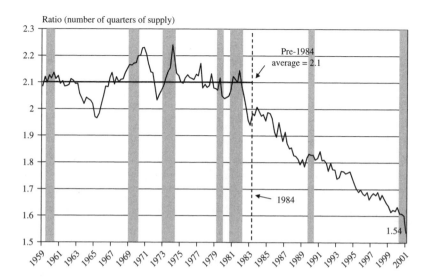

Figure 4.3   Inventory-to-sales ratio: goods sector

trough GDP decline of less than one-quarter of 1 per cent, clearly demonstrates the new recuperative powers of the US economy. Moreover, Figure 4.3 suggests that inventory policy played an important role. This is the only recession during which the inventory-to-sales ratio has fallen.

The change in inventory control policies is only one of several things contributing to the speedy recovery from the 2001 downturn. Changes in labor and financial markets also played a role in increasing the flexibility of the US economy. On the employment side, there has been a dramatic shift toward temporary help over the past decade. Figure 4.4 shows that the proportion of employees from temporary help agencies increased from ½ per cent of total nonfarm employment in 1983 to over 2½ per cent by 2000. At its peak in September 2001 over 3½ million workers were temporary. Not only that, but over the subsequent 16 months, the fall in temporary help accounted for 70 per cent of the nonfarm employment decline of 951 000 workers. The recession was concentrated to an extraordinary degree in this most flexible portion of the labor force, leaving 'permanent' employees in their jobs.

Turning to financial markets, we have seen significant innovation over the past decade as well. Once upon a time there were two sources for borrowing: direct debt issuance and bank borrowing. Most firms and households cannot issue marketable debt, and so were dependent on banks for financing. Beginning with the creation of mortgage-backed securities in the

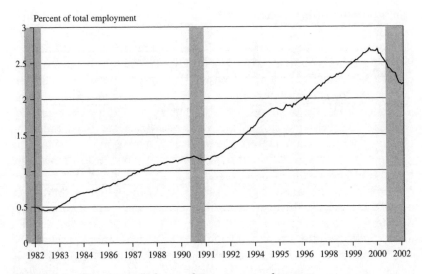

Figure 4.4   Temporary help supply services employment

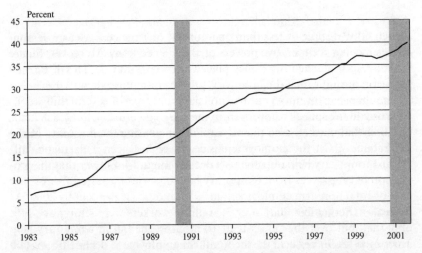

Figure 4.5   Asset-backed securities as a percentage of total liabilities

early 1970s, things started to change. Today the list of asset-backed securities now includes home mortgages, car loans, credit card debt, student loans, equipment leases, movie box-office receipts, and even the future revenues from British pubs.

Figure 4.5 plots total asset-backed securities (from both private and government issuers) as a percentage of debt that was typically issued by the banking system (this includes loans, mortgages and consumer credit).[3] Starting at close to zero in 1983, by the end of 2001, asset-backed securities accounted for 40 per cent of what had previously been credit held on the balance sheets of financial intermediaries.[4] This shift from bank to marketable debt is important for two reasons. It makes financing more flexible in response to external shocks, and it makes banks less important. The following example demonstrates what has happened. During the winter of 2001 as the US economy slowed, the credit-rating agencies downgraded the large automobile manufacturers, increasing their borrowing costs. Since the demand for cars was falling, this was potentially disastrous. How were Ford, GM and DaimlerChrysler going to offer the financial incentives needed to move the cars off of the dealers' lots? Without high credit ratings, it was too expensive for them to borrow directly and make the loans that were needed to sell the cars. And yet, in the fall of 2001 automobile sales hit record highs, as buyers were offered very attractive loans to purchase the cars. How did they do it? The answer is that the car companies created pools of car loans and securitized them. These car-loan-backed securities had better credit ratings – they were AAA – than the car companies themselves! (See Ip and Gold 2002.)

This new financial intermediation – through asset-backed securities – gives us all direct access to capital markets. By finding a broker who will put me into a pool, I now have direct access to capital markets, and no longer have to rely on a bank. The broker takes a fee for this service, but I don't need to worry about the availability of bank credit. Not only that, but I don't have to know it is happening to me, nor do I care!

These three changes – improved inventory control policies, the rise in the use of temporary help and the increase in the percentage of lending that is marketable – have each played a part in the improved performance of the US economy. They have made the economy more flexible in responding to unexpected events.

A Faster Growing Economy

Turning to the increase in the level of US growth, the first line of Table 4.1 gives us a sense of what happened over the last quarter of the twentieth century. The table shows raw average annual growth in business nonfarm output for the periods 1974 to 1990, 1991 to 1995, and 1996 to 1999. Growth in the last half of the 1990s was truly extraordinary. The increase over the first five years of the decade is in excess of two full percentage points *at an annual rate*.

By the end of the 1990s a consensus had developed that the sustainable growth rate of the US economy had reached at least 4 per cent. That is, with

*Table 4.1   Contributions to growth of real nonfarm business output, 1974
to 1999*

	1974–90	1991–95	1996–99
Growth of output	3.13	2.82	4.90
Contributions from			
Information technology	0.51	0.54	1.08
Hardware	0.28	0.24	0.62
Software	0.11	0.23	0.31
Communications equipment	0.12	0.07	0.15
Other capital	0.85	0.44	0.76
Labor hours	1.15	0.82	1.51
Labor quality	0.22	0.44	0.31
Multifactor productivity	0.44	0.57	1.25
Growth rate of inputs			
Hardware	31.4	17.5	36.0
Software	13.2	12.8	13.1
Communications equipment	7.7	3.6	7.1

Source: Oliner and Sichel 2000.

the unemployment rate steady, American GDP could grow at a rate that
was now 1½-percentage points higher than previously. Labor productivity
growth had risen by the same 1½ percentage points and was rising at a rate
of at least 3 per cent per year.[5]

What were the sources of this astonishing performance of the US
economy in the latter half of the 1990s? To get some idea we can turn to the
Oliner and Sichel's (2000) estimates of the sources of growth, reproduced
in Table 4.1. From their accounting we learn that the two-percentage-point
rise in US growth had three primary sources: higher labor inputs, higher
investment in information technology capital, and increases in multifactor
productivity. The increase in labor inputs mirrored the decline in the US
unemployment rate from over 5½ per cent in 1995 to 4 per cent five years
later. What is most striking is the importance that Oliner and Sichel ascribe
to the increase in IT investment. By their estimates, IT investment alone
accounted for 0.54 of the 2.08 percentage-point rise in growth, fully one-
quarter of the increase in growth. Increased multifactor productivity
growth accounts for 0.7 percentage points of the remaining change. This is
the part of the change that is left unexplained by standard growth accounting. There are a number of possible interpretations of this increase, one of

Table 4.2   The change in the 1990s (average annual percentage growth)

	1991–95	1996–99
Nonfinancial corporate business		
Labor productivity	1.61	3.55
Unit labor costs	1.36	0.52
Unit non-labor costs	0.75	−0.50
Real investment in computer hardware*	29.0	45.9
Prices of computer hardware	−14.8	−23.4

Note: *National income and product accounts basis.

Source: US Bureau of Economic Analysis, National Income and Product Accounts.

which is that it represents the increased productivity arising from the efficient use of technology in production.[6]

It is worth looking at the IT data a bit more closely. Table 4.2 reports that, between the first and second half of the 1990s, the growth rate in computer hardware inputs increased from an already impressive 29 per cent to a phenomenal average annual growth rate of 46 per cent. As a simple matter of accounting, this acceleration in equipment installation is responsible for all of the increase in productivity growth attributed to information technology.

Digging deeper, we see that the increased growth in computer equipment investment came from the intensification in the US of computer price declines during this period. The deflator for information technology equipment used by the Bureau of Economic Analysis (BEA) to calculate US GDP went from an average of about −15 per cent in the first half of the decade of the 1990s to an average of nearly −25 per cent in the second half. If, from 1995 to 1999, the hardware deflator had continued to decline at the more modest −15 per cent rate, then US growth would have averaged between 0.25 and 0.50 percentage points less than it was.[7] The clear implication is that a significant share of the increase in the American productivity growth rate is a consequence of measured improvements in the *quality* of computer hardware installed by businesses.[8]

Before turning to the recent inflation record, it is worth digressing briefly to bring up the possibility that we are overinvesting in information technology equipment. After the NASDAQ finished its slow motion crash in mid-2001, newspapers and magazines were cluttered with pictures of surplus computers piled in warehouses. This 'refuse' came from bankrupt Internet companies that had been able to obtain financing because of the bubble in the NASDAQ. Because it was too cheap to obtain financing, the economy invested too heavily in computers. Since investment in IT equipment was so big a part of the New Economy productivity acceleration, if it was unjustified then the measured increase in growth was a mirage.

Overinvestment in IT equipment may be more than just a one-time problem arising from a stock 'bubble'. The possibility comes from what I think of as the dark side of network externalities. A network externality arises when the usefulness of a product to you depends on how many other people have it. If you have the only fax machine, it is useless. But if everyone has a fax machine, that is a different story. The same is true of computer software. I am typing this document using Microsoft Word 2000 version 9.0.3821 SR-1. I don't really know what all of that means, but I do know that if I send the document to someone using a sufficiently antiquated version of Microsoft Word that this document will not display or print properly. In other words, to take advantage of the network externality that comes from using this word processing software, we all have to keep our software sufficiently up to date. This means more than buying updates. As we have all learned, updates are designed to run on the newest, fastest, more memory-intensive, machines and so the upgrading of the software often forces us to buy new hardware quite frequently – probably more frequently than we really need!

I believe the GDP numbers produced by the Bureau of Economic Analysis, but if we are replacing our computers too frequently, investment and growth may be overestimated. This will show up mainly in the price deflator, as the true quality of computers may not be increasing as fast as the official estimates suggest.

Lower Inflation

Beyond the increase in productivity growth, a second important aspect of recent experience in the US has been the behavior of inflation. Through the latter half of the 1990s, inflation in the US was both low and falling.

Figure 4.6 plots the 12-month changes in headline inflation as measured by the All-Items Consumer Price Index (CPI) and two measures of core inflation, the CPI excluding food and energy, and the Median CPI.[9] Inflation in the US dropped steadily throughout the 1980s and into the 1990s, hitting a low in 1999. But the most striking fact about this picture is the pattern over the latter part of the 1990s. Here we see that both the headline CPI and the two core measures actually fell as growth was rising. During this entire period, the vast majority of analysts inside and outside of the government were forecasting that inflation would be one-half to one percentage point higher than it turned out to be. It was only in the year 2000 that inflation began to rise to levels in excess of 2½ per cent.

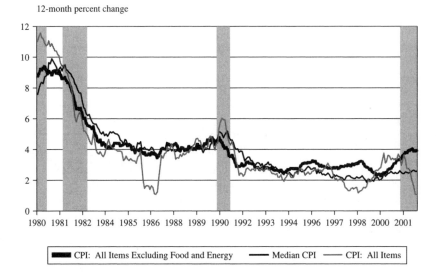

12-month percent change

Note: * Based on current methods.

*Figure 4.6   US consumer prices, headline and core measures**

How can we account for this inflation experience? There are several explanations. The most obvious is that in the late 1990s, the US economy experienced two beneficial supply shocks that reduced inflation. These came in the form of the restructuring of the system for the delivery of medical care and the reduction of oil prices. Figure 4.7 reports the 12-month change in the consumer price index for medical care commodities and services. As the data clearly show, inflation in medical costs declined significantly throughout the 1990s, falling from nearly 10 per cent at the beginning of the decade to a low of 2½ per cent in late 1997. But through the latter half of the 1990s, medical care cost inflation remained below 4 per cent per year.

Turning to oil prices, Figure 4.8 reports the price *level* of West Texas Intermediate crude oil. Through 1998, oil prices fell from $25 per barrel at the beginning of the year, to a low of just over $10 by the end of the year. This significant reduction in energy prices had a clearly beneficial effect on the US economy, helping to both raise growth and lower inflation.

Has the advance of information technology changed the inflation process itself? While its possible to argue that the product markets have become more competitive, as it is now easier to sample the prices of many suppliers at lower cost, there is no reason to believe that inflation has changed in any material way. The Internet, and the low cost of communicating prices to potential customers has certainly improved the efficient operation of the

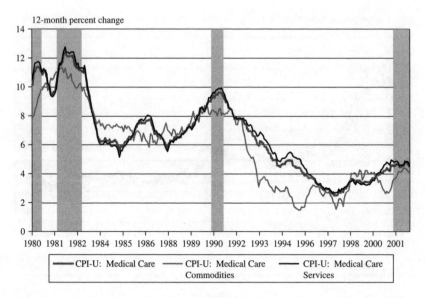

Figure 4.7   US consumer prices: medical care

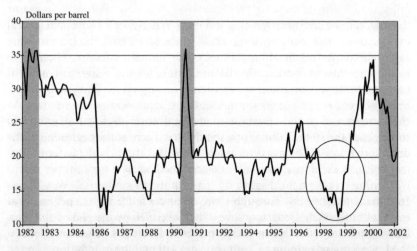

Figure 4.8   Domestic US spot oil prices: West Texas Intermediate crude oil

price system in allocating resources, but it has not changed the way in which overall price inflation occurs. The New Economy has affected inflation in the same way that it has influenced output – by making short- and medium-term forecasting more difficult. The difficulty in forecasting inflation and growth over the medium term is the primary challenge for policy-makers posed by the New Economy for monetary policy-makers, and I take that up next.

MACROECONOMIC POLICY IN THE NEW ECONOMY

The two pillars of modern macroeconomic policy are the government's tax and expenditure decisions and the determination of short-term interest rates by the central bank. In the past we have thought of fiscal and monetary policy as sharing responsibility for short-term stabilization and having somewhat different roles in insuring long-term growth. Does the New Economy imply a new macroeconomic policy as well? Things have certainly changed. Let's see how.

Fiscal Policy

Over the past 50 years we have come to think of fiscal policy as an important source of stimulus during a general slowdown. People turn to their elected officials for help, demanding that they set things right with new programs that bring some combination of lower taxes and higher government spending. Payments to the unemployed and lower income tax bills create a social safety net that automatically stabilizes modern market-based economics. We believe that this reduces the overall amplitude of cyclical downturns while at the same time insuring that the burden is not overly concentrated on the unlucky few.

But when things start going bad, the natural reaction is to want to do something, and in the fiscal arena that means discretionary tax and expenditure programs tailor-made for the problem at hand. These can work. But just because something can work, it does not follow automatically that it will or that it is the right thing to do. There have always been flaws with discretionary fiscal policy, and the more flexible goods, labor and financial markets of the New Economy have only made these worse. The problem is that fiscal policy is both slow and hard to do sensibly. Look at a few facts.

Most recessions are short, lasting a year or less. The longest recession in the US after the Second World War lasted 16 months. Furthermore, because data are only available with several months' lag, a recession is often half way through before there is consensus that a recession has started.

Timing presents a considerable challenge. I know of no government that has an agreed-upon economic stimulus legislation waiting to be implemented. In fact, given both the shifting environment and the changing cast of characters, such a thing is both economically undesirable and politically inconceivable. Instead, someone has to write new legislation every time a recession comes along. This takes several months even under the best of circumstances. The most recent example is instructive. Serious Congressional efforts to pass stimulus legislation in 2001 began only after September 11, six months after the recession 'officially' started, [10] and were completed in early March 2002, when economic recovery was already underway.[11]

As if that were not enough, policies take time to have any impact. Even after legislative action is complete, changes in taxes do not increase individual consumption or corporate investment immediately. By the time the spending starts, the chances are the coming boom will be in full swing.

The main problem is with the substance of economic stimulus packages. Economists do not write economic stimulus packages, politicians do! And fiscal stimulus is one place where economics and politics collide. Economists prefer policies that focus attention on getting a few important people to do something they were not planning to do while avoiding paying for others to do what they would have done anyway. Temporary incentives to spur investment and income tax reductions for the less well off who will spend what they get are good examples. Politicians, by contrast, look for programs that reward the largest number of people possible in order to win support and ensure re-election.

The Bush administration's decision in 2001–02 to try to sell a capital gains tax reduction as part of their anti-recession program is a particularly egregious example of an expensive proposal that will have virtually no impact on the problem at hand. I guess reducing the tax burden on some wealthy people when they chose to sell appreciated stock might lead them to buy a few more Mercedes and BMWs, but I'm not exactly sure what it has to do with improving the prospects for short-run economic growth. The proposal to cut the taxes big companies pay on past profits is another example. I do not hold opportunism against elected public officials, but we all need to recognize that it exists. We elect politicians to do things that are popular. Economic slowdowns, when some people are suffering and the rest are worried, play to their worst instincts.

The fact that the economy has become more flexible in adjusting to shocks has made all of these problems worse. To the extent the economy's natural recuperative powers are improved, there is now even less time to get the job done. This increases the odds that any legislatively-based stimulus program will come on line too late to do what was intended. Add to this the fact that markets, through mechanisms like asset-backed-securities and temporary help, have made it easier to circumvent roadblocks put up by governments trying to distort economic incentives, and many things look even more pointless.

All of this means that discretionary fiscal policy is a poor stabilization tool. While it might be possible to design economically sensible stimulus legislation, we need to realize that it will not be enacted. Instead, legislators should focus their attention on building solid foundations for long-term growth. This means creating structural tax and spending policies that encourage investment, innovation and hard work. It may mean eliminating the corporate income tax and the individual tax on capital gains. This should be debated. In the meantime, the New Economy has made fiscal policy an even worse stabilization tool than it was a decade ago.

Central Bank Policy

The changes wrought by the advances of the 1990s pose both immediate and long-run challenges for the operations of central banks. In the short term, these are really just the same old problems that monetary policy-makers have faced for decades: stabilization requires distinguishing transitory from permanent shifts in productivity growth. The long-term threat is rather different. There, central banks are threatened by the possibility that the disappearance of the demand for the monetary base – the thing only they can supply – will render their policy tools impotent. We will consider each of these in turn.

Immediate Challenges

The objective of most of the central banks of the world is to stabilize inflation about some low level while maintaining growth at near its sustainable rate. One way of expressing this is that monetary policy seeks to minimize a weighted average of inflation and output variability. Variability is usually measured as the squared deviation from the target. In the case of inflation, there is general agreement that target levels should be in the range of zero to 2 per cent per year. The exact value depends on a number of considerations that are likely to be unique to the conditions within the region that the central bank operates as well as the manner in which inflation is measured.[12] The problem is the target for output, where policy-makers require an estimate of the sustainable rate of growth, or potential output.

In practical terms, the difficulty is that central bankers should react differently to *transitory* movements in productivity than to *permanent* ones. If a productivity shock is transitory, then policy-makers will attempt to stabilize output about its permanent growth path, allowing prices to deviate somewhat from their long-run target path. By contrast, if productivity growth shifts permanently, then the appropriate policy response is to stabilize inflation while allowing output to move to its new long-run growth path.

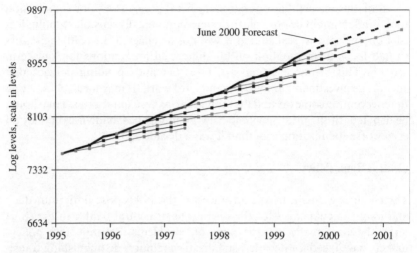

Figure 4.9   Blue chip forecasts of real GDP relative to actual

Telling the difference between changes in productivity growth that are temporary and those that are not has proven to be extremely difficult. To see the point, first look back to Figure 4.2 where I have plotted output per hour in the nonfarm business sector and ask how long it would take to tell that the second half of the 1990s is different from the first half. In hindsight we can see it. But to do their job, the FOMC needed to divine this change in 1997! Our good fortune is that they were able to see the productivity acceleration in its early stages.

Private sector economists as a group failed to realize that the sustainable growth rate of the economy had risen. Figure 4.9 is a plot of the log of GDP together with a series of consensus forecasts from the Blue Chip survey. For each quarter, the chart shows the forecast out several years. For example, for the first quarter of 1996, I plot the actual data point, plus the forecast for the next few years. The actual level of GDP follows a path that is steeper than the forecasts throughout the period, meaning that the forecasters consistently underestimated growth. The systematic underestimates of the growth rates were a clear sign that forecasters were slow to learn that a significant part of the productivity acceleration was permanent.

The continuous underestimates of GDP growth were accompanied by a series of overestimates of future inflation. Figure 4.10 plots the log of the consumer price index together with the series of forecasts. Until oil prices began to rise in early 1999, professional forecasters were consistently overestimating future levels of inflation. (Core inflation forecast errors continued to be positive through the end of the decade.) Interestingly, the combination

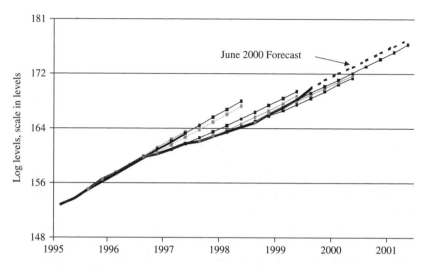

Figure 4.10   Blue chip forecasts of the CPI relative to actual

of the real GDP and inflation forecast errors suggest that forecasts of *nominal* GDP were approximately correct.

It is interesting to note that if we were to collect data for the latter half of the 1970s, we would be able to produce very similar charts, although the labels would be switched. That is, forecasts of GDP would have been consistently too high, and forecasts of inflation would have been systematically too low.

But the problem of estimating trend growth extends beyond the tumultuous periods of the late 1970s and late 1990s. Athanasios Orphanides (1998) has compared real time estimates (i.e. those used by a putative inflation forecaster) for 1980 to 1992 of the output gap in the United States with subsequent revisions, and arrives at astonishing conclusions. During this period, the real time estimates of the gap (measured as output minus potential output divided by potential) averaged −3.99 per cent with a standard deviation of 3.46. Subsequent revisions in measures of both actual and potential output led to changes in the estimated gap such that by 1994 the revised figures for the 1980–92 period implied a gap of only −1.64 per cent with a standard deviation of 2.44! In other words the revised gap was on average 2.35 percentage points lower than the real-time estimates, which presumably were used in the preparation of inflation forecasts and as inputs into the formulation of monetary policy at the time.

Turning to monetary policy, we can look to the work of Jordi Galí to help us to understand the challenges posed by shifts in trend productivity. Galí (2002) compares the behavior of inflation following a move in productivity in the Volcker-Greenspan period (1979–99) with that in the pre-Volcker (1954–79) period. He finds that during the 1980s and 1990s, a negative productivity shock left inflation unchanged, while in the earlier period, inflation rose significantly. The explanation for this is that the FOMC of the 1960s and 1970s did a poor job of distinguishing transitory from permanent changes in growth, and tried to keep a decline in productivity from affecting output. The result was inflation. In the more recent period, with an increased focus on inflation, the FOMC has not made the same mistakes.

Overall, the message is clear. During periods when the productivity growth trend is changing, central bankers face challenges that are more daunting than the usual ones. Failing to react to a decline in productivity growth, as the US did in the 1970s, can result in an extended episode of higher than desired inflation, which is then costly to eliminate. Alternatively, a central bank that tightens policy when faced with a permanent increase in its economy's sustainable rate of growth risks not allowing the growth to occur in the first place. In the end, though, the challenge is to figure out as quickly and accurately as possible the trend growth rate of productivity.[13]

Long-term Challenges

While technological progress poses clear short-run and medium-run challenges for monetary policy, they can all be studied and discussed using the now common vocabulary of central bankers. We talk about the impact of the change in an interest rate instrument on output and inflation as transmitted through the financial system.

But when we think about the long-run challenges posed by technological advance, we must think critically about the nature in which the transmission mechanism will change. Will the central bank continue to be able to control an interest rate? How will they do it? What will the consequences of changes in the system of financial intermediation be for system stability?[14]

These are all difficult questions, and they have elicited a variety of answers in past years. At the heart of the issue is whether technological advance will ultimately eliminate completely the private sector demand for central bank liabilities. Today, this demand is split between two groups. First, there is the demand for currency to be used in daily transactions by individuals, and second, financial intermediaries demand reserves for their daily clearing operations through the payments system that is maintained by the central bank. In some countries, intermediaries hold reserves to meet regulatory requirements, but in most instances, this demand is being eliminated by technological advance and so I will ignore it here.[15]

Monetary policy operates by adjusting the level of the central bank's liabilities. If the demand for these liabilities goes to zero, then the leverage of policy-makers will disappear as well. But is the time approaching when individuals will no longer hold currency and financial firms will no longer hold central bank reserves? Let us take each of these in turn.

First, consider the demand for currency. The claim is that privately issued store-value cards and the like will replace the functions of officially issued paper money. Currency provides finality, security, and anonymity in transactions. Surely, we will want all of these and so any adequate substitutes will need to have all of these characteristics. It is difficult to conceive of privately issued substitutes with all of these. Specifically, the risk-free nature of central bank liabilities is something that private money will have a very difficult time emulating.

To see the point, think of the example of stored-value cards issued by a telephone company. These exist in many countries, are easy to purchase, and convenient to use. The cards have value because they can be exchanged for phone-company provided services, something that is in nearly universal demand.

Can we imagine the cards, or their electronic equivalent, replacing central bank liabilities in the payment and settlement of transactions? There are several reasons to be skeptical. First, there is the fact that the government is unlikely to accept payment of taxes in telephone company liabilities. This alone is probably enough to sustain the existence of central bank money. But beyond that, there is the fact that the probability of phone company default is likely substantially higher than that of the central bank.

But even in the absence of actual default, the phone company can partially default by inflating the price of its services. This possibility means that it is unlikely that phone company 'money' will always trade at par.[16] Central bank money has no such problem. The central bank can always guarantee that a dollar is one dollar.

In fact, the private issuer need not actually threaten bankruptcy to partially default on its liabilities. If, as in the case of the phone company, the 'money' is backed by services rendered by the issuer, then raising the price of the services is partial default on the nominal value of the money. While central banks surely have defaulted on the value of their liabilities through aggregate inflation, a credible commitment to price stability is now the norm.

Information technology may well eliminate demand for central bank issued *paper* currency. But if the central bank adapts and issues e-money, then the official e-money seems very likely to dominate that of all private issuers.

It is worth pausing to comment on the demand for cash for illegal and underground transactions. Some people have noted that so long as this demand remains, monetary policy will retain its efficacy. But if the only remaining demand for currency were to come from drug dealers and the

Mafia, surely we would all agree that the proper policy response would be to eliminate its issuance.

This brings us to the demand for central bank reserves used in the payments system. We have already reached the point in most central bank systems where the intra-day demand far exceeds the overnight demand for these balances. In the US, for example, the overnight level of clearing balances is now well below $10 billion. Meanwhile, the gross level of *daily* transactions on the Fedwire exceeds $2 trillion. During any given day, cumulative overdrafts of banks that are executing these clearings can easily exceed $40 billion at any given instant. The overdrafts arise from the timing mismatch of incoming and outgoing payments at the largest banks, and attract a charge of less than 50 basis points at an annual rate (measured by the minute). But the point is that this system is very heavily used, and it runs largely on intra-day credit.

The details of these payments systems, including charges for intra-day credit and remuneration for overnight balances, differ. But several things look as if they are similar. In particular, the payments system run by the central bank usually entails some form of subsidization. This can be in the form of the provision of intra-day credit, or the implicit guarantees, or the network externalities of letting everyone connect for a nominal (or zero) charge. Given the existence of the central bank's payment system and the use of central bank liabilities in clearing, it seems that the demand for reserves is likely to continue long into the future. Since the leverage of monetary policy is a consequence of the central bank being the monopoly supplier of these reserves, my prediction is that the leverage to influence economic activity will continue long into the future.

CONCLUSION

The rapid advance of information and communication technology has brought with it changes in virtually every sector of the economy. This New Economy is growing more quickly and is more stable than the old one. I have argued that these changes have been the result of a series of changes to the structure of production, labor markets and financial intermediation. Using new ideas and technologies, firms are now able to manage their inventories of goods more accurately and so need less of them, temporary workers increase the flexibility of the labor force, and the increased reliance on asset-backed securities to finance credit has made us less dependent on banks.

The improved recuperative powers of the New Economy mean that policy-makers must change the way that they do their jobs. I have argued that fiscal policy, never a particularly good stabilization tool, should now focus exclusively on providing a foundation for long-term stable growth. The job of short-term policy adjustments should be left to central bankers. They are not only independent from the political considerations that make it difficult for legislators to do the right thing, but they can respond quickly to changed economic conditions. But I have emphasized that the New Economy poses particularly difficult challenges for monetary policy-makers for several reasons. First, the changes in the financial sector may well have blunted the impact of monetary policy. Interest rate changes affect growth and inflation through the banking system. As banks have become less relevant to credit creation, monetary policy may well have become less effective. The second challenge comes from the fact that it appears to have become more difficult to differentiate between transitory and permanent shifts in productivity growth. When the trend is shifting around, as it has been for some years now, historical patterns are a poor guide to the future, making a central banker's job even more difficult. It is worth noting that to the extent that structural changes have made the economy more stable, monetary policy is less important than it once was – and the risks from policy mistakes are also smaller.

In considering the long-run impact of information and communication technology on monetary policy, the concern is over the potential disappearance of the demand for central bank liabilities. Since monetary policy acts through changes in the quantity and interest rate charged for central bank liabilities, if the demand evaporates, monetary policy goes with it. My conclusion is that perfect substitutes for all of the functions of central bank money are extremely unlikely to arise, and so the central bank will retain some leverage.

We can only hope that each new day continues to bring with it a New Economy and that the challenges of the future are as pleasant as those of the recent past have been.

NOTES

*   Professor of Economics, The Ohio State University, and Research Associate, National Bureau of Economic Research. This paper was prepared for the conference 'The New Economy: What's new about it?', George Bush School of Government and Public Policy, Texas A&M University, 19 April 2002. An early version of this paper was prepared for the conference on 'New Technologies: Consequences and Challenges for Central Banks', Banque de France, 1–9 February 2001. I would like to thank Stefan Krause and Roisin O' Sullivan of Ohio State; Richard Peach, Donald Rissmiller and Simon Potter of the Federal Reserve Bank of New York; and Guhan Venkatu of the Federal Reserve Bank of Cleveland; for assistance in helping me clarify ideas, collect data, and construct charts.
1. DeLong and Summers (2001) place the most recent New Economy into historical perspective.
2. This topic has been the subject of heated debate over the past few years. The papers on 'The future of monetary policy' by Charles A.E. Goodhart, Michael Woodford, Charles Freedman and Benjamin Friedman that have appeared in the July 2000 issue of the journal *International Finance* provide a comprehensive summary of the issues.

3. The data are from the Federal Reserve's Flow of Funds Accounts See Teplin (2001). The numerator of the series is Table L125 line one plus L126 line one, financial assets of federally related mortgage pools plus financial assets of private issuers of asset-backed securities. The denominator is the sum of lines 6, 7, 8 and 9 from Table L4, credit market debt included bank loans not elsewhere classified, other loans and advances, mortgages and consumer credit.

4. Estrella (2002) provides a summary of the increase in asset-backed securities and its likely impact on monetary policy effectiveness.

5. At the time of writing this, early 2002, disagreements had resurfaced and estimates of the sustainable growth rate ranged from 3 to 4 per cent.

6. Before continuing, it is worth pointing out that Robert Gordon has looked at these same numbers and come to somewhat different conclusions. Gordon makes two points. First, he notes that evaluation of the changes in the productivity trend requires careful treatment of cyclical factors. From this he concludes that this accounts for part, but not all of the acceleration of the late 1990s. Second, Gordon's analysis shows that the productivity growth increase is concentrated in the durable manufacturing sector. That is, the improvement in productive efficiency has not been shared across the entire economy, but has been entirely in less than one-tenth of the economy (measured by employment). See Gordon (2000).

7. It is important to note that in the US, the Bureau of Economic Analysis (BEA) employs hedonic adjustments, which incorporate improvements in processing speed and memory, for example, directly into the construction of price indices. Furthermore, because these adjustments have become more important in recent years and they are not made in most European countries, the differences have increased. During the first half of the 1990s German and US computer price deflators showed roughly equivalent declines. It is over the past five years that the two have diverged significantly, with the German deflator showing a decline of less than 10 per cent on average.

8. I have argued elsewhere that the computers generate monopoly rents for the producers that need not be shared with the users, and so the economic benefits generally may accrue to the individuals (and countries) that are making chips and IT hardware. This has two implications. First, aggregate improvements in productivity will flow to the computer makers, and second that the productivity growth increases will accrue to the countries that produce computers.

9. The Median CPI is computed by the Federal Reserve Bank of Cleveland, and is available on their web site, http://www.clev.frb.org/Research/index.htm#cpi. The computation is based on work that first appeared in Bryan and Cecchetti (1994).

10. The official arbiter of recessions, the NBER Business Cycle Dating Committee, could have easily picked an early beginning for the recession, as employment and production seem to have peaked in late 2000.

11. At the time of writing, the dating of the end of the recession was not yet official.

12. See Cecchetti (2001b), for a detailed discussion of this, and other issues regarding policy objectives.

13. It is interesting to note that the debate over the distribution of increased US growth between its permanent and transitory components continues in the form of trying to cyclically adjust productivity. Robert Gordon (2000) suggested that a significant part of the acceleration has been cyclical.

14. These questions are in addition to the ones raised by the change in the financial intermediation system. Estrella (2002) discusses how the increase in securitization has decreased the effectiveness of monetary policy. He estimates a rather dramatic decline in the interest elasticity of GDP growth.

15. The US is a case in point, where very few banks are bound by their reserve requirements. Regional banks hold ATM cash and money center banks hold clearing balances in the Federal Reserve accounts that both exceed their respective required reserve levels.

16. If you believe that this is far-fetched, consider the example of the California energy utility Pacific, Gas and Electric during the year 2000. At the beginning of the year, PG&E bonds were very high grade. By the end of the year, the firm was nearly bankrupt.

REFERENCES

Bryan, Michael F. and Stephen G. Cecchetti (1994), 'Measuring core inflation', in N. Gregory Mankiw (ed.), *Monetary Policy*, Chicago: University of Chicago Press for NBER, pp. 195–215.

Cecchetti, Stephen G. (2001a), 'Is the New Economy contagious?', *Financial Times*, January 3.

Cecchetti, Stephen G. (2001b), 'Making monetary policy: objectives and rules', *Oxford Review of Economic Policy*, **16** (4), 43–59.

DeLong, J. Bradford and Lawrence H. Summers (2001), 'The "New Economy": background, historical perspective, questions and speculations', in *Economic Policy for the Information Economy*, Proceedings of a Symposium Sponsored by the Federal Reserve Bank of Kansas City, Jackson Hole, Wyoming, August 30, pp. 11–45.

Estrella, Arturo (2002), 'Securitization and the efficacy of monetary policy', Federal Reserve Bank of New York *Economic Policy Review*, **8** (1), 243–55.

Freedman, Charles (2000), 'Monetary policy implementation: past, present and future – will the advent of electronic money lead to the demise of central banking?', *International Finance*, **3**, 211–27.

Friedman, Benjamin M. (2000), 'Decoupling at the margin: the threat to monetary policy from the electronic revolution in banking', *International Finance*, **3**, 261–72.

Galí, Jordi (2002), 'The conduct of monetary policy in the face of technological change: theory and postwar US evidence', *Stabilization and Monetary Policy: The International Experience*', proceedings from a symposium sponsored by the Banco de Mexico, Mexico City, November 14, 2000, 407–44.

Goodhart, Charles A.E. (2000), 'Can central banking survive the IT revolution?', *International Finance*, **3**, 189–209.

Gordon, Robert, J. (2000), 'Does the 'New Economy' measure up to the great inventions of the past?' *Journal of Economic Perspectives*, **14**, 49–74.

Ip, Greg and Russell Gold (2002), 'Shock absorbers: lessons of expansion are helping economy beat recession', *Wall Street Journal*, March 4, p. A1.

McConnell, Margaret Mary and Gabriel Perez Quiros (2000), 'Output fluctuations in the United States: what has changed since the early 1980s?' *American Economic Review*, **90**, 1464–76.

Oliner, Stephen D. and Daniel A. Sichel (2000), 'The resurgence of growth in the late 1990s: is information technology the story?', unpublished manuscript, Board of Governors of the Federal Reserve System.

Orphanides, Athanasios (1998), 'Monetary policy evaluation with noisy information', *Finance and Economics Discussion Paper 1998–50*, Board of Governors of the Federal Reserve System.

Teplin, Albert M. (2001), 'The US flow of funds accounts and their uses', The Federal Reserve Bulletin, July, http://www.federalreserve.gov/pubs/bulletin/2001/0701lead.pdf.

Woodford, Michael (2000), 'Monetary policy in a world without money', *International Finance*, **3**, 229–60.

5. Competition policy in network industries: an introduction

Nicholas Economides*

INTRODUCTION

Network industries are a large part of the world economy. A key network industry is telecommunications, providing voice and data services, including the Internet and World Wide Web. Another key network industry is computer software and hardware. These two sectors, telecommunications and computers, have been the engines of fast growth of the world economy. In the news and entertainment sector, network industries include broadcasting and cable television, which in recent years have been reaching into traditional telecommunications services. In transportation, networks include airlines, railroads, roads, and shipping, and the delivery services that 'live' on these, such as the postal service and its competitors. In the financial sector, networks include traditional financial exchanges for bonds, equities, and derivatives, clearing houses, B2B and B2C exchanges, credit and debit card networks, as well as automated transactions banking networks, such as ATM networks.

Besides traditional network industries, many of the features of networks apply to *virtual networks*. A virtual network is a collection of compatible goods that share a common technical platform. For example, all VHS video players make up a virtual network. Similarly, all computers running Windows 95 can be thought of as a virtual network. Compatible computer software and hardware make up a network, and so do computer operating systems and compatible applications. More generally, networks are comprised of complementary components, so they also encompass wholesale and retail networks, as well as information networks and servers such as telephone Yellow Pages, Yahoo, Google, etc.

Adding to the importance of networks from a public policy point of view is the fact that network industries often provide necessities. Monopolization in such a setting can have significant social and political implications.

There may be a number of anti-competitive concerns in a network industry. The focus of this chapter is the question: Since network industries have special common features, are there special competition policy issues arising out of key features of network industries? If yes, what is the framework of the public policies that can be pursued to address these issues?

THE LOGIC OF COMPETITION LAW

The logic of competition and antitrust law in the United States and the European Union is to guard against restrictions and impediments to competition that are not likely to be naturally corrected by competitive forces. Although some disagree, I will posit that the maximization of efficiency (allocative, productive, and dynamic) is the desired outcome of competition and antitrust law, and that competition is the means of achieving efficiency.

As an alternative to antitrust and competition law, economic regulation have been established in three exceptional cases: (1) for those markets where it is clear that competition cannot be achieved by market forces; (2) where deviation from efficiency is deemed socially desirable; and (3) where the social and private benefits are clearly different. In each of these cases, it is clear that a market without intervention will not result in the desired outcome. In the first case, this is true by the definition of the category. In the second case, markets may lead to efficiency, but society prefers a different outcome and intervention is necessary to achieve this. In the third case, maximization of social surplus does not coincide with maximization of the sum of profits and consumers' surplus because of 'externalities'.

Some key network industries are regulated in at least part or in some aspects. Telecommunications has very significant regulation in both the federal and state level. Railroads, electricity, air and ground transportation are also heavily regulated. Financial exchanges are under 'light' regulation and to a significant extent under self-regulation. In contrast, B2B exchanges, credit card, and banking networks, as well as computers and their virtual networks are almost completely deregulated.

A full discussion of the merits and problems with regulation of each of these network industries is impossible in the context of this chapter. Instead, I will outline the parameters that would necessitate regulation or deregulation based on the broad features of network markets. In future work I will examine the full application of these principles on all network industries. I expect to observe that the principles of economic regulation are not applied equally to all industries, and, in a number of cases, the present regulatory regime is based on historical reasons (political, social, and technological) and cannot be justified based on the application of the economic principles of the present technology.

SPECIAL FEATURES OF MARKETS WITH NETWORK EFFECTS

Sources of Network Effects and the Reversal of the Law of Demand

Many network industries exhibit increasing returns to scale in production: unit (average) cost decreases with increasing scale of production. Often incremental cost is negligible (for example in software). However, these are also features of non-network industries and are *not* the defining feature of network industries. Thus, increasing returns to scale in production is also not the defining feature of the competition policy issues that are rooted in the existence of networks.

Networks are composed of complementary nodes and links. The crucial defining feature of networks is the complementarity between the various nodes and links. A service delivered over a network requires the use of two or more network components. Thus, network components are complementary to each other.

A common and defining feature of network industries is the fact that they exhibit increasing returns to scale in consumption, commonly called 'network effects'. The existence of network externalities is the key reason for the importance, growth, and profitability of network industries and the New Economy. A market exhibits network effects (or network externalities) when the value to a buyer of an extra unit is higher when more units are sold, everything else being equal.

Network effects arise because of complementarities. In a traditional network, network externalities arise because a typical subscriber can reach more subscribers in a larger network. See Figure 5.1, which depicts a traditional telecommunications network where customers A, B, . . ., G are connected to a switch at S. Although goods with 'access to the switch' AS, BS, . . ., GS have the same industrial classification and traditional economics would classify them as substitutes, they are used as complements. In particular, when customer A makes a phone call to customer B, he uses *both* AS and BS.

In a *virtual network*, externalities arise because larger sales of components of type A induce larger availability of complementary components B_1, . . ., B_n, thereby increasing the value of components of type A. See Figure 5.2. The increased value of component A results in further positive feedback. Despite the cycle of positive feedbacks, it is typically expected that the value of component A does not explode to infinity because the additional positive feedback is expected to decrease with increases in the size of the network.

In traditional non-network industries, the willingness to pay for the last unit of a good decreases with the number of units sold. This is called *the*

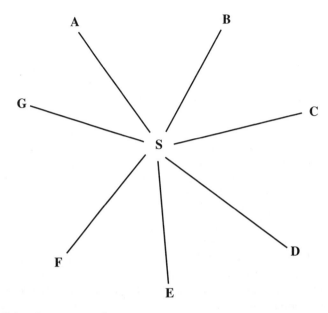

Figure 5.1   A star network

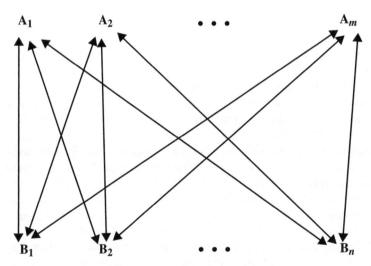

Figure 5.2   A virtual network of complementary goods

law of demand, and is traditionally considered to hold for almost all goods.[1] However, the existence of network effects implies that, as more units are sold, the willingness to pay for the last unit may be higher. This means that for network goods, the fundamental law of demand is violated: for network goods, some portions of the curve demand can slope upwards. This means that, for some portions of the demand curve, as sales expand, people are willing to pay more for the last unit.

The law of demand is still correct if one disregards the effects of the expansion of sales on complementary goods. But, as increased sales of a network good imply an expansion in the sales of complementary goods, the value of the last unit increases. Combining the traditional downward-sloping effect with the positive effect due to network expansion can result in a demand curve that has an upward-sloping part.

The key reason for the appearance of network externalities is the complementarity between the components of a network. Depending on the network, the network effect may be direct or indirect. When customers are identified with components, the externality is direct. Consider for example a typical two-way network, such as the local telephone network of Figure 5.1. In this n-nodes 2-way network, there are $2n(n-1)$ potential goods. An additional ($n+1$th) customer provides direct externalities to all other customers in the network by adding $2n$ potential new goods through the provision of a complementary link (say ES) to the existing links.

In typical one-way networks, the network effect is only indirect. When there are m varieties of component A and n varieties of component B as in Figure 5.2 (and all A-type goods are compatible with all of B-type), there are mn potential composite goods. An extra customer yields indirect externalities to other customers, by increasing the demand for components of types A and B and thereby (because of the presence of economies of scale) potentially increasing the number of varieties of each component that are available in the market.

Exchange networks (financial networks such as the NYSE and NASDAQ, commodities, futures, and options exchanges as well as business-to-business 'B2B' exchanges) also exhibit indirect network externalities. There are two ways in which these externalities arise. First, externalities arise in the act of exchanging assets or goods. Second, externalities may arise in the array of vertically related services that compose a financial transaction. These include the services of a broker, bringing the offer to the floor, matching the offer, etc. The second type of externalities are similar to other vertically-related markets. The first way in which externalities arise in financial markets is more important.

The act of exchanging goods or assets brings together a trader who is willing to sell with a trader who is willing to buy. The exchange brings together the two complementary goods, 'willingness to sell at price p' (the 'offer') and 'willingness to buy at price p' (the 'counter-offer') and creates a composite good, the 'exchange transaction'. The two original goods were complementary and each had no value without the other one. Clearly, the availability of the counter-offer is critical for the exchange to occur. Put in terms commonly used in finance, minimal liquidity is necessary for the transaction to occur.

Financial and business-to-business exchanges also exhibit positive size externalities in the sense that the increasing size (or thickness) of an exchange market increases the expected utility of all participants. Higher participation of traders on both sides of the market (drawn from the same distribution) decreases the variance of the expected market price and increases the expected utility of risk-averse traders. *Ceteris paribus*, higher liquidity increases traders' utility. Thus, financial exchange markets also exhibit network externalities.

As we have noted earlier, network externalities arise out of the complementarity of different network pieces. Thus, they arise naturally in both one- and two-way networks, as well as in vertically-related markets. The value of good X increases as more of the complementary good Y is sold, and vice versa. Thus, more of Y is sold as more X is sold. It follows that the value of X increases as more of it is sold. This positive feedback loop seems explosive, and indeed it would be, except for the inherent downward slope of the demand curve.

To understand this better, consider a fulfilled expectations formulation of network externalities. Let the willingness to pay for the nth unit of the good when n^e units are expected to be sold be $p(n; n^e)$. In this formulation, n and n^e are normalized so that they represent market coverage, ranging from 0 to 1, rather than absolute quantities. Willingness to pay $p(n; n^e)$ is a decreasing function of its first argument because the demand slopes downward. $p(n; n^e)$ increases in n^e; this captures the network externalities effect, i.e., that the good is more valuable when the expected sales n^e are higher. At a market equilibrium of the simple single-period world, expectations are fulfilled, $n = n^e$, thus defining the fulfilled expectations demand $p(n, n)$.

Figure 5.3 shows the construction of a typical fulfilled expectations demand in a network industry. Each willingness-to-pay curve $p(n, n_i^e)$, $i = 1, 2, \ldots$, shows the willingness to pay for a varying quantity n, given an expectation of sales $n^e = n_i^e$. At $n = n_i^e$, expectations are fulfilled and the point belongs to $p(n, n)$ as $p(n_i^e, n_i^e)$. Thus $p(n, n)$ is constructed as a collection of points $p(n_i^e, n_i^e)$. It is reasonable to impose the condition $\lim_{n \to 1} p(n, n) = 0$. This means that, as the market is more and more covered, eventually we reach consumers who are willing to pay very little for the good, despite the fact that they are able to reap very large network

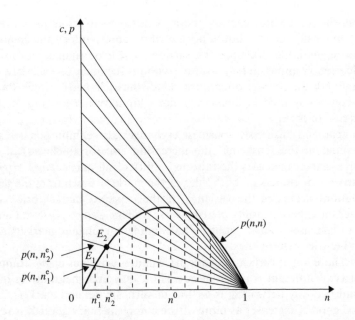

Figure 5.3   Willingness to pay as a function of expected quantity, and the locus of market equilibria where expectations are fulfilled

externalities. It follows that $p(n, n)$ is decreasing for large n. In Figure 5.3, the fulfilled expectations demand at quantity zero is $p(0, 0) = 0$. This means that consumers think that the good has negligible value when its sales (and network effect) are zero. Although this is true for many network goods, some network goods have positive inherent value even at zero sales and no network effects. If the good has an inherent value k, $p(0, 0) = k$, the fulfilled expectations demand curve in Figure 5.3 starts at $(0, k)$.

Economides and Himmelberg (1995) show that the fulfilled expectations demand is increasing for small n if either one of three conditions hold:

1.   The utility of every consumer in a network of zero size is zero; or
2.   There are immediate and large external benefits to network expansion for very small networks; or
3.   There is a significant number of high-willingness-to-pay consumers who are just indifferent on joining a network of approximately zero size.

The first condition is straightforward and applies directly to all two-way networks, such as the telecommunications and fax networks where the good has no value unless there is another user to connect to. The other two conditions are a bit more subtle, but commonly observed in networks and vertically-related industries. The second condition holds for networks where the addition of even a few users increases the value of the network significantly. A good example of this is a newsgroup on an obscure subject, where the addition of very few users starts a discussion and significantly increases its value. The third condition is most common in software markets. A software application has value to a user even if no one else uses it. The addition of an extra user has a network benefit to other users (because they can share files or find trained workers in the specifics of the application), but this benefit is small. However, when large numbers of users are added, the network benefit can be very significant.

Critical Mass

When the fulfilled expectations demand increases for small n, we say that the network exhibits a positive critical mass under perfect competition. This means that, if we imagine a constant marginal cost c decreasing as technology improves, the network will start at a positive and significant size n^0 (corresponding to marginal cost c^0). For each smaller marginal cost, $c < c^0$, there are three network sizes consistent with marginal cost pricing: a zero size network; an unstable network size at the first intersection of the horizontal through c with $p(n, n)$; and the Pareto optimal stable network size at the largest intersection of the horizontal with $p(n, n)$. The multiplicity of equilibria is a direct result of the coordination problem that arises naturally in the typical network externalities model. In such a setting, it is natural to assume that the Pareto optimal network size will result.

Features of Markets with Network Effects

Ability to charge prices on both sides of a network
There are a number of fundamental properties of network industries that arise out of the existence of network effects.

First, a firm can make money from either side of the network. For example, a telecommunications services provider can charge subscribers when they originate calls or when they receive calls or for both.[2] When a network consists of software clients and servers, both provided by the same firm, the firm can use the prices of the client and server software to maximize the network effect and its profits. For example it can distribute the client at marginal cost (free) and make all its profits from the server. In a similar vein, Adobe distributes the 'Acrobat Reader' free while it makes its profits from the 'Acrobat' product that allows the creation of files that can be read by the Acrobat Reader. The availability of prices on both sides of the network allows for complex pricing strategies, and, depending on the dynamics and market shares in the two sides of the market, can be used strategically to enhance and leverage a firm's strong strategic position on one side of the network.

Externalities internalized or not

Second, in network industries, the additional subscriber/user is often not rewarded for the benefit that he/she brings to others by subscribing. Hence typically there are 'externalities', i.e., benefits not fully intermediated by the market. However, firms can use price discrimination to make favorable terms available to large users to maximize their network effect contribution to the market. For example, a large customer in a financial market can be given a very low price to be compensated for the positive network effect it brings to the market.[3]

Fast network expansion

Third, generally, the pace of market penetration (network expansion) is much faster in network industries than in non-network industries. In the earlier discussion on critical mass, we saw that, in a one-period model, as unit cost decreases, the network starts with significant market coverage. In the presence of frictions and imperfectly elastic supply, the network expansion is not instantaneous from 0 to n^0 but rather is a very fast expansion following and S-shaped curve, as seen in Figure 5.4. This figure compares the market share expansion of a new good (diffusion) in presence (delta = 1) and absence (delta = 0) of network effects. The self-reinforcing nature of network effects leads to a much faster expansion when they are present.[4]

Inequality of market shares and profits

Fourth, markets with strong network effects where firms can chose their own technical standards are 'winner-take-most' markets. In these markets, there is extreme market share and profits inequality. The market share of the largest firm can easily be a multiple of the market share of the second largest, the second largest firm's market share can be a multiple of the market share of the third, and so on. This geometric sequence of market shares implies that, even for a small number of firms n, the nth firm's market share is tiny. At equilibrium, there is extreme market share and profits inequality.[5]

The reason for the inequality is straightforward. A firm with a large market share has more complementary goods and therefore its good is more valuable to consumers. Good examples of this are PC operating systems market and specific software applications markets.

To understand the extent of market share, price, and profits inequality in network industries, we provide results from Economides and Flyer (1998). As a benchmark, they assume that all firms produce identical products,

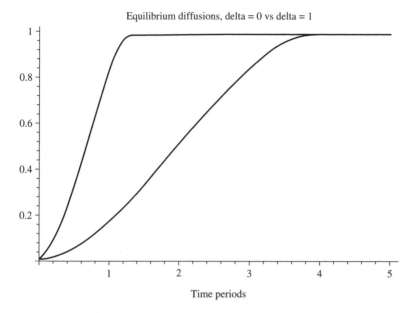

Figure 5.4   Diffusion in the presence of network effects (delta = 1) and in their absence (delta = 0)

except for whatever quality is added to them by network externalities. They also assume that no firm has any technical advantage in production over any other with respect to any particular platform and that there are no production costs. We consider here only the extreme case of 'pure network goods' where there is no value to the good in the absence of network externalities. The summary of the equilibria under total incompatibility (which can be enforced when firms have proprietary standards) is in Tables 5.1 and 5.2. Firm #1 has the largest sales, firm #2 is the second largest, etc.

Even with no fixed costs and an *infinite* number of firms, the Herfindahl–Hirschman index (HHI) = 0.464, which corresponds to between two and three firms of equal size.

The market equilibria exhibit extreme inequality. The ratio of outputs of consecutive firms is over 2.6. Ratios of prices of consecutive firms is at least 7. The ratio of profits of consecutive firms is about 20. This means that a firm has about 38 per cent of the sales of the immediately larger firm, can charge only 15 per cent of the price of the next larger firm, and receives only 5 per cent of the profits of the immediately larger firm. Entry after the third firm has practically no influence on the output, prices, and profits of the top three firms as well as the consumers' and producers' surplus. From the fourth one on, firms are so small that their entry hardly influences the market.

Table 5.1   Quantities, market coverage, and prices under incompatibility

Number of firms I	Sales of largest firm q_1	Sales of second firm q_2	Sales of third firm q_3	Market coverage $\Sigma^I_{j=1}q_j$	Price of largest firm p_1	Price of second firm p_2	Price of third firm p_3	Price of smallest firm p_I
1	0.6666			0.6666	0.222222			2.222e-1
2	0.6357	0.2428		0.8785	0.172604	0.0294		2.948e-2
3	0.6340	0.2326	0.0888	0.9555	0.170007	0.0231	0.0035	3.508e-3
4	0.6339	0.2320	0.0851	0.9837	0.169881	0.0227	0.0030	4.533e-4
5	0.6339	0.2320	0.0849	0.9940	0.169873	0.0227	0.0030	7.086e-5
6	0.6339	0.2320	0.0849	0.9999	0.169873	0.0227	0.0030	9.88e-11
7	0.6339	0.2320	0.0849	0.9999	0.169873	0.0227	0.0030	0

Note: q_1 indicates sales of firm 1, where the sum of sales of all firms is normalized to be less than or equal to one. Prices are in dollars. The ith firm produces quantity q_i at price p_i, and firms are ordered in decreasing quantity so that $q_1 > q_2 > q_3$, etc.

Source: Economides and Flyer (1998).

Table 5.2   Profits, consumers' and total surplus under incompatibility

Number of firms I	Π_1	Π_2	Π_3	Profits of last firm Π_1	Total industry profits $\Sigma^I_{j=i}\Pi_j$	Consumers' surplus CS	Total surplus TS
1	0.1481			0.1481	0.1481	0.148197	0.29629651
2	0.1097	7.159e-3		7.159e-3	0.1168	0.173219	0.29001881
3	0.1077	5.377e-3	3.508e-4	3.508e-4	0.1135	0.175288	0.28878819
4	0.1077	5.285e-3	3.096e-4	1.474e-5	0.1132	0.175483	0.28868321
5	0.1077	5.281e-3	2.592e-4	8.44e-7	0.1132	0.175478	0.28867817
6	0.1077	5.281e-3	2.589e-4	1.18e-14	0.1132	0.175478	0.28867799
7	0.1077	5.281e-3	2.589e-4	0	0.1132	0.175478	0.28867799

Note: Profits of firm 1 are Π_1. All variables are in dollars. Subscripts indicate firms; Π signifies profits.

Source: Economides and Flyer (1998).

Monopoly may maximize total surplus

Fifth, in industries with significant network externalities, under conditions of incompatibility between competing platforms, monopoly may maximize social surplus. This is because, when strong network effects are present, a very large market share of one platform creates significant network benefits for this platform which contribute to large consumers' and producers' surpluses.

It is possible to have situations where a breakup of a monopoly into two competing firms of incompatible standards *reduces* rather than increases social surplus because network externalities benefits are reduced. This is because de facto standardization is valuable, even if done by a monopolist.

In the Economides–Flyer model, although consumers' surplus is increasing in the number of active firms, total surplus is decreasing in the number of firms. That is, the more firms in the market, the lower is total welfare. This remarkable result comes from the fact that when there are fewer firms in the market there is more coordination and the network effects are larger. As the number of firms decreases, the positive network effects increase more than the dead weight loss, so that total surplus is maximized at monopoly! Thus, total surplus is highest at monopoly while consumers' surplus is lowest at monopoly. This poses an interesting dilemma for antitrust authorities. Should they intervene or not? In non-network industries, typically both consumers' and total surplus are lowest at monopoly. In this network model, maximizing consumers' surplus would imply minimizing total surplus.

Compared to the market equilibrium under compatibility, the incompatibility equilibrium is deficient in many dimensions. Consumers' and total surplus are higher under compatibility; the profits of all except the highest production firm are lower under incompatibility; and prices are lower under compatibility except for duopoly.

No anti-competitive acts are *necessary* to create market inequality
A sixth implication of network effects is that, because inequality is natural in the market structure of network industries, there should be no presumption that anti-competitive actions are responsible for the creation of market share inequality or very high profitability of a top firm. Thus, no anti-competitive acts are *necessary* to create this inequality. The 'but for' benchmark against which anti-competitive actions in network industries are to be judged should be not be 'perfect competition' but an environment of significant inequality and profits.

In network industries, free entry does not lead to perfect competition
A seventh implication of network effects is that, in network industries, free entry does not lead to perfect competition. In a market with strong network effects, once a few firms are in operation, the addition of new competitors, even under conditions of free entry, does not change the market structure in any significant way. Although eliminating barriers to entry can encourage competition, the resulting competition may not significantly affect market structure. This implies that, in markets with strong network effects, antitrust authorities may not be able to significantly affect market *structure*

by eliminating barriers to entry. See earlier example where the addition of the fifth firm hardly changes the output of the first four firms.

The remarkable property of the incompatibility equilibrium is the extreme inequality in market shares and profits that is sustained under conditions of free entry. Antitrust and competition law have placed a tremendous amount of hope on the ability of free entry to spur competition, reduce prices, and ultimately eliminate profits. In network industries, free entry brings into the industry an infinity of firms but it fails miserably to reduce or to flatten the distribution of market shares. Entry does not eliminate the profits of the high production firms. And, it is worth noting that, at the equilibrium of this market, there is no anti-competitive behavior. Firms do not reach their high output and market domination by exclusion, coercion, tying, erecting barriers to entry, or any other anti-competitive behavior. The extreme inequality is a natural feature of the market equilibrium.

At the long-run equilibrium of this model, free entry is present and an infinity of firms have entered, but the equilibrium is far from competitive. No anti-competitive activity has led firms to this equilibrium. Traditional antitrust intervention cannot accomplish anything because the conditions such intervention seeks to establish already exist in this market. Unfortunately the desired competitive outcome does not.

Can there be an improvement over the market incompatibility equilibrium? Yes, a switch to the compatibility equilibrium which has higher consumers' and total surpluses for any number of firms. Is it within the scope of competition law to impose such a change? It depends. Firms may have a legally protected intellectual property right that arises from their creation of the design of the platform. Only if anti-competitive behavior was involved, can the antitrust authorities clearly intervene.

Imposing a 'competitive' market structure is likely to be counterproductive
The eighth implication of network effects is that antitrust interventions may be futile. Because 'winner takes most' is the natural equilibrium in these markets, attempting to superimpose a different market structure (say one of all firms having approximately equal market shares), may be both futile and counterproductive.

Nature of competition is different in network industries
A ninth implication of the network effects is that competition *for the market* takes precedence over competition *in the market*. The fact that the natural equilibrium market structure in network industries is winner-take-most with very significant market inequality does not imply that competition is weak. Competition on which firm will create the top platform and reap most of the benefits is, in fact, very intense. In network industries, there is typically a very

intense race to be the dominant firm. In network industries, we often observe Schumpeterian races for market dominance.

A good recent example of Schumpeterian competition is the competition among dot-coms in 1999–2000. As explained earlier, economic models imply very high valuation of the dominant firm compared to other firms in the same network industry. The same perception prevailed in Wall Street. During that period, dot-com firms advertised very intensely and subsidized consumers to be able to achieve the coveted dominant position in the market. The easy availability of capital for dot-coms at the time made it easy to observe their behavior as they 'burned' almost all the cash they had to get the top market share. Many of the dot-coms failed because demand for their services was much lower than predicted or because of flaws in their business models. However, all the successful dot-coms, such as eBay, Amazon, and Yahoo, also followed this strategy.

Generally, in network industries, the costs of entry may be higher but the rewards of success may also be higher compared to non-network industries.

Path dependence
A tenth implication of network effects is the importance of *path-dependence*. Path-dependence is the dependence of a system or network on past decisions of producers and consumers. For example, the price at which a VHS player can be sold today is path-dependent because it depends on the number of VHS players sold earlier (the installed base of VHS players). The existence of an installed base of consumers favors an incumbent. However, competitors with significant product advantages or a better pricing strategy can overcome the advantage of an installed base.

For example, in the market for video players, VHS overcame Beta after six years of a higher installed base by Beta. This was an implication of:

1. Sony's mistakes in disregarding network externalities and not licensing the Beta format;
2. Matsushita's widespread licensing of VHS;
3. The fact that one low-end low-price VHS player can contribute as much to the network effect as a high-end high-price Beta player.

In the Beta/VHS case, it is clear that Sony mistakenly disregarded the network effects that arose from the availability of rental tapes of pre-recorded movies. The main function of video recorders was originally thought to be 'time delay' in watching material recorded from the TV. The pre-recorded market emerged later, first as a market where movies were sold, and later as a movies rental market. The emergence of markets for 'movies for sale' and 'movies for rent', which had to be recorded in particular format, created a significant complementary good for Beta and VHS players. The significant cost of physical distribution of tapes throughout the country and the costs of carrying a significant inventory of titles made the choice of what movies to bring and in what format crucially dependent on present and forecast demand which was closely correlated with the present and forecast installed base of video players in each format. Thus, although network effects and path dependence played a crucial role in determining the fate of Beta, the outcome was far from predetermined. Early, more aggressive licensing of the Beta format by Sony or the early promotion of low-end Beta players could have reversed the demise of the Beta format.[6]

COMPETITION POLICY ISSUES IN NETWORK INDUSTRIES

One-sided Bottlenecks

Interconnection issues in telecommunications, railroads, airline, and other transportation networks are very common. Often one company has exclusive control of part of the network, which is required by others to provide services. We call this network part 'a bottleneck.' Generally, bottlenecks can be divided into two categories: one-sided and two-sided. A one-sided bottleneck is monopolized by a firm and this firm does not require the use of a different bottleneck. An example of such a bottleneck is shown as link AB in Figure 5.5. An example of such a bottleneck is the connection of local service telecommunications subscribers to a switch. This is typically called 'the last mile', and often called 'the local loop'. After the 1984 breakup of AT&T, the local loop has been monopolized by the local exchange carrier, typically a Regional Bell Operating Company ('RBOC') or GTE (General Telephone and Electronics). The local loop is a required input in the production of

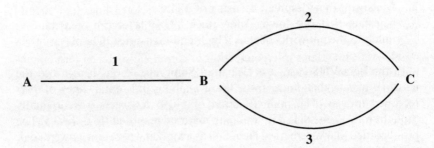

Figure 5.5   A one-sided bottleneck

long-distance services, and typically long-distance companies do not have a comparable local loop. Similarly, such a one-way bottleneck can arise when a firm monopolizes a railroad track such as AB. In telecommunications, the local exchange bottleneck has traditionally resulted in high prices for use of the bottleneck to originate ('access origination') or terminate calls ('access termination').

The potential anti-competitive consequences of a one-sided bottleneck are obvious, and have been understood since the early days of the telecommunications network when AT&T enjoyed a monopoly in long distance (say here AB) but faced competition in local markets. In the context of Figure 5.5, the early AT&T was in possession of links 1 (long distance) and 2 (local), but did not allow an independent firm which possessed link 3 to interconnect at B and provide part of the long-distance service CBA. For over two decades in the beginning of the twentieth century, AT&T refused to interconnect independent local telecommunications companies to its long-distance network, unless they became part of the Bell System, which essentially meant unless they were acquired.[7]

The early AT&T foreclosure of independents through a refusal to interconnect shows the importance of complementarities in networks and the way that companies can leverage dominance in one market to create dominance in a market for complementary goods, especially when the complementary good requires the monopolized input (to provide a final service). In this case, AT&T monopolized long distance and was able to leverage its position in long distance (through the refusal to interconnect of independent locals) and gain a dominant position in local telecommunications markets throughout the country.

The continued foreclosure of the independents by AT&T and its 'refusal to deal' with them caused regulation to be established at the state and Federal levels in the 1930s. The 1934 Federal Communications Act ('1934 Act') imposed mandatory interconnection in an attempt to stop the foreclosure of independents and stabilized the market share of local lines held by AT&T. However, at that point AT&T's market share of local lines had already reached close to the 89 per cent that AT&T had at its breakup in 1981.

A major revision of the 1934 Act, the Telecommunications Act of 1996 ('1996 Act') mandates interconnection of all public switched telecommunications networks at any technically feasible point. The 1996 Act and similar European Union regulations attempt to solve the problem of the monopolization of the key parts of local telecommunications network. They impose unbundling of the network and forced lease to entrants of some of the monopolized parts of the network, including the local loop. The goal is to make mix and match entry strategies feasible for local voice telephone service as well as broadband Internet access through DSL that utilizes high frequencies transmission though copper local loops. Thus, they mandate alternative access prices for unbundled parts of the network (unbundled network elements 'UNEs') at cost-based prices. The Federal Communications Commission (FCC) and state Public Utilities Commissions (PUCs) accepted the view that lease prices should be based on *forward-looking* costs rather than on historical, accounting, or embedded costs (which was favored by RBOCs). In setting prices for unbundled network elements, the FCC and state PUCs also rejected the relevance of prices based on *private* opportunity cost, such as the 'Efficient Components Pricing Rule', ('ECPR'). Such rules derive prices for components from the monopoly end-to-end prices. Thus, the ECPR and its varieties would guarantee the monopolist's profits despite market structure changes in the markets for components that are used to create final services (see Economides and White 1995; Economides 2003). The 1996 Act also imposes a number of rules to prevent anti-competitive actions in telecommunications, such as number portability, mandatory resale of services, transparency, non-discrimination, etc. A full discussion of these rules can be found at Economides (1999). Still, the 1996 Act missed opportunities to define technical standards. Unfortunately, legal maneuvers by the incumbent local exchange carriers and high prices for the unbundled network elements considerably delayed significant entry into local telecommunications markets.

Two-sided Bottlenecks

In a two-sided bottleneck, each of two firms is monopolist, each with a different bottleneck, and each firm requires the other's bottleneck to produce its output. For example, suppose there are two local telephone companies, each customer subscribes only to one local telephone company, and each company requires the other's network to complete calls. This could be represented in Figure 5.5 with the second link BC (number 3) removed, and considering AB to belong to firm 1, BC to belong to firm 2, firm 1 selling service ABC and firm 2 selling service CBA. In the context of this example, each of firms 1 and 2 buys *access termination* from the other. If each firm $i = 1, 2$, sells both services ABC and CBA, then each firm buys both *access origination* and access termination from the other.

Many of the issues of traditional bottlenecks have been dealt with by regulation in the United States and the European Union. In monopolized one-way bottlenecks, such as access origination and termination used in the creation of long-distance calls, there has been a tendency to decrease the regulated prices, but prices are still high. In the two-way bottleneck of access used in the creation of local calls by competing local exchange carriers, the

Telecommunications Act of 1996 ('1996 Act') imposes cost-based reciprocal fees and allows the possibility of 'bill and keep', i.e., zero prices. If cost-based reciprocal compensation were not the rule, and firms were able to set termination at profit maximizing levels, Economides et al. (1996a, 1996b), have shown that a large network will try to impose very high termination charges on an opponent small network so that no calls terminate from the small network to the large one. Without the possibility of such across-networks calls, a small network will only be able to provide within-the-network calls, and, being small, will add little value to potential subscribers. As a consequence, large networks are able to provide more value to subscribers, and the small network is foreclosed. Starting from a regime of large local incumbent and a small local entrant, the large incumbent can set up termination access fees so that the entrant is driven out of the market.[8]

In summary, in the absence of specific regulatory rules, two-sided bottlenecks can lead to foreclosure of competitors, even when each firm requires use of the bottleneck of the other to complete calls or provide a service.

Market Power Creation Specific to Networks: Technical Standards

The early AT&T refusal to deal (interconnect) with independents (and with interconnected networks of independents) can arise in milder terms when a firm X that has a significant position in its industry insists that firms that provide products Y that are complementary to X do not also provide them for any competitor of X. For example, in the mid-1980s Nintendo refused to allow third-party games (software) to play on its game console (hardware) unless the software manufacturers agreed not to write a similar game for two years for competing game systems. Faced with this condition imposed by Nintendo, software developers had to make a choice to either write a game for Nintendo or for the competing platforms of Atari and Sega. Clearly this restriction reduced the potential revenue of a game developer who would like, for a small additional cost, to port its game to the alternative systems. But, also, more important, the restriction forced developers to predict which game system would have higher sales, and create software just for this system. Thus, Nintendo used the dominance of the game market at that point in time to coerce developers to write software just for its platform, and thereby increased the value of the Nintendo virtual network (of hardware and software). Nintendo abandoned this requirement under an antitrust challenge.

Because of the extreme inequality of market shares, prices, and profits in a network industry, restriction to the installed base of a firm in a network industry can be very detrimental since it can push a firm to a lower rank with significantly lower profits, or, in extreme cases, push a firm to such a low market share that it has closed down because it cannot recover fixed costs.

Another example from the computing industry illustrates a situation of market power creation specific to networks. Suppose that firm A chooses to make its product A incompatible with the products of other firms that perform similar functions, and it also subsidizes firms that produce complementary goods B to its product A.[9] Alternatively, we may assume that firm A subsidizes its own division that sells complementary goods B. As a result:

1. The value of firm A's product increase;
2. The entry hurdle of firm A's rivals increases;
3. There is possible creation of market power.

Firm A's defense will be that its actions are pro-competitive since their primary cause is the enhancement of value of product A. For the point of view of A's competitors, the actions of A look very much anti-competitive since the abundance of complementary goods B for product A puts them at a competitive disadvantage.

Note that the existence of incompatibility is a *necessary* condition for possible creation of market power. Moreover, the key to increasing social welfare is a potential move to compatibility. That is, assuming that innovation and product availability would not be reduced, the best of all worlds is to have public standards and full compatibility. However, it is very difficult for US antitrust authorities to intervene and/or define standards.

Besides the use of technical standards, firms can also use bundling and other pricing strategies as well as non-price discrimination strategies to leverage market power across markets.

In networks, as in other settings, there are potentially anti-competitive issues arising from the possibility of vertical integration and the behavior of vertically integrated firms. These may include, first, the bundling of components through vertical integration contracts, or manipulation of technical standards so that an entrant will not be able to enter in only one of the components markets, but will have to enter in both. Often firms have expertise or a technical advantage in only one component, and would like to enter only in the market for that component. An incumbent can strategically alter the market environment through acquisition or contract so that the entrant can only be successful if it enters more than one market. This increases the financial hurdle for an entrant, and it also forces it to sell components where it does not have expertise. Thus, it makes it more likely that entry will not occur.

A vertically integrated firm can also use discrimination in prices charged to a subsidiary compared to prices charged to a downstream competitor, or discrimination in quality provided to a subsidiary compared to quality provided to a downstream competitor, that is raising rivals' costs. These issues are discussed in more detail in Economides (1998).

Firms in network industries can also use a variety of ways to manipulate technical standards in joint ventures to achieve market power. The issue of market power also arises in 'aftermarkets', where consumers are 'locked in' to a durable good or a service that arises out of commitments of a durable nature. For example, in an important case that reached the Supreme Court, Kodak refused to supply parts to independent firms that serviced Kodak photocopiers. Although one could argue that there was significant competition in the market for new photocopiers and Kodak did not have a dominant position in that market, once customers had bought a Kodak photocopier, they were locked in, and faced significant costs to buy a new photocopier of a different brand. So, Kodak's actions could be anti-competitive in the 'aftermarket' for repair services of consumers who have already bought Kodak photocopiers. A similar case of anti-competitive actions can be made in aftermarkets where consumers are locked-in by having made an investment in a durable good that is incompatible with other comparable durable goods, or are locked-in in other ways. For example, consumers without number portability in wireless cellular and PCS markets may be locked-in the service of a particular provider or network.

B2B and Other Exchanges Issues

The world of business to business exchanges lacks the regulation of traditional financial and commodity exchanges. Many proposed B2B exchanges are run by the firms that also are trading. For example, Enron was proud of the fact that it was participating as a trading party in B2B exchanges that it organized and ran. Such a situation would be strictly prohibited in traditional financial and commodity exchanges because of the possibility that the organizer of the exchange would take advantage of the information created in the trading process to fashion privately beneficial trades. In another example, COVISINT, an exchange for automobile parts organized by automobile manufacturers has been accused of acting to consolidate the monopsony power of car manufacturers. In general, B2B exchanges can provide substantial benefits by consolidating trades, increasing market liquidity, improving standardization, and reducing search costs.[10] But B2B exchanges also have the potential of creating significant antitrust issues.

Dynamic Efficiency Issues

The world of networks and dynamic effects brings to the forefront the fact that behavior that exhibits static efficiency may lack dynamic inter-temporal efficiency. The possibility exists of a lock-in to a technology and a path which, when decisions taken in every period, looks optimal given past decisions, but is sub-optimal if earlier investment decisions had been delayed and all the decisions were taken at once. In a world with network effects a lock-in in an inferior technology can easily occur as firms (and countries) find it more desirable to invest further in the technology in which they already invested. This can occur under perfect competition. The problem can easily become much more important under oligopoly, as firms race to become the dominant firm, given the importance of dominance in a network industry.

Innovation Issues

An important antitrust issue is the speed of innovation in a network industry as affected by strategic decisions of firms and potentially anti-competitive actions. The effects of actions on innovation are important because innovation affects the welfare of future consumers, and this should be taken into consideration in an antitrust action. The difficulty in dealing with innovation issues in an antitrust action arises from the fact that the efficiency and intensity of innovation in monopoly compared to perfect competition and oligopoly are open questions in economics. Thus, it is very hard to make general statements on innovation in an antitrust context.

Criteria to be Used for Antitrust Intervention in Network Industries

When an antitrust intervention is considered in a network industry, a number of considerations that arise out of the nature of network industries have to be taken into account. These are explained in detail in earlier sections. First, the benchmark of the 'but for' world that should be considered should be a network industries equilibrium with significant inequality, rather than a perfectly competitive equilibrium. Second, competitors' harm should not be a sufficient reason for intervention. The right question is, 'were consumers (past, present, future) harmed by specific actions?' Third, uncertainty should be taken into account, and caution should be used in guessing how a high-tech industry would have evolved but for the anti-competitive action(s). Fourth, it is possible that monopoly may maximize total surplus. Fifth, that it will not be possible to sustain a long-term equal-market-shares equilibrium, and a short-term equal-market-shares equilibrium may have low total surplus. Sixth, path dependence and the value of the installed base are limited by Schumpeterian competition, and upheavals are not uncommon in network industries. Seventh, especially in software industries, the extent and functionality of products is flexible. This can help an incumbent because it can expand the functionality of its product, but can also help its rivals as they may incorporate functionalities of the incumbent's product in theirs.

Criteria to be Used for Remedies

When a remedies phase is reached, a liability finding has already been made. The objective of remedies is to stop practices that were found to be illegal, prevent the recurrence of such practices, and deal with any recurring threat posed by such practices.

Any intervention by antitrust authorities creates a disruption in the workings of markets. The objective of the remedial relief is to accomplish the objectives mentioned in the previous paragraph without damaging efficient production and competition in the market. The potential damage that antitrust intervention can produce is larger when it is applied to an industry with fast technological change, where leaps to new and more efficient technologies are expected, while the specific nature of the future winning technology is unknown. Often, it is plainly difficult to predict future winning technologies and therefore it is very hard to fashion an antitrust remedy with an accurate prediction of its effect on industry structure and competition a few years down the road. Of course, this uncertainty is multiplied when the remedy creates a significant intervention in the industry. Therefore, lacking the knowledge of the effects of their actions, it is in the public interest that antitrust authorities and courts avoid very extensive intervention in industries with fast technological change. It is best to intervene only to the extent that (1) intervention reverses the effects of actions for which liability was established; and (2) the effects of the intervention are predictable.

The existence of network effects has crucial implications for market structure and the ability of antitrust authorities to affect it. Even in the absence of anti-competitive acts, the existence of strong network effects in a market, can result in very significant inequalities in market shares and profits. The resulting equilibrium market structure can be called a *'natural oligopoly'* where very few firms dominate the market. The structural features of natural oligopoly for software markets cannot be altered by antitrust intervention without very significant losses for society. The very nature of markets with network effects implies that the ability of antitrust authorities to alter market stricture in such industries is limited, as discussed above.

As an alternative to antitrust and competition law, economic regulation can and has been established in three exceptional cases: (1) for those markets where it is clear that competition cannot be achieved by market forces; (2) where deviation from efficiency is deemed socially desirable; and (3) where the social and private benefits are clearly different, since in each of these cases, it is clear that a market without intervention will not result in the desired outcome. I will leave case (2) aside, since a discussion of it would lead us to a detailed discussion of specific industries. The requirements for case (3) are typically met in many network industries, since expansion of the network creates network effects that are typically not fully internalized by markets. However, it would be foolish to advocate regulation as the standard solution in network industries because of the existence of network effects. Often, a much smaller intervention, such as subsidization of the network to help network effects will be enough.

In case (1), where it is clear that competition and its benefits cannot be achieved by market forces, regulation may be a solution. The significant advantage of industry-specific regulation is that it can be tailored to the specifics of the industry, and specify rules on pricing and availability of particular products and services. Regulators, such as the FCC, also have staffs that can provide impartial technical advice that would be unavailable to a court.

However, regulation has a number of drawbacks. First, it is best suited for industries with well defined and not changing products and services. With stable product definitions, rules can be devised and specific pricing can be implemented if necessary. Second, as a corollary to the first observation, regulation is not well suited in industries with high technological change and frequently changing product definitions. Moreover, in an industry with fast technical progress, regulation can be used by the regulated companies to keep prices high, as exemplified by telecommunications regulation. Third, often regulators are very close to the interests of the regulated parties rather than to the interests of the public. Fourth, experience has shown that often regulators are not well informed about key variables as well as changes in the industry. Fifth, regulators at both the state and federal levels are under pressure and influence by both the executive and the legislative part of government, and cannot be as impartial as a court. These drawbacks can create significant surplus loss due to regulation.

In summary, regulation should be used sparingly in industries with stable products, if it is clear that antitrust action has failed, and keeping in mind that regulation can also cause a significant surplus loss.

CONCLUSION

This chapter is a start of an in-depth discussion of public policy in network industries. I believe that it is fair to say that the legal system does not yet have a framework for analysis of competition policy issues in network industries. This was to a large extent exemplified in *United States* v. *Microsoft*. I will not go into the details of this case, but will use it as an example of a case that failed to create such a framework.[11]

The Microsoft case has certainly been the most important antitrust case of the 'New Economy' this far. Unfortunately, its legal battle was fought to a very large extent without the use of the economics tools discussed above that are at the foundation of the New Economy and were key to the business success of Microsoft. There are a number of reasons for this. First, legal cases are often created and filed before an economist is found who will create the appropriate economic model to support the case. Second, the economic theory of networks is so inadequate and unsettled that there is no commonly accepted body of knowledge on market structure with network externalities, based on which one could evaluate deviations toward anti-competitive behavior. Third, the legal system has tremendous inertia to new ideas and models. Fourth, the legal system is ill-equipped to deal with complex technical matters. Fifth, given all these facts, lawyers on both sides find it easier to fight the issues on well-trodden ground even if the problems are really of a different nature. It is as if there is a dispute between two parties in the middle of a heavily forested area, but the lawyers of both parties fight it as if the dispute happened on the open plains, because they know the way disputes on the plains are resolved while the law of dispute resolution in forests has yet to be established.

I hope that, with further academic analysis of antitrust issues, when the next major New Economy antitrust case appears, there will be a deeper understanding and application of the economics of networks and of the way the law should apply to network industries.

NOTES

*   Stern School of Business, New York University, New York, NY 10012, (212) 998–0864, fax (212) 995–4218, http://www.stern.nyu.edu/networks/, email: neconomi@stern.nyu.edu.
1. More precisely, the law of demand is true for *normal* goods, that is, for goods for which an increase in income leads to a higher quantity of sales. For *inferior* goods an increase in income leads to a lower quantity of sales. If this effect is strong enough, the possibility of a *Giffen good* arises where sales increase as prices increase. Giffen goods are truly exceptional and rarely observed.
2. The pricing schemes used vary considerably depending on the telecommunications service. Traditionally, in fixed networks, in most places in the United States, local calls are free with a local connection that requires a fixed monthly fee. Long-distance subscribers were traditionally charged only for outgoing calls. In the last two decades 800, 866, 877, 888–prefix 'toll free' services allow for no charge to the calling party, while 900-prefix services allow the receiving party to charge a positive price. In wireless cellular and PCS telecommunications, United States subscribers pay for both incoming and outgoing calls, while in most of the rest of the world, wireless subscribers pay only for outgoing calls. On the Internet, retail subscribers pay a flat fee irrespective of the amount of time they use the service, the number of bits exchanged, whether they are incoming or

outgoing, and irrespective of the destination. Similarly, Internet service providers buy backbone connectivity at rates that depend just on the size of the pipe they utilize and irrespective of whether they are incoming or outgoing, and of the destination.

3. It is anecdotally known that Cantor Fitzgerald, which has a 70 per cent market share in the secondary market for US government 30 year bonds, offered to Salomon (the largest 'primary dealer' and trader of US bonds) prices equal to one tenth to one fifth of those charged to small traders. This is consistent with profit maximization by Cantor Fitzgerald because of the liquidity (network effect) brought to the market by Salomon which is by far the largest buyer ('primary dealer') in the auctions of US government bonds.

4. For a detailed discussion, see Economides and Himmelberg (1995).

5. If the distribution of the willingness to pay is distributed away from 0, an industry with network effects exhibits the finiteness property (Shaked and Sutton 1983), with a finite maximum number of active firms despite positive profits.

6. An often-cited example on path dependence is the prevalence of the QWERTY keyboard despite claims of more efficient function by the alternative Dvorak keyboard. For many business applications, and for antitrust purposes, the QWERTY example is not crucial because there was no significant strategic business interest in the success of either design.

7. AT&T claimed that the main reason for its refusal to interconnect was the low technical standards of the independents, as well as incompatibilities, that would jeopardize AT&T's network after interconnection. While there is some truth to those claims, it is unlikely that they applied to all independents. Moreover, once acquired by AT&T, independents were interconnected with AT&T's network, after some modifications. This shows that the refusal to interconnect was mainly a strategic and commercial decision rather than a technical one.

8. This is not just a theoretical possibility. Telecom New Zealand ('TNZ'), operating in an environment of weak antitrust and regulatory intervention (so-called 'light-handed regulation') offered such high termination fees that the first entrant into local telecommunications, Clear, survives only by refusing to pay interconnection fees to TNZ, while the second entrant, BellSouth New Zealand exited the local telecommunications market.

9. For example, one can think of A as a computer operating system, and B as an application. OS manufacturers can and do embed software routines that are useful to application software developers since they reduce the cost of writing applications.

10. See Economides and Siow (1988) for a discussion of the benefits of B2B and other exchanges.

11. For a discussion of the Microsoft case, see Economides (2001a, 2001b, 2002) and http://www.stern.nyu.edu/networks/.

REFERENCES

Economides, Nicholas (1996), 'The economics of networks', *International Journal of Industrial Organization*, **16** (4), 675–99.

Economides, Nicholas (1998), 'The incentive for non-price discrimination by an input monopolist', *International Journal of Industrial Organization*, **16** (May 1998), 271–84.

Economides, Nicholas (1999), 'The Telecommunications Act of 1996 and its impact', *Japan and the World Economy*, **11**, 455–83.

Economides, Nicholas (2001a), 'The Microsoft antitrust case', *Journal of Industry, Competition and Trade: From Theory to Policy*, **1** (1), 7–39.

Economides, Nicholas (2001b), 'The Microsoft antitrust case: rejoinder', *Journal of Industry, Competition and Trade: From Theory to Policy*, **1** (1), 71–9.

Economides, Nicholas (2002), 'Amicus brief of Nicholas S. Economides on the revised proposed final judgment in the Microsoft case', submitted to the United

States Department of Justice, available at http://www.usdoj.gov/atr/cases/ ms_tuncom/major/mtc-00022465.htm.

Economides, Nicholas (2003), 'The tragic inefficiency of M-ECPR', in A. Shampine (ed.), *Down to the Wire: Studies in the Diffusion and Regulation of Telecommunications Technologies*, New York: Nova Science Publishers, pp. 142–54.

Economides, Nicholas and Fredrick Flyer (1998), 'Compatibility and market structure for network goods', discussion paper EC-98-02, Stern School of Business, New York. University, available at http://www.stern.nyu.edu/networks/98-02.pdf.

Economides, Nicholas and Charles Himmelberg (1995), 'Critical mass and network evolution in telecommunications', in Gerard W. Brock (ed.), *Toward a Competitive Telecommunications Industry: Selected Papers from the 1994 Telecommunications Policy Research Conference*, Mahwah, NJ: Lawrence Erlbaum Association, pp. 47–63.

Economides, Nicholas and Aloysius Siow (1988), 'The division of markets is limited by the extent of liquidity', *American Economic Review*, **78** (1), 108–21.

Economides, Nicholas and Lawrence J. White (1994), 'Networks and compatibility: implications for antitrust', *European Economic Review*, **38**, 651–62.

Economides, Nicholas and Lawrence J. White (1995), 'Access and interconnection pricing: how efficient is the efficient component pricing rule?', *Antitrust Bulletin*, **XL** (3), 557–79.

Economides, Nicholas and Lawrence J. White (1998), 'The inefficiency of the ECPR yet again: a reply to Larson', *Antitrust Bulletin*, **XLIII** (2), 429–44.

Economides, Nicholas, Giuseppe Lopomo and Glenn Woroch (1996a), 'Regulatory pricing policies to neutralize network dominance', *Industrial and Corporate Change*, **5** (4), 1013–28.

Economides, Nicholas, Giuseppe Lopomo and Glenn Woroch (1996b), 'Strategic commitments and the principle of reciprocity in interconnection pricing', discussion paper EC-96-13, Stern School of Business, New York University, available from http://www.stern.nyu.edu/networks/96-13.pdf.

Posner, Richard A. (2000), 'Antitrust in the New Economy', *Tech Law Journal*, at http://www.techlawjournal.com/atr/20000914posner.asp.

Shaked, Avner and John Sutton (1983), 'Natural oligopolies', *Econometrica*, **51**, 1469–84.

6. Persistent price dispersion in online markets

Michael R. Baye, John Morgan, and Patrick Scholten

INTRODUCTION

The failure of the 'law of one price' has been widely observed in non-Internet markets. In his seminal paper, Hal Varian quipped that when it came to prices for identical products in conventional retail markets, '. . . the "law of one price" is no law at all' (Varian 1980, 651). Beginning with Stigler (1961), a large and successful theoretical literature has arisen explaining how dispersed prices can comprise equilibrium in the presence of price-sensitive consumers and homogeneous products. One approach generates price dispersion in pure strategies, where different firms charge different prices because of heterogeneities in costs or service levels. The other approach generates price dispersion through randomized pricing strategies by firms.[1] As Varian points out, the former type of price dispersion is unlikely to be long-lived, as consumers will eventually learn which firms are charging the best prices and shop from them exclusively. Varian argues that the latter type of price dispersion will persist over time.

Price dispersion has also been observed in Internet markets (see Smith et al. 1999 for a useful survey of results[2]); however, little is known about the empirical persistence of this price dispersion over long periods of time. In contrast to Varian's explanation, Brynjolfsson and Smith (2000) argue that price dispersion is largely due to retailer heterogeneity with respect to branding, awareness, and trust. If this is the case, price dispersion should be modest after controlling for such heterogeneities.

This chapter examines the persistence of price dispersion in a well-established online retail market. Using data collected over an 18-month period from one of the leading price comparison sites on the Internet, we show that prices for identical consumer electronics products listed by multiple retailers display considerable and persistent price dispersion. On average, the highest price for a consumer electronics product is 57 per cent above the lowest available price. The savings to a consumer simply from consulting the comparison site are also significant – on average, the difference in prices paid by consumers shopping at a randomly selected firm rather than from the firm offering the lowest price is about $31 in 2002.

Price dispersion persists across products and across time. We find no convergence to the 'law of one price' over an 18-month period even after controlling for differences in shipping charges and inventories. We also use time variation in the data to make an additional inference. Specifically, we show that Varian's model implies that as the reservation value of consumers seeking to purchase an item decreases, (1) the number of firms listing the product declines and (2) the range of prices offered decreases. The methodology we employ to test these predictions is to use the short life cycles of consumer electronics products as a means of obtaining variation in consumer reservation values. Reservation values are presumably lower later in the product lifespan. Empirically, we find evidence consistent with these hypotheses. The number of competing firms declines by over 60 per cent in the final seven months of our dataset. Over this same period, the average range in prices decreases by $31 or 54 per cent of the range at the start of the sample period.

We find that even after controlling for differences in costs, reputation, awareness, and trust, a significant fraction of the observed price dispersion is unexplained. Specifically, regressions controlling for the presence of banner ads, consumer feedback ratings, firm disclosures about shipping costs, and inventory availability as proxies for these factors explain only about 17 per cent of the observed dispersion in prices. Further, regressions using individual firm dummies and allowing the coefficients on these dummies to vary across multiple products offered by the same firm still leave 28 per cent of price dispersion unexplained.

The nearest antecedent to this chapter is Sorensen (2000).[3] Sorensen showed that there was considerable price dispersion in retail prescription drug markets in upstate New York. Moreover, this dispersion cannot be accounted entirely for by firm heterogeneities.[4] He finds that, consistent with equilibrium search models such as Burdett and Judd (1983), prescriptions that consumers purchase more frequently display less dispersion than those that are purchased less frequently. Our approach is similar in that we too seek to establish the empirical importance of price dispersion unaccounted for by firm heterogeneities.

It is important to stress that our data comes from online markets where consumers have access to a list of prices. In this setting, information flows are 'costless' inside the market. This suggests that models such as Varian (1980) or Baye and Morgan (2001) are probably more appropriate for generating testable implications for our data than models such as Reinganum

(1979) or Burdett and Judd (1983) where equilibrium price dispersion stems from costly sequential or fixed-sample search.

The remainder of the chapter proceeds as follows. The next section derives three empirically testable implications of the Varian model. The third section describes our dataset, while the fourth section presents the analysis of the persistent price dispersion hypothesis. The fifth section examines the alternative hypothesis: that price dispersion is mainly due retailer heterogeneities. Finally, the final section is a conclusion.

THEORY

Unlike costly search models, which generate price dispersion from consumers' positive search costs, the model of Varian postulates that I 'informed' consumers have access to the complete list of firm prices for some homogeneous product, as would be the case were these consumers to consult a price comparison site. The remaining consumers, perhaps unaware of the site or without Internet access, simply shop at a randomly selected firm and purchase from it if the price offered is less than the reservation value, r. There are M of these 'uninformed' consumers in this market. All consumers have unit demand.

Firms are assumed to be identical, there is free entry, and all firms have declining average cost curves.[5] We make the additional assumption that average cost curves are convex.[6] Since firms pricing at the reservation price sell only to uninformed consumers at a price of r each, free entry implies that:

$$r = AC(M/n) \tag{6.1}$$

where $AC(\ )$ is the average cost function of each firm and n is the equilibrium number of firms. Since average costs are declining, this implies:

Hypothesis 1 As the reservation value decreases, the equilibrium number of firms declines.

Intuitively, a shrinking reservation value reduces the overall surplus in the market. As a consequence, the market can support fewer firms' fixed costs, and the equilibrium number of competing firms declines.

Varian shows that in a symmetric equilibrium, prices are dispersed over the interval $[p^*, r]$, where:

$$p^* = AC(M/n + I). \tag{6.2}$$

The convexity of the average cost curves together with equilibrium conditions (6.1) and (6.2) implies:

Hypothesis 2 As the reservation value decreases, the range in prices declines.

The intuition for the decrease in the range in prices is as follows. As the reservation value decreases, the lowest price a firm is willing to charge if it is assured of attracting all shoppers declines, since the opportunity cost of this discount in terms of forgone revenue to loyal customers is reduced. This lowest price is p^* in equation (6.2) above. However, because of equilibrium exit, a larger fraction of a firm's fixed costs are being covered by uninformed consumers; hence, the gains in terms of reduced average costs from selling to informed consumers is smaller when reservation values are lower than when they are higher. The upshot is that the range of prices offered is reduced under this circumstance.

Finally, in Varian's model, the symmetric equilibrium consists of all firms pricing according to an atomless cumulative distribution function over the range $[p^*, r]$. This implies:

Hypothesis 3 Price dispersion for products will persist over time.

In the sequel, we examine empirically these three hypotheses.

DATA

Tests of the above hypotheses require data from an environment where some consumers have access to the complete list of prices while others do not. Further, products sold must be fairly homogeneous and (for the symmetric equilibrium to be appropriate) the firms must have similar costs. While none of these conditions is likely to be exactly met in field data, Internet price comparison sites offer a reasonable approximation of these conditions. To this end, we assembled a dataset consisting of monthly price observations for 36 consumer electronics products offered for sale at the price comparison site Shopper.com for the period from November 1999 through May 2001. Initially, we collected these data by saving web pages for each of the products listed. After August 2000, we automated this process by constructing an Internet 'spider' written in the PERL programming language to automatically download this information.

The set of products in our dataset were selected because they were the 36 highest ranked products, in terms of popularity, at the Shopper.com site at the start of the study. We inferred that the markets for these products were likely to be thick on the consumer side. Thus, the incentives for sellers to balance between posting a high price to make higher margin sales to uninformed consumers versus selling at a low price to attract the informed consumers at Shopper.com were likely to be large. The product rankings given at Shopper.com are a function of the number of unique consumer requests for either product or price comparison information from the Shopper.com site. This amounts to a 'click through' from a general Shopper.com page to a specific product information page.

One potential problem in studying price dispersion on a product-by-product basis is that the relevant consumption component for consumers might be a bundle of products rather than an individual product. For two reasons, this problem is mitigated in our data. First, the products we study do not have obvious purchase complementarities. Indeed, many of the products listed in Table 6.1 (such as the Palm III, IIIx, and Palm V) are in fact substitutes. Second, the products we study are fairly expensive (averaging about $500), so consumers are unlikely to purchase multiple products at the same time in order to economize on shipping costs. This aspect of our data differs from earlier studies of less expensive items, such as books and CDs, where these effects might be more important.

We grouped products into one of three broad categories: software, peripherals, and accessories. Software is self-explanatory. Peripherals were items that would typically be installed as part of an existing PC. Video boards are a representative item in this category. Finally, accessories are consumer electronics items that are usable with or without a PC. The Palm handheld is a typical item in this category.

The cost structure of Shopper.com provides disincentives for dishonest or otherwise obfuscating pricing strategies.[7] A firm pays Shopper.com a fixed monthly fee plus an additional fee per 'qualified lead' (defined as a click through by a consumer from the Shopper.com site to the merchant's site). Thus, the strategy of posting a low price for a product which is unavailable in hopes of driving consumer traffic to one's site does not come without cost. An additional concern is that merchants might choose to price discriminate between consumers coming to their website from Shopper.com and those accessing it directly. To deal with these issues, we conducted random audits of merchant listings. We found no obfuscation strategies being employed for the products we studied nor did we find evidence of discriminatory pricing. Hence, we are confident that the prices listed on Shopper.com represent actual prices for actual products that can be obtained.[8]

There were a few instances of prices that were obviously inputted incorrectly by firms. Specifically, there were a couple of prices that were listed at $0 on the site. To deal with this issue, we dropped all prices of $5 or less from the sample. This eliminated six observations from the sample of 9441 observations. Results presented below are robust to a variety of different approaches to 'cleaning' the data.[9]

The information returned to a consumer searching for a specific product (associated with a unique manufacturer part number) at Shopper.com includes a tabular list of all firms in the Shopper.com marketplace selling that specific product, along with their price, shipping cost, Cnet Certified Store status, Gomez merchant rating, product availability, and the date on which the firm last updated its information. Consumers can sort the relevant information by clicking on the column header. For example, a consumer wanting to sort the firms by price can click on the price column header.

Further product information and how to purchase an item from a particular firm can be obtained by 'clicking' either the 'Buy info,' 'firm name,' or 'price' link.[10] Consumers can access information about a firm's return policies, acceptable methods of payment, delivery options, and other special features by clicking the 'Company info' link below a firm's name. Also, clicking the Certified Store logo brings up the requirements firms must meet in order to maintain its certified status. Finally, consumers can view the criteria on which a firm was evaluated and read the overall review by clicking on the stars from the Gomez.com firm review.

Branding, Reputation and Trust

Shopper.com provides firms with other opportunities to distinguish themselves in the market. For an additional fee, a firm can complement its merchant name with its company logo or participate in a revolving targeted banner advertising campaign in several locations.

Shopper.com provides two firm quality ratings with each product search. The first is the Cnet Certified Store rating. All firms displaying the Cnet Certified Store logo have met a set of seven criteria that include: providing Cnet with up-to-date pricing, shipping cost, and stock information; providing Cnet with a customer service policy; honoring prices displayed on the firm's web site; using encryption technology so all transactions are made in a secure environment; providing order confirmation within one business day of order and process orders promptly; providing professional packaging; and responding to customer service emails and phone calls within two business days. It would seem that stores that are Cnet certified are likely to be perceived as more reputable than those who are not.

Shopper.com also retains the services of an independent firm rating service. During the early part of our study, Shopper.com used Bizrate.com to survey consumers shopping experience with firms advertising on its web site and compiled ratings of the firms in several areas. An overall rating, between 1 and 5 stars (in half-star increments) was assigned to each firm and displayed next to the firm's name. This allowed consumers to assess overall firm quality. Bizrate.com's services are provided for free to consumers and retail Internet firms. Bizrate.com provided these services for a fee to Shopper.com. In November 2000, Shopper.com terminated its relationship with Bizrate.com.[11]

Firms may differ not only with respect to their use of banner ads, Cnet certified merchant status, and Bizrate ratings, but also with respect to their disclosure policies regarding shipping and inventory.

In principle, all of these variables represent observable heterogeneities among firms. In the following analysis, we examine how much of the observed price dispersion these heterogeneities explain.

ANALYSIS

Summary of Price Variation

Table 6.1 presents a list of prices for products offered in common by the four merchants covering the largest number of products in our dataset at the beginning of the dataset. The first column of the table lists the 27 products sold by all four firms on 5 November 1999. The type of product (S for software, P for peripherals, A for accessories) is listed in the second column. The last four columns show the listed price by the four firms on this date.

The price dispersion observed for these products on this date is representative of the entire dataset. A consumer shopping for a digital camera, the Nikon Coolpix 950 can save about $100 by simply buying from the lowest rather than the highest priced of these four merchants. Among these four firms, pcWonders offers the low price for 24 out of the 27 products on this date. Interestingly, pcWonders is the high-price seller among the four for the remaining three products for which it lists a price. Likewise, there is no firm among the four that is the high price seller for all products, but McGlen Micro comes close – its price is the highest for 19 out of the 27 products. The remaining two sellers split second and third place fairly evenly. It is important to stress that none of these four firms consistently offers the lowest price across all products and time.

Table 6.2 presents summary statistics of various measures of price dispersion for the entire period of the study. The results here confirm the impressions in Table 6.1 – price dispersion is a significant and persistent phenomenon in these markets. Table 6.2 shows that the range in prices is $75.99 on average. The table also shows that a consumer shopping from the low-price firm, rather than from a firm charging the average price, stands

Table 6.1 *Sample prices posted by four firms on 5 November 1999*

Product	Type	AccessMicro.com ($)	Computer 411 ($)	McGlen Micro ($)	pcWonders.com ($)
3Com Homeconnect	P	120.42	131.40	128.42	115.89
Adobe Acrobat V4.0	S	210.42	221.32	218.42	196.89
ATX Motherboard	P	134.98	136.72	150.95	117.89
Cassiopeia E-105	A	530.73	537.13	534.73	579.95
Creative Labs 3d Blaster Riva TNT2 Ultra	P	162.07	164.95	170.07	146.89
Creative Labs PC-DVD Encore 6x	P	202.37	199.95	210.37	183.95
Creative Labs Video Blaster Webcam 3	P	59.66	64.95	67.66	53.89
Diamond Viper V770 Ultra	P	162.29	151.95	170.29	149.89
Epsonstylus Color 740	P	194.19	196.00	202.19	179.89
Frontpage 2000	S	122.65	124.95	130.65	109.89
Half Life	S	33.47	31.95	39.00	24.95
HP CD-Writer Plus 8200i	P	191.44	194.95	199.44	185.89
Intellimouse Explorer	P	50.99	63.23	58.99	45.89
Money Deluxe 2000	S	46.94	49.95	54.94	44.89
Matrox Millennium G400 Max	P	200.29	208.88	208.29	197.88
Nikon Coolpix 950	A	851.28	879.52	855.28	786.95
Olympus C-2000Z	A	784.79	779.95	788.79	698.89
Olympus D-340R	A	258.82	264.95	266.82	298.95
Pentium III 450 Chip	P	189.95	184.95	209.95	172.89
Pentium III 500 Chip	P	231.95	229.95	254.95	224.89
Palm III	A	247.00	219.95	255.00	189.89
Palm IIIx	A	330.00	249.95	338.00	209.50
Palm V	A	381.95	339.95	389.95	279.89
Quicken Deluxe 2000	S	45.25	49.95	53.25	42.89
Star Wars Episode I: Racer	S	35.13	35.55	39.13	27.95
Star Wars X-Wing Alliance	S	24.75	23.95	26.02	31.95
Virusscan Classic V4.0	S	12.85	13.95	48.57	9.95

Table 6.2   Summary statistics for dispersion measures

	Average	Std. dev.	Selected percentiles				
			5%	25%	50%	75%	95%
Absolute measures of price dispersion							
Range in prices ($)	75.99	97.1	6.12	21.89	38.70	89.05	312.17
Difference between average and lowest price	30.70	39.3	2.60	8.78	15.36	36.32	107.61
Gap (difference) between lowest two prices	8.52	22.6	0.00	0.20	1.94	6.25	40.80
Relative measures of price dispersion							
Range in prices (as a percentage of lowest price)	57.1	52.8	7.6	24.4	42.7	67.0	176.4
Coefficient of variation	12.6	9.0	3.6	6.8	9.7	15.6	32.5
Gap between lowest two prices (as a percentage of lowest price)	6.2	12.8	0.0	0.2	2.0	6.3	28.6
Difference between average and lowest price (as a percentage of lowest price)	21.8	18.5	3.5	10.1	17.4	26.9	59.2

to save $30.70 on a purchase. Even a conservative measure of price dispersion, the difference between the two lowest listed prices, shows an average gap between these two prices of $8.52. The coefficient of variation – a unit-free measure of price dispersion defined as the ratio of the standard deviation to the mean – averages 12.6 per cent. Thus, the price dispersion is substantial, although somewhat lower than that found by Sorensen in conventional retail markets for prescription drugs.[12]

Price Dispersion over Time

In Figures 6.1 through 6.3, we present evidence of persistent price dispersion over the 18-month period covered in our dataset using three measures of price dispersion. Two of the measures, the coefficient of variation and range, were discussed earlier. In this case, the range in price is reported as a percentage of the lowest price offered for each product. Figure 6.1 also shows the difference between the two lowest price listings, expressed as a percentage of the lowest listed price. This measure, which we shall refer to as the *gap* between the two lowest prices, is a very conservative measure of price dispersion. Moreover, it places no weight on high price outliers, which would affect the other two measures.[13]

Panel 6.1a   Average percentage gap over time

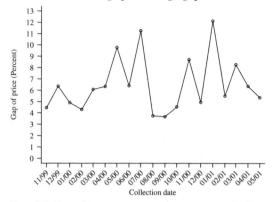

Panel 6.1b   Average percentage range over time

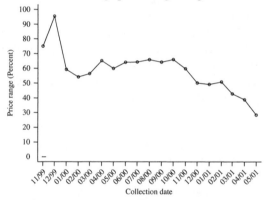

Panel 6.1c   Average coefficient of variation over time

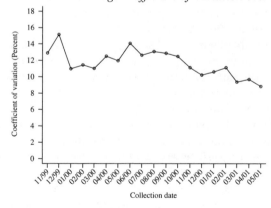

Figure 6.1   Raw measures of price dispersion over time

In Figure 6.1, we show the average level of price dispersion giving equal weight to each product date in our dataset over the 18-month period of our study. As the three panels of the figure show, there is persistent price dispersion using all three measures. Panel 6.1a displays the percentage gap over the 18-month period covered by our dataset. The percentage gap starts at around 5 per cent and ends at slightly above this level. In between, the measure displays considerable volatility with upward spikes reaching over the 10 per cent level in the middle of 2000 and the beginning of 2001. If anything, there is a slight upward trend in this measure.

Panel 6.1b displays monthly percentage range figures. Unlike the percentage gap, this measure of price dispersion displays a distinct downward trend starting at between 70 per cent and 80 per cent and ending under 30 per cent by May 2001. The trend in this measure of dispersion is consistent with the theoretical prediction of hypothesis 2 derived in the previous section. Finally, panel 6.1c displays the coefficient of variation on a monthly basis. There is a slight downward trend in this measure of dispersion. At the start of our study, coefficient of variation averages around 13 per cent whilst it falls to around 9 per cent by May 2001. Despite the downward trend displayed in the coefficient of variation and percentage range measures of price dispersion, prices are still significantly dispersed even after 18 months of price discovery by consumers and rival firms.

The panels shown in Figure 6.2 display the same three dispersion measures adjusted for shipping costs. While the prices used to compute the price dispersion measures in Figure 6.1 and elsewhere are based on list prices, in Figure 6.2 we adjust the prices for shipping and handling charges. Specifically, we divide the dataset into firms that report shipping and handling charges and those that do not. Of those firms that do report a shipping cost, if they suggest a range of prices, we take the midpoint of the range. Otherwise, we adjust the listed price for the shipping charge shown on the site and compute dispersion with these adjusted prices.

It is theoretically possible to observe persistent dispersion in list prices, yet for all firms to be charging the same 'full price' once one accounts for shipping costs. Figure 6.2, however, shows that this is not the case. Including shipping charges lowers the coefficient of variation, but typically by less than 1 per cent. Shipping adjusted prices also lower the price range by less than 5 per cent for each monthly period. Shipping adjusted prices have the least effect when one looks at the gap between the lowest two prices. Here, there is little to distinguish between dispersion using the adjusted and unadjusted prices.

Figure 6.3 examines these same dispersion measures dividing firms into those that positively disclose that a particular item is in stock and those that do not. The idea is that firms that do not have an item in stock may list a

Panel 6.2a   *Percentage gap of firms disclosing full price (list price + shipping
cost) compared to firms that do not disclose shipping cost*

Panel 6.2b   *Average percentage range of prices for firms disclosing full
price (list price + shipping cost) compared to firms that do not
disclose shipping cost*

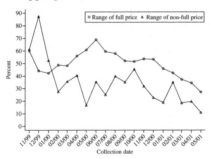

Panel 6.2c   *Average coefficient of variation for firms disclosing full price
(list price + shipping cost) compared to firms that do not
disclose shipping cost*

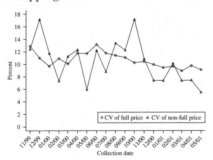

Figure 6.2   *Measures of price dispersion controlling for differences in
shipping*

Panel 6.3a   Average gap for firms disclosing inventory compared to those not disclosing inventory

Panel 6.3b   Average percentage range of prices for firms disclosing inventory compared to those not disclosing inventory

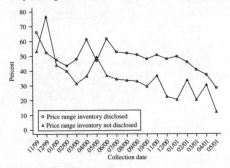

Panel 6.3c   Average coefficient of variation for firms disclosing inventory compared to those not disclosing inventory

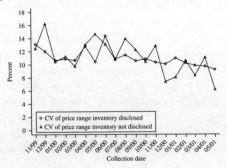

Figure 6.3   Measures of price dispersion controlling for inventory differences

price simply as a device to divert traffic to their site in hopes consumers will buy some other, presumably higher margin item. This could cause various measures of price dispersion to indicate dispersion even though all of the firms that actually have goods to sell charge the same price. As Figure 6.3 shows, focusing solely on firms positively having the item in stock slightly decreases the coefficient of variation and range measures of price dispersion and does little to affect the gap measure. Regardless of the measure used, persistent price dispersion remains.

To summarize, we find evidence of persistent price dispersion using a variety of dispersion measures and controlling for differences in shipping costs and whether the item is in stock. This is consistent with hypothesis 3.

TESTING COMPARATIVE STATIC IMPLICATIONS

We now turn to hypotheses 1 and 2, which predict that as reservation values decline, the equilibrium number of firms and the range in prices should both decline. Our data tracks 36 products over an 18-month period, starting at the point when they were the most popular products listed at Shopper.com. As products get older in our sample, one would expect consumer reservation values to decline. To get at this effect, we run the following regression:

$$\text{RANGE}_{it} = \beta_0 + \beta_1 D_1 + \beta_2 D_2 + \beta_3 MSRP_{it} + \gamma X_i + \varepsilon_{it}. \qquad (6.3)$$

RANGE_{it} is the range in prices for product i on date t expressed in dollars. D_1 is a dummy for whether the observation comes six to ten months from the end of the dataset. D_2 is a dummy for whether the observation comes from the last five months of the dataset. The variable $MSRP_{it}$ is the manufacturers suggested retail price for product i on date t. The vector X_i consists of dummies for the type of product (software, peripherals, or accessories). The idea behind these controls is that if demand or costs vary systematically with product type, this variation will be absorbed.

Using GLS to correct for the presence of heteroskedasticity in the error term, Table 6.3 presents the coefficient estimates for equation (6.3). The first column of the table displays the estimates of equation (6.3) when the dependent variable is simply the range in prices expressed in dollars. The coefficient associated with D_1 is -4.576 indicating that the range in prices is compressed by about \$4.58 within ten months of the end of the dataset. The compression in the range of prices approximately doubles to \$12.59 in the last five months of the dataset. Both coefficients are of the sign predicted in Hypothesis 1 and are significant at conventional levels. Moreover,

Table 6.3   Product life cycle and range of prices

	Range in prices	Range in residuals	Number of firms
Jun 00 to Oct 00	−4.576	−11.859	−4.623
	(2.310)	(1.907)	(1.072)
Nov 00 to May 01	−12.585	−19.282	−12.957
	(2.361)	(1.973)	(1.079)
MSRP	0.237	−0.008	0.003
	(0.013)	(0.005)	(0.003)
Software	−12.004	−0.939	−3.73
	(2.509)	(2.242)	(1.278)
Accessories	−6.078	−10.021	−10.908
	(3.624)	(2.178)	(1.290)
Constant	18.959	73.42	29.274
	(2.930)	(2.39)	(1.364)
Number of observations	427	427	427
Log likelihood	−2057.902	−1841.891	−1638.909

Notes:
GLS estimates with heteroskedastic error structure across panels
Asymptotic standard errors in parentheses

both coefficients display the expected magnitudes – coefficient D_1 is statistically significantly smaller than the D_2 coefficient.

The second column of Table 6.3 displays the coefficients when we estimate the 'corrected' range in prices using the procedure described in Sorensen (2000) to control for the effects of observable firm heterogeneities. Following Sorensen (2000), we estimate the range of the residuals from a fixed effects regression of price on product dummies and dummies for product type, certified merchant status, banner status, whether shipping cost and product availability were disclosed. The coefficient associated with the period from June to October 2000 indicates a compression of this 'corrected' range measure of \$11.86 while the coefficient for the final five months of the dataset shows compression of \$19.28. Once again both coefficients are of the expected sign and significant. Also, the magnitudes of the coefficients are in the expected pattern; that is, we reject the null hypothesis that the coefficients $D_1 = D_2$ against the one-sided alternative that D_1 is smaller than D_2. Taken together, the results are supportive of Hypothesis 1.

Next, we examine the relationship between the age of the product and the number of listing firms. We do this by estimating the following regression:

$$NUMFRM_{it} = \beta_0 + \beta_1 D_1 + \beta_2 D_2 + \beta_3 MSRP_{it} + \gamma X_i + \varepsilon_{it}, \quad (6.4)$$

where NUMFRM$_{it}$ denotes the number of firms listing prices for product *i* on date *t*.

Once again, we estimate this regression using GLS and correcting for heteroskedasticity. The estimated regression coefficients are reported in the third column of Table 6.3. The number of competing firms declines by about 4.6 firms, as the coefficient on the dummy variable for the period June 2000 through October 2000 indicates. Similarly, from November 2000 until the end of the dataset, the table shows that the number of firms further declines by about 13 firms. Both coefficients are of the expected signs and magnitudes and both are significant at conventional levels. Thus, the results of the fourth column of Table 6.3 are consistent with hypothesis 2.

Neither hypothesis 1 nor hypothesis 2, are made in isolation in Varian's model. Indeed, that model predicts that changes in the range of prices and numbers of listing firms should be correlated with one another. This suggests that a more efficient estimation approach is to use Zellner's Seemingly Unrelated Regressions to simultaneously estimate equations (6.3) and (6.4). The results of this approach are shown in Table 6.4. The first two columns of this table present the coefficient estimates using the raw dollar value of the range in prices. The second two columns present the coefficient

Table 6.4 Product life cycle, range of prices, and number of firms

	Range in prices	Number of firms	Range in residuals	Number of firms
Jun 00 to Oct 00	−21.608	−8.041	−15.345	−8.041
	(6.722)	(0.997)	(1.801)	(0.997)
Nov 00 to May 01	−30.569	−18.08	−25.588	−18.08
	(7.340)	(1.089)	(1.967)	(1.089)
MSRP	0.337	0.031	0.124	0.031
	(0.022)	(0.003)	(0.020)	(0.003)
Software	−17.747	−20.872	67.147	−20.872
	(24.039)	(3.565)	(17.619)	(3.565)
Accessories	−16.246	−0.946	74.045	−0.946
	(17.083)	(2.533)	(14.528)	(2.533)
Constant	21.112	29.964	−15.980	29.964
	(14.426)	(2.139)	(17.451)	(2.139)
Number of observations	427	427	427	427
R^2	0.6773	0.6772	0.5385	0.6772

Notes:
SUR estimates
Asymptotic standard errors in parentheses

estimates using the 'corrected' price range using the residuals from the fixed effects regression described earlier.

Once again, the coefficients on D_1 and D_2 are of the expected signs and magnitudes and are significant at conventional levels. The correlation coefficient between these two variables is estimated to be 0.3783, which is positive and significant, again consistent with the theoretical predictions.

FIRM HETEROGENEITY AND PRICE DISPERSION

The analysis above indicates not only that price dispersion persists over time, but that the pattern of observed dispersion is consistent with predictions of the Varian model. In this section, we examine alternative explanations based on differences in branding, reputation, and trust as well as cost heterogeneities.

For a given product listed at Shopper.com, all retailers are offering the same item. Yet, retailers do differ in their restocking policies, exchange policies, shipping speeds, and so on. Thus, it is possible that the observed price dispersion merely reflects quality differences among retailers, although the differences in the price rankings of the portfolio of products offered by the same retailer does cast some doubt on this explanation.

Brynjolfsson and Smith (2000) identified branding, reputation, and product awareness as key factors in generating price dispersion on the Internet. To quantify the impact of these factors on the dispersion observed in our dataset, we consider the following model separately for each product in our dataset:

$$\text{PRICE}_{jt} = \beta_0 + \beta_1 CNET_{jt} + \beta_2 \text{BANNER}_{jt} + \beta_3 \text{SHIP}_{jt} + \beta_4 \text{STOCK}_{jt} + \varepsilon_{jt} \qquad (6.5)$$

As equation (6.5) shows, for each product, we regress the list price of firm j in period t on dummy variables for whether firm j is a Cnet certified merchant (the variable $CNET_{jt}$), whether it posted a banner ad on that date (BANNER_{jt}), whether it disclosed shipping costs on that date (SHIP_{jt}), and whether it had the item in stock on that date (STOCK_{jt}). The resulting R^2 values are reported in the first column of Table 6.5 (model 1).

Notice that the R^2 values reported for model 1 represent the percentage of the total variation in the prices charged for each product that can be explained purely by observable differences in these firm characteristics. The R^2 values range from 2 per cent to 100 per cent. The average value is 17 per cent, indicating that 83 per cent of the variation in the prices for these products *cannot* be explained by observable differences in firms' reputations,

Table 6.5   *Percentage of price dispersion explained by observable and unobservable firm heterogeneities*

Product name	Model 1 R^2	Model 2 R^2
3Com Homeconnect	0.03	0.59
Adobe Acrobat V4.0	0.08	0.63
Adobe Photoshop V5.0.2	0.91	0.98
ATX Motherboard	0.02	0.70
Cassiopeia E-105	0.04	0.58
Creative Labs 3d Blaster Riva TNT2 Ultra	0.06	0.83
Creative Labs Blaster CDRW 4224	0.13	1.00
Creative Labs CDRW 6424	0.13	0.92
Creative Labs PC-DVD Encore 6x	0.05	0.85
Creative Labs PC-DVD RAM 5.2gb SCSI-2	0.08	0.47
Creative Labs Sound Blaster Live Value	0.26	0.79
Creative Labs Video Blaster Webcam 3	0.13	0.50
Diamond Viper V770 Ultra	0.02	0.75
Epsonstylus Color 740	0.07	0.44
Frontpage 2000	0.08	0.64
Half Life	0.10	0.95
HP CD-Writer Plus 8200i	0.08	0.76
Intellimouse Explorer	0.04	0.66
Intel Create & Share Camera Pack USB	0.99	1.00
Money Deluxe 2000	0.04	0.84
Matrox Millennium G400 Max	0.07	0.61
Nikon Coolpix 950	0.10	0.61
Official Red Hat Linux V6.0	0.17	0.78
Olympus C-2000Z	0.25	0.85
Olympus D-340R	0.17	0.82
Paint Shop Pro V5.0	0.03	0.53
Pentium III 450 Chip	0.18	0.79
Pentium III 500 Chip	0.17	0.51
Palm III	0.05	0.73
Palm IIIx	0.12	0.56
Palm V	0.07	0.55
Quicken Deluxe 2000	0.03	0.76
Star Wars Episode I: Racer	0.13	0.48
Star Wars X-Wing Alliance	0.26	0.69
Upgrade Windows 98	1.00	1.00
Virusscan Classic V4.0	0.02	0.73
Average	0.17	0.72

advertising strategies, or disclosure policies regarding shipping costs or product availability. If price dispersion were an artifact purely of these observable differences, the R^2 values would all have been close to 1.

Model 1 controls only for firm heterogeneities that are observable to consumers visiting the Shopper.com site. One might speculate that unobserved heterogeneities in firms' costs or other factors explain the observed price dispersion. In order to quantify the impact on price dispersion of both observed and unobserved firm heterogeneities, we also regressed the list price of firm j in period t on dummy variables for each firm j. The R^2 values from this specification (model 2) are given in column 2 of Table 6.5.

The R^2 values reported for model 2 represent, for each product, the percentage of the total variation in prices explained by both firm differences observable by looking at the Shopper.com site as well as heterogeneities not directly observable (such as cost differences). Not surprisingly, including all of these dummy variables greatly increases the percentage of the observed price dispersion that can be explained. However, even with individual dummies for every firm in the sample and controls for each product in our sample, 28 per cent of the dispersion in prices remains unexplained.

To summarize, after accounting for firm heterogeneities in costs, branding, reputation, trust, product availability and shipping costs, 28 per cent of the variation in prices charged for homogeneous products remains. This finding is consistent with Hypothesis 3.

DISCUSSION

George Stigler noted that in practice there is never absolute homogeneity of commodities in naturally occurring markets. However, Stigler was loathe to attribute all of observed price dispersion to heterogeneities. He writes: 'a portion of the observed dispersion is presumably attributable to such [product] differences. But it would be metaphysical, and fruitless, to assert that all dispersion is due to heterogeneity' (Stigler 1961, p. 214).

The primary purpose of this chapter is to assess whether a significant fraction of the price dispersion observed on a leading Internet price comparison site owes its existence to forces of persistent price dispersion hypothesized in Varian as opposed to being an artifact of differences in costs, branding, reputation, or trust among competing retailers. Our central finding is that price dispersion is remarkably persistent over the 18-month period of our study – even after controlling for shipping costs and firm heterogeneities.

If temporal price dispersion, as hypothesized by Varian, is indeed an empirically important component of observed price dispersion, then an important implication of that model is that both the number of firms listing prices for a given product and the range of prices offered should decline as the product ages. We find evidence consistent with this prediction.

Finally, we note that while a fraction of observed price dispersion may be explained by appealing to firm heterogeneities, 28 per cent of the observed dispersion remains unexplained. We contend that this is further evidence in support of the empirical relevance of equilibrium models of persistent price dispersion.

NOTES

1. Typical of the first approach are Salop and Stiglitz (1977), Reinganum (1979), and Spulber (1995). Typical of the second approach are Shilony (1977), Rosenthal (1980), Varian (1980), Narasimhan (1988), Baye and Morgan (2001), and Baye and Morgan (2002). Stahl (1989) and Janssen and Moraga (2000) combine both approaches.
2. See also Brynjolfsson and Smith (1999), Stahl (2000), and Bakos (2001).
3. This chapter is also in the spirit of Villas-Boas (1995), who looks at prices for coffee and saltine crackers and examines whether the empirical distribution of prices is consistent with the theoretical distribution induced by Varian's model. Baye et al. (2001, 2002a, 2002b) also examine comparative static implications of mixed strategy models of price dispersion using data from Internet price comparison sites.
4. See Pratt et al. (1979) and Carlson and Pescatrice (1980) for additional studies of price dispersion in conventional retail markets. See Brynjolfsson and Smith (2000) and Scholten and Smith (2002) for a studies comparing conventional retail markets and Internet markets.
5. Shapiro and Varian (1999) argue that declining average cost curves are characteristic of many aspects of Internet markets.
6. Shapiro and Varian (1999) argue that cost curves consisting of a fixed cost and a constant (and low) marginal cost characterize many online markets. This type of cost function satisfies the convexity assumption.
7. Ellison and Ellison (2001) find considerable evidence of the use of obfuscation strategies in selling computer memory on a rival price comparison site.
8. Of course, the listed price is not the final price that a consumer pays for the item. This final price will typically include shipping and handling charges and possibly tax depending on the state in which the consumer resides. Both of these costs are variable depending on the bundle of items purchased by the consumer and his or her state of residence. Thus, we treat the listed price as the relevant price. Calculations of price dispersion where we assume consumers buy only a single item, do not live in the state where the retailer is located, and use the information about shipping costs available on the Shopper.com site to calculate the final purchase price do not lead to qualitatively different results regarding price dispersion nor are the magnitudes of the observed dispersion much affected. See Figure 6.3 for some evidence on this.
9. While we have 9441 individual price observations, our unit of observation in examining summary statistics of price dispersion is the product-date. This pools all price observations for a given product on a given date. There are 427 product-dates in our dataset.
10. Each firm's web site also provides consumers with different information. Some firms include a photograph and detailed description of the product offered for sale, while others list only the price and shipping information.
11. On 20 December 2000, Cnet announced that Gomez.com would serve as its new, independent rating service. This ranking is similar to Bizrate.com, with the exception that Gomez.com's overall rating systems are based on a three-star scheme in full-star increments.

12. As a basis for comparison, Sorensen observes a coefficient of variation of 22 per cent in retail prescription drugs markets.
13. See Baye et al. (2001) for a discussion of the theoretical rationale for using the gap measure of price dispersion. Some other researchers use the trimmed range to deal with outliers. Note, however, that the trimmed range has the undesirable property of dropping low-priced outliers, which presumably get a large volume of sales.

REFERENCES

Bakos, Yannis (2001), 'The emerging landscape of retail e-commerce', *Journal of Economic Perspectives*, **15**, 69–80.

Baye, Michael R. and John Morgan (2001), 'Information gatekeepers on the Internet and the competitiveness of homogeneous product markets', *American Economic Review*, **9**, 454–74.

Baye, Michael R. and John Morgan (2002), 'Information gatekeepers and price discrimination on the Internet', *Economics Letters*, **76** (1), 47–51.

Baye, Michael R., John Morgan and Patrick Scholten (2001), 'Price dispersion in the small and in the large: evidence from an Internet price comparison site,' mimeo, Princeton University.

Baye, Michael R., John Morgan and Patrick Scholten (2002a), 'Pricing and reputation in an online consumer electronics market', mimeo, Princeton University.

Baye, Michael R., John Morgan and Patrick Scholten (2002b), 'The value of information in online markets: theory and evidence', mimeo.

Brynjolfsson, Erik and Michael D. Smith (1999), 'The great equalizer? Consumer choice behavior at Internet shopbots', MIT Sloan School of Management Working Paper.

Brynjolfsson, Erik and Michael D. Smith (2000), 'Frictionless commerce? A comparison of Internet and conventional retailers', *Management Science*, **46**, 563–85.

Burdett, Kenneth and Kenneth L. Judd (1983), 'Equilibrium price dispersion', *Econometrica*, **51**, 955–69.

Carlson, John A. and Donn R. Pescatrice (1980), 'Persistent price distributions', *Journal of Economics and Business*, **33**, 21–7.

Ellison, Glenn and Sara Fisher Ellison (2001), 'Search, obfuscation, and price elasticities on the Internet', mimeo, MIT.

Gatti, J. Rupert J. (2000), 'Equilibrium price dispersion with sequential search', mimeo, Cambridge University.

Janssen, Maarten and Jose Luis Moraga (2000), 'Pricing, consumer search and the size of Internet markets', mimeo, Tinbergen Institute.

Narasimhan, Chakravarthi (1988), 'Competitive promotional strategies', *Journal of Business*, **61**, 427–49.

Pratt, John W., David A. Wise and Richard Zeckhauser (1979), 'Price differences in almost competitive markets', *Quarterly Journal of Economics*, **93**, 189–211.

Reinganum, Jennifer F. (1979), 'A simple model of equilibrium price dispersion', *Journal of Political Economy*, **87**, 851–8.

Rosenthal, Robert W. (1980), 'A model in which an increase in the number of sellers leads to a higher price', *Econometrica*, **48**, 1575–80.

Salop, Steven C. and Joseph E. Stiglitz (1977), 'Bargains and ripoffs: a model of monopolistically competitive price dispersion', *Review of Economic Studies*, **44**, 493–510.

Scholten, Patrick and Adam Smith (2002), 'Persistent price dispersion', *Advances in Applied Microeconomics*, **11**, 63–88.

Shapiro, Carl and Hal R. Varian (1999), *Information Rules: A Strategic Guide to the Network Economy*, Cambridge, MA: Harvard Business School Press.

Shilony, Yuval (1977), 'Mixed pricing in oligopoly', *Journal of Economic Theory*, **14**, 373–88.

Smith, Michael D., Joseph Bailey and Erik Brynjolfsson (1999), 'Understanding digital markets: review and assessment' in E. Brynjolfsson and Kahin (eds), *Understanding the Digital Economy*, Cambridge, MA: MIT Press, 99–136.

Sorensen, Alan (2000), 'Equilibrium price dispersion in retail markets for prescription drugs', *Journal Political Economy*, **108**, 833–50.

Spulber, Daniel F. (1995), 'Bertrand competition when rivals' costs are unknown', *Journal of Industrial Economics*, **43**, 1–11.

Stahl, Dale O. II. (1989), 'Oligopolistic pricing with sequential consumer search', *American Economic Review*, **79**, 700–12.

Stahl, Dale O. II. (2000), 'Strategic advertising and pricing in E-Commerce', *Advances in Applied Microeconomics*, **9** (79), 69–100.

Stigler, G. (1961), 'The economics of information', *Journal of Political Economy*, **69**, 213–25.

Varian, H. (1980), 'A model of sales', *American Economic Review*, **70**, 651–9.

Villas-Boas, M. (1985), 'Models of competitive price promotions: some empirical evidence from the coffee and Saltine crackers markets', *Journal of Economics and Management Strategy*, **4**, 85–107.

7. Network meltdown: the legacy of bad economics

Stan Liebowitz

WHAT'S NEW ABOUT THE NEW ECONOMY?

Although the Internet and the information economy are not really one and the same, the Internet seems to have become the embodiment of the information economy in the eyes of many individuals. For that reason, I plan to make it the central focus of this chapter.

The Internet creates value by reducing the costs of transmitting information. That, in a nutshell, is all the Internet does. I put it this way not to belittle what the Internet accomplishes. After all, automobiles and airplanes merely lowered the costs of transportation, and language merely lowers the cost of communication, though they are all monumental achievements. But it is important to strip away myth from reality. Information transmission is very important. The Internet is a terrific advance in lowering the cost of information. But, and this is most important, information transmission does not change the laws of economics.

Transmitting information is one of the most valuable functions in an economy. But it is a useful comparison to contrast the Internet with other technologies that have reduced the cost of transmitting information, namely, telephones and television.

Telephones allowed instantaneous voice communication, whereas the technologies prior to the telephone allowed very slow written communications (the mail) or faster but limited communication via the telegraph and Morse code. Telegraph never made it into private homes, so communication using telegraphs required delivery of telegrams. Thus while it virtually eliminated the time to move the message from one city to another it still required a costly and time-consuming local delivery.

The telephone, therefore, was a tremendous improvement, in large part because it was intended to be used in homes and businesses, eliminating any delivery costs whatsoever. It required a new and very costly infrastructure to be built up – the ubiquitous telephone lines that cover the landscape and the wires leading into and through homes. This tremendous investment retarded its diffusion, but the value was so great that the diffusion became virtually complete and telephony completely transformed communication as it was then known.

Television, and radio before it, had a somewhat different impact. Television offers one-way communication. Information along with entertainment is transmitted from broadcasting studios to consumers possessing television or radio receivers.

What were the precursors to radio and television? Live entertainment, theatrical releases of movies, and in the home a fledgling phonograph industry. Television and radio greatly enhanced the choices available to consumers. These technologies brought entertainment into the home and automobile. They greatly magnified the audience that could enjoy any given performance, whether by a singer, comedian, or actor. They allowed the virtually instantaneous transmission of news and information.

How does the Internet compare? It is based largely on the same transmission mechanism as cable television and telephones, two prior technologies capable of going into people's homes and offices. The reception is largely confined to computers, which needed only minor modifications to provide Internet access. Although broadband required serious new investment in infrastructure, much of the infrastructure was already in place and much of the new infrastructure can be thought of as more of an upgrade than a brand new investment. So the Internet is more evolutionary, in terms of infrastructure, than were radio and television, which required new transmitters, cameras, and receiving equipment.

As far as content, the Internet is also less revolutionary. It allows for two-way communication, entertainment and information. So far, it doesn't sound like much of an advance, since television, radios and telephones, taken together, did the same things. What distinguishes the Internet from the prior technologies, however, is its ability to quickly retrieve information stored on computers, something that telephones and television couldn't do. Television couldn't because it is a one-way medium. Telephones cannot because they are analog devices intended to have sound come out the speaker of the receiving end and users are not computers that can 'remember' information and manipulate it as it comes across the line.[1]

By combining the two-way transmission mechanism of the telephone with the informational display of the television and the database capability of computers, the Internet does provide a new experience. The crude intelligence of computers, which will only improve over time, can be used to tailor information to specific users or needs. Users can quickly find information and retrieve it for instantaneous or later use. Some of the uses are extraordinary, others are quite mundane.

But all is not necessarily good for the business firm. The reduction in transmission costs, while creating value, should reduce the ability of firms participating on the Internet to take advantage of what we would otherwise call 'locational' monopolies, the monopoly from being physically close to the customers. Less clear is the impact on 'brand name' loyalty. The Web makes it very easy to explore new locations and to get feedback on the web locations. This should ease entry since incumbents would be thought harder pressed to take advantage of consumer ignorance and inertia than they might in the brick-and-mortar world. One might also think that it will be more difficult for price spreads to exist, and for firms to engage in differential pricing since consumers should be able to do price comparisons at lower costs. Ratings on the reliability of retailers can be determined with the click of a mouse.

If, on the one hand, these improvements in retrieving information come to pass, we can expect profitability of Internet firms to be affected – negatively. Firms that are outstanding, however, should rise to prominence more rapidly. On the other hand, many consumers tire of providing their credit card information over and over again, and tend to stay with one or two sites instead of continuously trying new ones. If this behavior is similar enough to what one finds in the brick-and-mortar world then the performance of Internet firms may not be all that different from their brick-and-mortar counterparts.

BAD ECONOMICS LEADS TO BAD BUSINESS STRATEGY

I would like to frame the issues by examining what was said about the 'information' economy at the peak of its market lunacy. Although I presume that those individuals responsible for the more egregious statements would like to deny having made them, these statements represent a type of thinking that is always just below the surface. There is one article that I find contains so many juicy nuggets that I will use it to represent this whole class of thought.

On 3 January 2000, the first work day of a new millennium, the *Wall Street Journal* published an entire multi-page section of the newspaper that should be a collector's item to those interested in following the fads in business thinking. Ironically, most of the claims that were made in these articles were only months away from being unraveled by the events that were soon to unfold. One of the articles that I am sure appeared extremely profound to the hordes of business readers mesmerized by 'Who moved my cheese' was authored by Thomas Petzinger with the provocative title 'So long supply and demand' (2000). Being the neolithic Chicago School economist that I am and a believer that the major economic insights come from simple supply and demand, I tend to take titles like that one personally.

The supposed death of supply and demand was born of monumental hubris championed most fervently by those largely unschooled in economic analysis. But some economists get to share at least some of the blame for these foolhardy theories.

Petzinger provided several illustrations of how this belief had entered managerial thinking. He quoted Mark McElroy, a principal in International Business Machines Corp.'s Global Knowledge Management Practice as saying: 'Conventional economics is dead. Deal with it!' He also quoted Danny Hillis, vice-president of research and development at Walt Disney Co. as saying that the New Economy 'is actually much broader than technology alone. It is a new way of thinking.'

Petzinger explains that mainstream economists were loathe to accept that their prized theories were no longer applicable to the New Economy:

> You can understand why economists throw cold water on the new-economy concept, since accepting it would require them to abandon many of their dearest tools and techniques. It has become clichéd to cite the historian Thomas Kuhn's 40-year-old concept of a 'paradigm shift' – a revolution in knowledge that forces scientists to give up the beliefs on which they have staked their careers. But that's exactly what economics and accountants could be facing.

It is ironic that accountants were included in the list of Luddite professions, particularly given the newfangled and creative accounting techniques that have now received so much attention in the Enron/Anderson imbroglio. Still, it is instructive (and amusing) to follow Petzinger's thought process. What did he believe was causing the concepts of supply and demand to be overturned? He provides several factors.

First, he claims, the sources of wealth had changed.

> On an economywide level, these accelerating improvements may now be entering a supercritical phase in which they compound exponentially. Inventories, which once triggered or prolonged recessions, are not just declining but in many places evaporating . . . 'Economists fail to realize that these improvements are reducing costs so radically as to enable entirely new ways of doing business,' says telecom consultant David Isenberg of isen.com, Westfield, N.J. . . . Creativity is overtaking capital as the principal elixir of growth. And creativity, although precious, shares few of the constraints that limit the range and availability of capital and physical goods. 'In a knowledge-based economy, there are no constraints to growth,' says Michael Mauboussin, CS First Boston's managing director of equity research. 'Man alive! That's not something new?'

Almost all the ideas in this paragraph are complete nonsense. But for many industry analysts prior to the Internet meltdown these claims seemed perfectly reasonable, and anyone who didn't believe them just 'didn't get it'. Economists often were accused of just that, in part because the basic premise of economics has always been that scarcity is an unfortunate fact of life, Internet or no Internet, and scarcity limits such things as the growth of the economy. This scarcity assumption, although a bit of a downer, is not going to be overturned. Note, as well, that some of the claimed new ideas in the above paragraph were not even new. For example, economists have long known that new knowledge and not capital was the major ingredient in economic growth.

The second major reason that the old economics failed, according to Petzinger, was that the fundamentals of pricing and distribution had changed.

> In his classic undergraduate text 'Economics,' Paul Samuelson noted that any second grader could figure out that increased supplies cause lower value. But that was before Windows 95, automatic teller machines and Nike shoes. Products used in networks – whether computing, financial or social – increase in unit value as the supply increases . . . Former Stanford economist W. Brian Arthur has popularized this more-begets-more concept under the banner of 'increasing returns.' The timeless notion of diminishing returns isn't dead, of course, but it applies to an ever-shrinking proportion of value-added activity, such as grain harvests and polyvinyl-chloride production . . . This explains why a seemingly insane strategy such as giving away your basic product has become a strategy of choice in the New Economy . . . [T]he vendor collects revenue from another source, such as from selling upgrades, support or advertising. (Radio and television broadcasters – networks, after all – have always operated this way.) Another network, the cell-phone system, exploded when telecom companies began providing phones for practically nothing, even free of charge, and reaping increasing returns from air-time charges.

The future for economists surely looked bleak to Mr Petzinger. Economists are relegated to studying those few markets like 'grain harvests and polyvinyl-chloride production' – whatever those two markets might have in common. Note that Mr Petzinger appears to assume that that television networks have network effects just because the term 'network' is part of their name. He also believed, incorrectly, that network effects somehow naturally led to advertising-based revenue models, apparently as a result of the facile comparison of Internet 'network' with that of television 'networks.' His claim that cell-phone systems reap 'increasing returns' from air-time charges revealed a lack of understanding of that concept as well.

He continues:

> Our 500-year-old system of accounting has grave limitations in this world. A few big companies, notably Skandia Insurance Co. of Stockholm, are trying to invent Information Age accounting tools that reflect knowledge assets and

long-term value creation. But for now, according to the CS First Boston atoms-to-bits report, 'there is a substantial and growing chasm between our accounting system and economic reality' . . . [I]n an economy awash in capital, the endgame, not the score at the end of each quarter, is all that counts . . . 'Earnings are a decision variable, not a requirement,' says Prof. Arthur, the economist. 'If everyone thinks you're doing fine without earnings, why have them?'

This is a truly great quote. Why have earnings? Can Professor Arthur be serious? Do we really need to ask? What, after all, is the value of a piece of stock if the underlying company to which the stock provides ownership doesn't have any earnings? As we shall see, Professor Arthur is a major player in my tale, and the proud creator of enough whoppers to give Burger King a run for its money.

And since adherents of traditional accounting practices didn't seem to agree with Professor Arthur that money-losing practices were the road to riches, they were to be thrown out along with all those other outdated ideas that old-fashioned economists were fond of.

THE GENESIS OF THESE NOTIONS

Where did these ideas come from? Why were they taken seriously? In short, they came from where most crazy ideas come from – the academy. And like most academic ideas, they were meant to be taken seriously. These concepts have received a tremendous amount of attention from mainstream economists. They came from a profession that is crazy about theory, that has a distaste for applications, but understands full well that practical applications are required to sell a theory to the public.

The building blocks of these new theories – concepts such as network effects, economies of scale, and winner-take-all – are all sound enough, which is not to say that there aren't errors made in discussing these concepts. But it is the final leap to a concept known as lock-in, or first-mover-wins, where the truly pernicious errors occurred and continue to occur.

SPECIAL ECONOMICS OF THE INTERNET, OR MAYBE NOT SO SPECIAL

Network Effects

Many products and firms associated with the Internet are thought to have an economic property known as 'network effects' (see Katz and Shapiro 1985; Liebowitz and Margolis 1998). Some products actually do have these effects, but many products that were involved in some way with e-commerce do not have even the slightest trace of network effects. Nevertheless, many business models applied to e-commerce were often based on unsupported and ultimately incorrect assumptions that *all* of e-commerce was subject to powerful network effects. How much of the recent Internet meltdown can be laid at the doorstep of these mistaken business strategies can not be ascertained with any precision, but certainly a substantial portion of the damage can be attributed to them.

The technical definition of network effects is fairly straightforward. Network effects are present when a product becomes more useful to consumers the more other people there are using it.[2] For example, the owner of a fax machine benefits from the fact that there are lots of other people with fax machines. If there were no other users of fax machines you couldn't send a fax to anyone, and its best use might be as a doorstop. Obviously, telephone and other *literal* networks where users are physically linked to one another exhibit network effects. Less obvious are what have been called *virtual* network, such as the network of WordPerfect users.[3] It *might* be that some, or even most, of the users of WordPerfect care about the number of other users. If WordPerfect users would pay more for their copy of WordPerfect as the number of other WordPerfect users increased, then WordPerfect would be said to embody network effects.

Note that there need not be anything particularly high-tech about network effects. Automobile owners benefit from having a ready supply of parts and mechanics that make it easier to have their cars repaired should they break down. The more units there are of a particular automobile model, the more likely that any single owner can find such repair facilities. Therefore, to the extent that consumers value the ease of repair, automobiles should have network effects. The same would be true for almost any product that needs repair facilities. These latter 'network effects,' therefore, have little or nothing to do with the 'information economy'.

Network effects clearly exist, but their strength is often overestimated.[4] Why is an overestimation of network effects so dangerous to the thinking of business managers? The answer has to do with business strategies that have been propounded based on network effects. These are theories that exhort firms to take advantage of network effects to lock-in winning positions. These are theories that suggest that getting to market first and generating a large market share and installed base is of the utmost importance. These are theories that imply that losing money to gain sales and share is a worthwhile investment because firms that succeed in generating large sales will have easy sailing in the future with their customers locked-in to their products. These are theories that make claims that are inconsistent with how markets have actually worked.

Before examining how those theories have been translated into business strategies we need to examine several other economic concepts that are closely related and in many cases more important than network effects.

Economies of Scale

Economies of scale, a concept that has been taught in microeconomics classes for many generations, imply that *average* costs decrease as the firm sells more and gets larger. Automobile companies experience significant economies of scale, which is one reason that a Rolls-Royce costs more to make than a Cadillac. There are large startup costs, more formally known as fixed costs, in designing a new automobile and in creating all the dies and assembly facilities to produce a particular model of a car. Almost all manufacturing exhibits some economies of scale. But usually, at some point, these economies tend to run out and are superseded by other components of production costs that raise the average cost of production as output increases.

Many new high-tech products are thought to have very significant economies of scale because they have very large startup costs. When a software product is developed, for example, the total cost of development is a fixed cost that does not depend on whether ten or ten million units are actually sold. The costs of duplicating, shipping, and servicing units that eventually land in the hands of consumers are often considered to be close to zero, a convenient though not necessarily accurate assumption.[5]

Still, it seems likely that software, microprocessors, and many other high-tech products do have substantial economies of scale. Although this concept has been given a role in business strategies that is far inferior to that of network effects, economies of scale are likely to have very similar impacts to network effects, and are frequently going to be more significant than network effects. Their somewhat neglected role in recent economic literature is probably due to the fact that the concept of economies to scale is not new and doesn't seem as sexy to academics who usually are looking for something new, even if it is just a new label on an old concept, or even if it turns out to be wrong.[6,7]

Winner Take All

Network effects and economies of scale have almost identical impacts. Each works to advantage large firms over small ones. Large networks, by definition, have stronger network effects than do small networks, meaning that consumers should be willing to pay more to join a large network, everything else equal. This should enhance the profitability of the large network relative to the small network. Similarly, economies of scale imply that large firms have lower costs than do small firms, providing them with larger profits. In terms of outcomes, these two economic forces are virtually indistinguishable from one another since each provides an advantage to large firms and networks relative to their smaller rivals.

This advantage of large over small is sometimes referred to as increasing returns (to scale). Increasing returns was normally thought to lead to winner-take-all results, particularly when products from different vendors were considered to be identical, as they are often modeled to be in economic theories. Some modern versions of this story, however, nodding to the reality that market shares are almost never 100 per cent, prefer the term 'winner-take-most.'

Increasing returns, therefore, was inconsistent with the idea of many competitors, one of the fundamental assumptions in economists' basic model of competition. It was also inconsistent with the observation that many industries had far more than a single dominant firm. For these and other reasons the concept of increasing returns was historically relegated to a relatively obscure position in economic analysis.[8]

Whenever large firms enjoy cost advantages that smaller firms do not enjoy, this could contribute to a winner-take-all result. But it need not, particularly if products are different from one another and appeal to different types of consumers. That is why the video format for camcorders (hi-8, before the advent of digital video camcorders) has mainly been different from the format for VCRs (VHS). VHS was successful against Beta in large part due to the longer playing time afforded by its larger cassette. The large cassette proved to be a disadvantage in the camcorder market where portability was very important.

Of course, many firms with large market shares, such as Packard-Bell in computers or General Motors in automobile manufacturing, did not have the cost advantages over their rivals that was expected of large firms. But, for some reason, this possibility was thought not to apply to Internet firms. Morgan Stanley, in a 1999 report opined:

> Owing in part to economics of increasing returns, the revenue/profit streams that accrue, in time, to the Internet leaders (defined as companies with the most/stickiest customers) should be broad-based and recurring and the user reach supported by the leaders may be impressive (of Microsoft-ian and ATT-ian proportions, or higher).[9]

This type of thinking led to Waterloo-ian type of results, but I will return to that later.

Nonetheless, there is yet one more factor that can also lead to winner-take-all results – instant scalability. Instant scalability is the ability of a firm to meet market demand in almost no time, tending to cause any favored product to get the lion's share of the market. Instant scalability arises when the production process requires non-specific inputs. For example, the production of copies of a piece of software such Quicken or Word requires disk duplication machinery (or web servers for software downloads). The machines that make copies of CDs are the same no matter what is on the CD being copied. Thus a machine making copies of Word could almost instantaneously be converted to start making copies of Quicken. Therefore, if demand shifts to favor one product over another, the facilities exist to very quickly start making copies of the now popular product. Note that this is not the same as saying that the cost of duplication is near zero. It could cost a million dollars for each CD (if the materials in a CD were very expensive) but the concept would still be the same and instant scalability would still exist in the industry.

Instant scalability does not necessarily lead to winner-take-all results. If consumers do not uniformly agree that one product in the market is superior to the others (in terms of bang for the buck) instant scalability will not lead to dominant market shares. For many information-based products, however, there will be fairly general agreement among consumers about product quality and large market shares will prevail. A common example of long standing can be found in the movie industry where in any given week one or two movies tend to take in a majority of box office receipts. Theatres, projectors, and movie duplication equipment are non-specialized, which has allowed these high shares to exist, even though they tend to be very short-lived.

Whether firms have the characteristics of economies of scale, network effects, or instant scalability depends on the specifics of their products and the manner in which they do business. The exact manner in which they use or do not use the Internet also can alter the existence or non-existence of these economic characteristics. One has to examine each industry on a case-by-case basis to determine whether winner-take-all is a likely result. For our purposes here, however, the question is more specifically how might using the Internet alter these characteristics for businesses. I turn to that now.

HOW THE INTERNET INFLUENCES THESE ECONOMIC FORCES

Could use of the Internet, or the transformation of a business model from brick-and-mortar to Internet based, turn an industry that was not previously winner-takes-all into one that was? This is really the central question in trying to understand how the embrace of the Internet will alter results in industries not previously thought to have increasing returns. What might be the expected impacts of converting a brick-and-mortar firm into one that uses the Internet to do business?

The creation of the web site is a fixed cost, so that this component of cost might produce an economy of scale effect. But if the cost of web site creation is small relative to other costs such as warehousing, shipping, production, sales, customer relations and so forth, then the fixed cost of web site creation is unlikely to result in much of a scale economy and thus unlikely to result in winner-takes-all.

It is commonly thought that most firms operating on the Internet are subject to network effects, presumably because the Internet itself is a network. This would seem naturally to lead to the conclusion that most e-commerce will be winner-takes-all.

This view is mistaken for a great number of firms classified as Internet firms, perhaps even a majority. The source of this error is due to a misunderstanding of network effects. Many Internet companies, when properly analysed, are seen to have few if any network effects – Amazon, Etoys, PeaPod, Priceline, and *most* other Internet retailers have (or had, since these firms are disappearing like flies) no network effects to speak of. Other firms, such as Ebay with its online auctions of used products, and the various Internet messaging services by the likes of AOL, Yahoo and Microsoft, do have strong network effects, but they seem to be more the exception than the rule for Internet companies.

What is noteworthy in all this is that there are important branches of e-commerce, perhaps the majority of e-commerce activities, that do not exhibit much in the way of network effects. Take the case of a consumer shopping for toys on the Internet. That consumer is likely to have very little interest in the number of other toy shoppers that will patronize a particular web e-tailer. Why should they? They want to buy the most appropriate products at the best price. Very little of that decision will depend on the number of other consumers patronizing a particular retailer. One exception to this, but I believe a minor exception, would be product reviews listed on the web site. One of the clever features of Amazon is its listing of product reviews conveniently accessible to users contemplating purchase of a product. Go and compare the number of reviews on Amazon versus that on Barnes and Noble's web site. Amazon seems to understand better that reviews are one of the few network features it can provide its customers.

But even this is a weak network effect, since consumers can go shopping at Amazon to get the product reviews and then go to another site that might have lower prices to make the actual purchase. In other words, other websites can 'free-ride' off of Amazon's product reviews, limiting the value of reviews as network effects. Consumers cannot free-ride on real network effects, such as AOL's Instant Messenger. If you want to have access to the many individuals who use the AOL product, you can only do so using the AOL product. AOL has fought hard to limit interoperability that would allow users of other instant messaging programs access to the large AOL Messaging subscriber base in order to keep the network effects for itself (Kapadia 2001).

Customers of most Internet retailers will be interested in the same general factors that they care about in the brick-and-mortar universe – price, return policy, whether the item is in stock, the firm's reputation for reliability, and so forth. The fact that business is taking place on the Internet does not introduce winner-takes-all characteristics into these markets. There is no reason to think that the biggest toy e-tailer would have a more significant advantage over other Internet toy stores than large brick-and-mortar toy stores have over their smaller competitors. Of course, if the brick-and-mortar world is winner-take-all, we might expect the Internet version of these firms to be the same.

RACING TO BE FIRST: FOOLISH BUT FORMERLY FADDISH

It is often asserted that being first is of paramount importance in the Internet age, far more important, say, than for brick-and-mortar industries. For example, the famous, or now infamous, Morgan Stanley stock-market analyst closely associated with the NASDAQ and Internet stock run-ups, Mary Meeker, said in a 1997 report:

> Our Internet team thinks first-mover advantage for Web retailers may be important. The retail group, by contrast, doesn't think being first matters much, since barriers to entry will likely remain low on the Web.[10]

What caused the Internet group to believe that first-mover-wins was an apt description of Internet retailing. What led the Internet group astray? Here is a hint from a January 1999 article (my italics):

> The notion of 'first-mover advantage' is gaining currency quickly and, in turn, influencing companies' chances for success . . . The idea of first-mover advantage seems to have become fashionable only recently. In a Dow Jones database search, the term appears 156 times in publications since the beginning of 1998, but only 28 times in the six years from 1988 through 1993. Much of its usage, before the rise of the Internet, *was in overseas business publications and academic journals*. (Mannes 1999)

The idea of first-mover-wins fits in neatly with a strain of economic thought that arose in the late 1980s and was nurtured, incubated and

proselytized to business audiences by academics. That is the subject of the
next few sections.

From Winner-take-all to First-mover-wins

If the market is going to become dominated by a small number of firms,
perhaps as few as one, how does a firm get to be that top dog? The typical
answer has been: 'Get established first. At any cost.'

This idea that being first is essential was a truly pernicious bit of faux
wisdom. This idea has helped firms madly throw themselves off a cliff like
lemmings, and to do so thinking they were bound for glory. Now I do not
wish to split hairs over the *first* mover versus say a *second* mover a week
later, for that is a distinction without a difference.[11] It is really the idea that
early movers have a *large* lead over later movers that deserves a good part
of the blame for appearing to give credence to these misguided business
plans of the e-commerce firms.

Finding examples of this view is easy. In a typical story of the time, a
company founder is quoted in the Wall Street Journal stating, 'Our biggest
competitor is time – being the first to market with this product' (Carlton
2000).

The generality of this claim is nicely illustrated in a column in eCompany,
(each of the companies mentioned in the quote soon went belly-up):

> 'We have the first-mover advantage,' Women.com CEO Marleen McDaniel told
> CNBC in June 1999. 'They have the first-mover advantage,' a Zona Research
> analyst told a reporter, explaining why eToys's stock was a steal. 'Eve.com is an
> outstanding e-commerce opportunity with a first-mover advantage,' Idealab
> founder Bill Gross bragged in a press release. As Draper Fisher Jurvetson
> partner Tim Draper told USA Today in October 1999, the first-mover is usually
> the (company) that's going to win it.[12]

Or this from *Information Rules*, in many respects one of the more reasonable books of advice for the information economy:

> First-Mover advantages can be powerful and long lasting in lock-in markets,
> especially those in information industries where scale economies are substantial.
> If you can establish an installed base before the competition arrives on the scene,
> you may make it difficult for later entrants to achieve the scale economies nec-
> essary to compete. (Shapiro and Varian 1998, p. 169)

Of course, as proper academics, Professors Shapiro and Varian, the
authors of *Information Rules*, are somewhat circumspect about overstating
the advantages of being first. They do not say that being first ensures an
advantage – only that it might. Still, for a business audience these nuances

are likely to be unnoticed. Furthermore, in the 'Lessons' section of their Chapter 6, which is where many busy readers are likely to gain their insights, we find the less circumspect: 'Be prepared to invest to build an installed base through promotions and by offering up-front discounts. You can't succeed in competitive lock-in markets without making these investments.' To a typical business reader it would certainly appear that one *needs* to initially lose money in order to gain the ever so important market share.

More exuberant still is Kevin Kelly in his book *New Rules for a New Economy*. Not only should you discount your product to get market share, Kelly tells businessmen, but you *need* to actually give it away. He has ten cutely named rules (chapters) in his book, the fourth of which is 'Follow the Free'. Here is a sampling:

> As crackpot as it sounds, in the distant future nearly everything we make will (at least for a short while) be given away free – refrigerators, skis, laser projectors, clothes, you name it. (Kelly 1998, p. 58)

> Talk of generosity, of information that wants to be free, and of virtual communities is often dismissed by businesspeople as youthful new age idealism. It may be idealistic but it is also the only sane way to launch a commercial economy in the emerging space. (ibid., p. 60)

At least he understood that giving nearly everything away sounded like a crackpot idea. The problem was that he didn't seem to understand that what he was putting forward didn't just sound like a crackpot idea but actually was one.

Last, but not least, we have Professor Brian Arthur, the pied piper of lock-in who provided the delicious quote from the Petzinger article. Arthur has received a blizzard of publicity and near-universal adoration from the media.[13] Arthur tells business strategists, in a 1998 *Harvard Business Review* article: 'Two maxims are widely accepted in knowledge-based markets: it pays to hit the market first, and it pays to have superb technology.' Yet that same year he discards even the importance of having good technology in an interview with Booze-Allen & Hamilton:

> If you are in a technically based industry, then it's not sufficient to think in terms of lowering your cost, improving your quality, keeping products moving out the door . . . business strategy has to go far beyond the usual adages about costs down, quality up, core competency. High tech adds a new layer of complication. You have to allow that you are playing games where the winner can walk off with a great deal of the market and the losers are left with practically nothing, even if their products are technically brilliant, and the cost is right. So basically the strategies are very much the strategies you would apply in presidential primaries. You want to build up market share, you want to build up user base. If you do, you can lock in that market.[14]

So there you have it. Technical brilliance, low prices and high quality are insufficiently important to lead to success. So much for the world beating a path to your door because you have built a better mousetrap. What could Emerson possibly have to tell us in our modern times? Instead, the winner might have mundane products, so-so quality and high prices. But this second-rate firm wins because it got to the starting line first and locked-in its customers, at least as Arthur tells it. And Arthur has not been shy about claiming that that traditional economic concepts were not relevant to high technology markets.[15]

Where are the intellectual underpinnings for this notion of the benefits of early entry? The answer has to do with the concept of lock-in, a relatively new concept in the thinking of economists.

THE CONCEPT OF LOCK-IN

In winner-take-all markets, it is possible that there will be swift leadership changes whenever a better challenger enters the market. Lock-in, however, suggests otherwise. The winner not only takes all, he can continue to keep taking all even in the face of a better rival. In this view of markets, lock-in works to keep the leading firm's customers immobile and the firm entrenched in the leading position.

In the telling of the lock-in story, network effects play the key role. Network effects lead to winner-take-all, and once the winner is established network effects keep competitors at bay. Just why this would be so has to do with a particular type of coordination problem.

Whenever consumers attempt to determine which brand or type of product to buy, they must go through (consciously or not) several internal calculations. Typically, they will compare the prices and qualities of products. They need to determine the costs of learning how to use a new product. And in network markets they would also have to take account of strength or size of the competing networks to gauge the size of the network effects that will be associated with the competing products. For example, a consumer in the early 1980s, when determining whether to buy a VHS or Beta VCR would normally consider the prospective size of the two networks.

It is this need to gauge what others are doing that leads to the theoretical possibility that consumers can in principle get locked-in to a product, seemingly unable to switch to something better. How that might work in theory is the subject of numerous economics papers. How it worked in the real world is the subject of a far smaller, and as we shall see, notably faulty, literature.

Lock-in costs can themselves be classified into two different types. First, there are the costs involved with just changing to another brand or version of a product, such as relearning old habits, becoming familiar with the new product, and also possibly being able to use the new product with old work-products, such as using a new word-processor to read your old documents. These are costs of being compatible with one's self.

Second, there are costs involved in possibly losing compatibility with others. This might be exemplified by someone wishing to switch from VHS to Beta and finding a dearth of pre-recorded Beta movies available at the video store, or someone switching to Lotus WordPro and finding they have trouble exchanging documents with their colleagues who use Microsoft Word.

These two different factors, being compatible with one's self and being compatible with others, play an important role in understanding how lock-in might work. And these two factors are essential in delineating the crucial distinction between *weak* and *strong* forms of lock-in. The strong form of lock-in supports the concept of first-mover-wins. The weak form does not.

This distinction is not one that is normally made in the literature.[16] Instead, all forms of lock-in are lumped together. Yet it is only the strong form of lock-in that leads to potential coordination problems, and only the strong form of lock-in that would lead to first-mover-wins. It is a failing of this literature that it hasn't distinguished between these two types of lock-in.

It is possible to imagine a situation where a newcomer firm produces a better product than an incumbent. A better product is defined as a product that a consumer would choose if he were starting from scratch and there was no concern with compatibility, either with oneself, or with others. Whether that product can break into the market depends largely on the type of lock-in involved.

Strong Lock-in

A *strong* form of lock-in exists when this better product is not adopted even though the superiority of the product can overcome any self-compatibility issues for consumers. In such a case, the switch would occur if consumers didn't care about compatibility with others. Network effects, if they exist in a market, bring compatibility with other consumers to the fore and there-fore the issue of whether superior products can overcome the lead of infe-rior incumbents or not has been closely associated with network effects.

Note that if the benefits of the new technology were not capable of over-coming learning costs and/or inability to use old work-product, then it would be inefficient for the new technology to replace the old. These costs of learning to use new products are real costs.

Most important, if strong lock-in exists, it might be wise for sellers to try to get a large market share even if the costs of doing so are very high. That is because challengers, even those with superior products, may not be able to overcome the lead of the early birds. This is the basis for the belief in first-mover-wins.

Potential incompatibility with other users can prevent a superior challenger from vanquishing an incumbent, at least in principle. With this strong form of lock-in, even though all consumers would like to switch if enough other users would also switch, a coordination failure among users prevents consumers from actually switching. In other words, we all would like to switch, say, from VHS to Beta. Beta, lets pretend, is universally acknowledged to be better than VHS. Because each individual consumer fears that others will not switch and that as a result most prerecorded movies will not be available on Beta, all consumers stick with VHS. This is a case where we would all be better off making the change, but we do not make the change because we can not coordinate our independent actions.

That is the strong lock-in story, and it has beguiled many an economist, particularly since at first there appeared to be some evidence to support it. It is not just a story of incompatibility with others, however. At its core, this strong lock-in story contains an assumption that each user believes that others will continue to use the inferior product even though everyone knows that the challenger product is superior.[17]

At the time the challenger enters the market, the two types of compatibility would appear to completely favor the incumbent. Compatibility with one's old behavior imposes costs on a change. And the incumbent has a larger market share, by definition. However, when consumers go through a calculation about the value of switching, it would be rational for them to try to project what the future will look like. Otherwise the first automobiles would never have been sold, since there weren't gas stations, and the first fax machines wouldn't have been sold, since there would be no faxes to receive and no one to send faxes to. It is the *expectation* of the size of networks that actually matters. If consumers believe the challenger will do well in the market, then the market shares at the time of purchase need not be particularly relevant.

So in fact, the importance of compatibility with others does not necessarily favor the incumbent. Challengers, who are able to demonstrate the superiority of their product, and gain momentum in the eyes of consumers, may very well prevail, as would be required if the market were working efficiently. Therefore, it is uncertain, in theory, whether strong forms of lock-in are likely to occur.

Real-world examples of strong lock-in have been put forward, such as the typewriter keyboard or video recorder format, but as I discuss below, these examples have been shown to be flat out wrong.

It might appear that winner-take-all brought about entirely by economies of scale might also be capable of strong form lock-in of an incumbent. After all, a new challenger, even with a better product, will have serious cost disadvantages relative to the much larger incumbent. However, the challenger has a straightforward task: investing sufficient resources to achieve a large enough scale in *new sales* so as to reach a low cost that will allow him to eventually prevail. The task facing a firm trying to overcome network effects appears less simple, because it would require overcoming the impacts of the *existing stock* of previous sales and influencing expectations about the market shares of future stocks of the competing formats.

Weak Lock-in

Alternatively, it is possible that a firm might produce a product that is superior to the incumbent, but is not sufficiently superior to cover the self-compatibility costs of switching to a new and different product. An example might be if a competitor to Zip drives were to produce at an identical cost an incompatible system with a minor improvement in capacity, say from 250 megs to 260 megs. Current Zip consumers are not likely to switch to the new system since the very small advantage of the new system is unlikely to make it economical to throw out the old Zip drives and disks for the new alternative.

These consumers of Zip drives can be thought of as *weakly locked-in* to the Zip system.[18] In this latter case it is inefficient for current consumers to switch to the new product, and although the term lock-in can and has been used to describe this situation, it is quite distinct from the strong form of lock-in. If the incumbent already dominates a mature market, then the incumbent will remain the dominant technology and it is efficient for it to remain the dominant technology. There is no necessity for network effects or coordination problems in order to have weak forms of lock-in.

There are many, many instances of weak lock-in. You are unwilling to purchase a new computer merely three months after buying one even though new ones are slightly better. You continue driving your no longer brand-new car. You continue to live in a five-bedroom house after the kids have grown up and left and the rooms largely sit empty. You continue to part your hair on the left. All of these, and millions of others, are examples of weak lock-in. All these examples provide some limited protection to incumbents.

Weak lock-in has nothing to do with network effects or economies of scale. Weak lock-in shouldn't require new business strategies since it has been around for so long that old business strategies should have taken it into account. Business strategies that neglected switching costs would be derelict strategies, and perhaps the current literature can have some salutary impact in that dimension. But weak lock-in has little to do with moving to an information economy unless we think that learning to use digital products is more difficult than learning to use old pen and paper systems.

The final difference between the two forms of lock-in is that it is efficient for the economy to stay with the incumbent while the incumbent is weakly locked-in. The costs of learning a new system are real costs, and if the new product is insufficiently better to outweigh those costs, then it is efficient for society to stick with the old. Strong lock-in, on the other hand, causes inefficiency. If we could get all the users to switch to the new product, they would all be better off even after the costs of switching are included.

IMPACTS OF LOCK-IN ON FIRST-MOVER-WINS

Proponents of the strong form of lock-in essentially assume that even if consumers wanted to switch to a better product, their fear that others might remain with the old product constrains them to remain with the old product as well. The challenger not only has to produce a better product that can overcome self-compatibility, but it also needs to overcome the consumer's cost of being incompatible with almost everyone else since it is assumed that no one else switches.[19] Critics of strong lock-in, on the other hand, believe that the expected market shares will depend mainly on self-compatibility. In other words, if the new product is sufficiently better when compared to the old product that it pays individuals to switch (ignoring network effects), then the expectations of consumers will be such that they will expect other consumers to switch for the same reasons that they would want to switch. The new superior product is thus able to dominate the market.

If the strong form of lock-in were to hold, the object lesson for firms would be to get to market first and largely ignore relative quality since even a significantly better product would not allow the challenger to dislodge the incumbent. This would be the claim of Brian Arthur and his followers.

The weak form of lock-in, on the other hand, gives little support for this tactic. The weak form of lock-in implies that the key to winning is to produce a product sufficiently better that it can overcome consumers' switching costs. Unless self-compatibility costs are very large, which is to some extent under the control of the challenger's product design, a better product will likely be able to overcome weak forms of lock-in. Emerson's dictum to build a better mousetrap would still work, in the sense that a better mousetrap was understood to be one that was sufficiently better that it would overcome the costs of self-compatibility. While it is possible that self-compatibility costs could be so strong that the original seller would retain all customers because no improvements to the product could be made by competitors that could overcome self-compatibility costs, this result, besides being perfectly efficient, lacks novelty and seems unlikely. It would hardly provide a sufficient basis for a claim that suddenly, in the new information-based economy, rushing to market will be a winning strategy whereas it wasn't in the past. Weak form lock-in has been around forever. It can be found in the most mundane activities.

I am used to going to a particular gas station. It is a habit. Even if the station across the street is a penny or two lower, I will continue going to the station at which I am comfortable. That makes it a weak form of lock-in. Does that mean that competing gas stations have to charge prices one half to two-thirds lower to get my business, a number that has been put forward as the percentage differential required to break out of lock-in?[20] Obviously not. Although the precise number will differ by driver, surely a very large majority of drivers would pick the gas station charging $1.00 a gallon, or even $1.35, compared to their old gas station charging $1.50 a gallon. It is difficult to imagine anyone going to their old station at $1.50 when a nearby station was charging $.90 a gallon.

Weak lock-in, therefore, seems an unlikely candidate to support first-mover-wins strategies.

WHAT DOES THE REAL WORLD TELL US ABOUT STRONG LOCK-IN?

The concept of first-mover-wins, if it is to be indicative of something new, of something central to the information economy, requires a strong form of lock-in. Yet, there is no evidence that strong form lock-in actually occurs. That explains why Altair, VisiCalc, and Ampex – the first firms to produce PCs, spreadsheets, and VCRs respectively – are not today the leaders in those markets. Neither are any of the other early leaders in these markets still entrenched.

This is not to say that no real world cases have been claimed as supporting strong form lock-in by the advocates of strong form lock-in. Paul David, Brian Arthur, and their students have put forward various claims of actual instances of strong form lock-in.

The two most popular examples of truly pernicious strong form lock-in, are the typewriter keyboard, and the VCR.[21] These examples are popular in the press and particularly among academic authors.[22] They are popular because they provide verisimilitude to what otherwise might appear to be purely theoretical abstractions about the world. The problem is that these stories are counterfeits.

My research with Stephen Margolis (that formed the subject of my book with him) found no support for these claims of strong lock-in. This severely weakens support for the first-mover-wins hypothesis. Additionally, our examination of software markets found the evidence to be in direct contradiction of the first-mover-wins concept.

The keyboard story is elsewhere described at great length.[23] The basic story that was first introduced to economists by Paul David and later repeated numerous times, as for example in Shapiro and Varian, starts with the claim that to prevent jamming of the mechanical keys, the typewriter mechanics who worked on the original QWERTY machine in the late 1800s came up with a design to slow typing down. Interestingly, not a shred of evidence has been brought forward to support this claim. Rather, it appears that to prevent jamming, the keyboard designers came up with a way to shift typing successive letters from left to the right hand through experimentation with the keyboard design. It also turns out that shifting successive letters between alternate hands also leads to faster typing speeds.

In the 1930s a professor of ergonomics at the University of Washington, August Dvorak, patented his own keyboard which was painstakingly created from a systematic examination of which letters and pairs of letters were most commonly used in English writing, and then applying this knowledge to position the keys to minimize the distance the fingers traveled. Dvorak's own research claimed that this keyboard design worked much better than the QWERTY design.

A study conducted by a component of the US Navy during World War II purportedly demonstrated that Professor Dvorak's design was indeed 40 per cent faster than the QWERTY design. If one examines the Navy study, as was not done by academic practitioners of lock-in theory,[24] one discovers several important irregularities in its conduct that biased the results in favor of the Dvorak keyboard and that make it unacceptable as a 'scientific' study.[25]

A more important problem with the claims of QWERTY's inferiority is that QWERTY detractors failed to discuss the most important study comparing the two keyboards. Professor Earl Strong, from Penn State, conducted a study in the 1950s for the General Services Administration (GSA), and his experiment and its results received a great deal of publicity both before and after its conclusion, including several articles in leading newspapers such as the *New York Times*.[26] Strong found that Dvorak was not superior to QWERTY.

Strong also reported that the studies conducted by the Navy during World War II were conducted by the Navy's chief expert in such matters, Lieutenant Commander August Dvorak, a fact that makes one suspicious, at least, of the impartiality of the earlier Navy study.

Amazingly, this GSA study, which was far more readily available in most academic libraries than the Navy study, was entirely neglected by the advocates of strong form path dependence even though Paul David was a former president of the American Economic History Association and might have been expected to have gotten the history correct. In fact, there were some criticisms of Strong's study in the ergonomics literature, but the QWERTY-as-lock-in advocates apparently never bothered reading any of these either. These criticisms of the GSA study, performed largely by supporters of Dvorak, do not seem terribly compelling and the consensus in that literature appears to be that there is little difference in performance between the two keyboard designs.[27]

It is also the case that modern ergonomic studies of the keyboard, and other experiments examining the costs of retraining typists to use the Dvorak keyboard, are consistent with the GSA results and inconsistent with those reported by the Navy Study.

This more complete history of the keyboards has been available to economists since 1990 but is almost never reported when lock-in advocates tell their version of the keyboard story. Instead, if they mention it at all, they usually bury it in a footnote stating that there appears to be some disagreement in the academic literature, as Shapiro and Varian did in their book. The intent seems clearly to leave the reader with the impression that the keyboard lock-in story is correct even though there has never been an academic presentation refuting the facts that we uncovered.[28]

The VHS/Beta story, as an example of first mover wins, is even more flawed.[29] First, it is important to note that the Beta format was first on the scene and had a head start of about a year and a half. It might be natural to ask where its first mover advantage was since it was soon routed from this market by its competitor, VHS. The proponents of lock-in report, with some justification, that the video recorder market wasn't yet very mature, and that the number of units sold was too small to give much of an advantage to Beta. But even more important, and perhaps the reason the video-recorder market didn't mature more rapidly under Sony's initial tutelage, was the fact that the initial Betamax could only record for one hour, eliminating the possibility of watching or recording movies on a single tape.

VHS had a larger cassette, but otherwise virtually the same technology as Betamax. The companies behind the two formats (Sony and Matsushita) had a patent sharing agreement as they had previously jointly produced a prior-generation video recorder. When Sony engineers saw the VHS machine they thought it was a clone of the Betamax, so similar was it in terms of technology. VHS's much bigger tape allowed a longer playing time for a given quality of picture. It was the inferior playing time that led to the demise of the Betamax, not the fact that it was first, or second, or third.[30]

Now you might expect that this strong form of lock-in, given its impact on current thinking (not just business strategy but antitrust prosecutions such as the Microsoft case) must depend on more than just these two quite feeble stories. And it does, but not much more. It survives mostly due to the popularity of the economic theory that demonstrates that it could happen, on a few other slightly more far-fetched examples, and on the hopes and wishes of those who put forward the theory in the first place.

So the claim has been made, by Brian Arthur and others, that the internal combustion engine was possibly a mistake that locked-out superior alternatives such as steam or electric (see Arthur 1990). If this seems pretty far-fetched, that is because it is far-fetched. But not too far fetched to avoid serious academic scrutiny, particularly by those hoping to find a strong form of lock-in.[31] But even with every incentive to conclude that the internal combustion engine was a terrible mistake, that research could not come to such a conclusion.

And there are other possibilities that have been suggested. Perhaps AM stereo radio should have replaced FM. Perhaps DC should have replaced AC as the standard for electrical generation. Perhaps quadraphonic sound of the 1980s should have replaced stereo. Perhaps the Macintosh operating system should have replaced DOS (a graphical operating system did, but it happened to be called Windows). Perhaps railroads used the wrong gauge tracks (distance between the track pairs) for the trains to run on.[32] These are all examples of possible instances of strong form lock-in. But upon closer scrutiny, these potential lock-in examples have all failed to make the case that their advocates were hoping to make.

There are as yet no real examples of strong lock-in. Someday, one or two might be found. But those will tend to be the exceptions that prove the rule.

Arthur and David have recently tried to turn the debate around by claiming that it is not they who should have to find strong forms of lock-in, but instead the critics of strong form lock-in should have to prove that every market has the most efficient product.[33] Arthur has said in several interviews that we (Liebowitz and Margolis) have not proven that QWERTY is the best possible keyboard.[34] Indeed, we have never made any such claim. Even if other keyboards were equally good or slightly better (which is what we actually concluded), that would not support claims of strong-form lock-in.

It is hard to provide better evidence of the difficulty of demonstrating strong form lock-in than the current claim by its proponents that it is not their scientific responsibility to actually find any examples.[35] This claim began to surface two or three years ago. If they believed this current claim of theirs, one wonders what was the purpose, during the prior 15 years, of their numerous attempts to find such examples? Why were they bothering?

In the lengthy examination of software markets that I conducted with Margolis we find, over and over again, that the product that wins also happens to be as good as or better than the others. Even though these markets appeared to be winner-take-all, having both network effects and economies of scale, and even though the leaders had very large market shares consistent with winner-take-all, good products pushed out lesser ones independent of which product was there first. VisiCalc, the first spreadsheet was supplanted by the superior 1–2–3, only to be replaced by the superior Excel. Managing Your Money was supplanted by Quicken, and so forth (see Lewin 2001 especially chs 7, 8, 9). This was true for markets where Microsoft was a player and in markets where it was not. It was true for Macintosh markets as well as Windows markets.

Finally, I have one more source of evidence. In 1999 I conducted a study for McKinsey trying to determine what causes firms to be successful.[36] I looked at twenty different markets, ranging from high tech, such as web portals, to low tech, such as athletic apparel and discount retailers. The results were very interesting and quite consistent with those found in software markets reported above.

There was a very strong relation between those firms producing the best quality product and those firms that were most successful, measured by either above normal profit, large market shares, or high stock market returns. Since PC manufacturers, software producers, and web site portals were all included in the study, they provide some specific cases to support the conclusion that building the being better mousetrap is an essential ingredient for success, even in high tech markets.

CONCLUSIONS

The general rules that have formed our understanding of markets have been developed over a period of centuries. Every now and then a new 'paradigm' is presented as a replacement. The death of supply and demand has been prematurely announced numerous times. The most recent new paradigm was the Internet economy, which was supposed to stand the old rules about markets and economies on their collective heads. The laws of supply and demand are not so fragile as to be overcome by anything so small as a new method of communicating with one another.

I do not want to diminish the fact that life changes, and technology along with it. That sometimes there is something new under the sun. That often, our theories and ideas turn out to be wrong. In this instance, however, the new theories and ideas that have been put forward are not more powerful alternatives that tell us something new and truthful about the world. Sometimes the new and intriguing ideas turn out to be wrong ideas. Probably more often than not. In this case, the new ideas had largely been demonstrated to be wrong before the Internet craze took off. But truth is often less important than glamour.

The old-fashioned ways of thinking warn against the expectations of easy and quick riches, of rushing off to catch the wave, of eschewing product quality because of the delay it might cause to product introduction. Old standards – such as slow and steady wins the race, build a better mousetrap, and there's a sucker born every minute – are standards for good reasons.

Readers should understand that business on the Internet is likely to be at least as competitive as business in the brick-and-mortar world. There will be no cornucopia of profits. Instead, firms will need to create superior and difficult-to-imitate business models. They must discover the products that work best being sold over the Internet. They must figure out efficient pricing mechanisms. They must not waste vast resources in a mad race to be first in a market since being first is not the key to long-term success. Faced with the choice of rushing a weak product or website to market in order to be first, or taking the necessary time to be best, firms should go with best. Similarly, a late start in a market is not an insurmountable obstacle. Good web businesses that continue to innovate may hold their positions for a long time, but they can't sit back in the expectation of milking those poor locked-in customers. That type of lock-in doesn't exist.

Finally, you can't correctly analyse a market by looking only at demand, or only at supply. And that you certainly cannot correctly understand a market by ignoring both. Even economists can get carried away with trendy ideas and forget to use the scientific method in judging theories. There is an important lesson here because the abandonment of sound economic principles in favor of faddish impulses has the potential to cause great damage to the economy. That is the most important lesson that was lost in the last few years.

NOTES

1. Of course, telephones can be hooked up to modems, but this is essentially a close cousin of the Internet, if not exactly the Internet itself.
2. Actually, network effects can be either positive or negative, meaning that the value consumers receive goes up or down as the number of other users changes. As more telephone users clog the lines, the network effects become negative. As it has been used in the literature, however, network effects are almost invariably positive.
3. This terminology is based on Liebowitz and Margolis (2002).
4. One needs to be very careful at this juncture. Literal network effects are often referred to as direct network effects and these are relatively straightforward. Indirect network effects have sometimes been defined broadly to include almost any impact that a firm or

consumer's behavior has on any other market participant. Down this path lies danger. Many 'indirect' network effects are pecuniary in nature, and as such are poor candidates for examples of network effects. (For example, a new firm enters the industry and takes away customers from the existing firms. We would not want the new firm to take account of its impact on other firms; otherwise we wind up with a cartel.) Calling these network effects can be very misleading. See Liebowitz and Margolis (1994).

5. Pedagogically convenient if one wishes to illustrate the workings of average costs and economies of scale. Theoretically convenient if one wishes to characterize the software industry as a natural monopoly without going to the trouble of examining the actual costs of support, shipping, and duplicating. The troublesome aspect of all this is the way a convenience is then, by force of repetition, taken as a factual representation of the industry, an activity of which I believe many economists in the area are guilty.

6. Of course, even network effects are not terribly new. A reader of current economic literature might be forgiven for thinking that the concept of network effects emerged *de novo* in the mid-1980s with the paper by Katz and Shapiro. In fact, these concepts had been around since at least the 1950s in a then influential paper by Harvey Leibenstein (1950).

7. For example, after Margolis and I had revealed that Paul David's QWERTY keyboard story was wrong (discussed below), Brian Arthur asked if we could give him, Arthur, credit for the story (claiming David got the story from him) in any future writings, even though we were claiming that the story was false.

8. Recently this concept has enjoyed a surge in popularity in several fields of economics. Our interest is in the usage found in the fields of industrial organization and economic history, where Brian Arthur and Paul David have played important roles. See Paul Krugman's writings in Slate, discussed in note 16 below, for more details.

9. Page 3 of slide show, 'The Internet company handbook', June 1999, Morgan Stanley Dean Witter. It can be found at: http://www.morganstanley.com/techresearch/netcomhdbook/ih6.pdf.

10. 'The Internet Retailing Report', page 3.1. Morgan Stanley, 28 May 1997, by Mary Meeker and Sharon Pearson, http://www.morganstanley.com/institutional/techresearch/pdfs/inetretail3.pdf. This thinking was repeated in the June 1999 slide show, page 63, with a bullet point 'First Mover Advantage is Key – whoever signs up the buyers and suppliers first will have good potential to keep them,' with the URL referenced in note 9.

11. There is a literature attacking the 'first mover' doctrine, but wishing to replace it with the second mover or third mover doctrine. See, for example, Freedman (2001).

12. See Freedman (2001). But do not think that Freedman doesn't buy most of the lock-in story, because he basically does. He reports that second or third mover may be the important starting position instead of just the first mover.

13. Arthur has been the subject of adoring stories in *Fortune* ('The theory that made Microsoft: it's called "increasing returns," and it's one of the hottest and most important ideas in economics today', James Aley and Lenore Schiff, 29 April 1996, p. 65); *The New Yorker* ('The force of an idea' 12 January 1998); *New York Times Magazine*, ('Why the best doesn't always win', Peter Passell 5 May 1996), *Boston Globe* ('Sitting alone at his table by the bar', David Warsh, 3 July 1994, p. 65 of the Business section); Britain's *Observer* ('Arthur's big idea: the prophet of profit; in the hi-tech future, punters like Bill Gates are poised to win the whole casino', Ed Vulliamy, 8 March 1998, p. 17), a chapter in Mitchell Waldrop's book (*Complexity*, Simon and Schuster, New York, 1992). In addition, he has had interviews with *Wired Magazine*, *Booze-Allen & Hamilton's Magazine*, and a somewhat more difficult interview in *Pretext Magazine*.

14. Interview with Brian Arthur by Joel Kurtzman, available from Strategy + Business; http://www.strategybusiness.com/press/article/16402?pg=0, 1998 second quarter.

15. There is an interesting debate about the novelty of the ideas that Arthur put forward and the putative intolerance of the economics profession to his ideas. See Krugman (1998). There were several interesting responses, including John Cassidy, the author of the flattering *New Yorker* piece about Arthur that stuck in Krugman's craw, and Mitchell Waldrop, the author of 'Complexity', http://slate.msn.com/Features/Krugman/Krugman.asp.

16. There are numerous inconsistent definitions of lock-in that can be found in the economics literature. Liebowitz and Margolis (1995a) attempt to put some order to this chaos by defining three different types of path dependence or lock-in. Here I have simplified it down to two types where the information possessed by consumers about the future is complete. In the terminology of Liebowitz and Margolis, these two types reflect first degree (weak) and third degree (strong) path dependence.

17. There is a debate about these topics in the economics literature. One of the more accessible versions of one aspect of these debates, with proxies often standing in for the main players, can be found at the economic history discussion groups: http://eh.net/FORUMS/PathDepe.html and http://eh.net/FORUMS/QWERTYSu2.html. Some of the important academic articles on network effects in addition to those already mentioned, are: Katz and Shapiro (1986). Farrell and Saloner (1985); Liebowitz and Margolis (1995b).

18. I am ignoring here the possibility that consumers might want to be compatible with one another. Since this new technology wouldn't replace the old technology (assuming that the incumbent already controlled a majority of potential consumers) even if there isn't any form of coordination problem, there is no need to examine coordination problems, even though coordination failures lie at the heart of the strong form of lock-in.

19. See Brian Arthur's example of decision-making among consumers that can be found in: 'Competing technologies, increasing returns, and lock-in by historical events'. Arthur (1989). His consumers are myopic and seem to live only for the moment since they do not look to the future at all.

20. Brian Arthur has claimed that a new product has to be 200–300 per cent better to break the grip of lock-in. This number seems to be taken entirely out of thin air, and it really is based on the strong form of lock-in although he has never made any distinction between strong and weak forms of lock-in. See, for example, his article in the Harvard Business Review where he states: 'A new product often needs to be twice or three times better in some dimension – price, speed, convenience – to dislodge a locked-in rival' (Arthur 1996, p. 100).

21. Technically, these are formats and not products. The QWERTY keyboard patent expired before the market matured but many, in fact virtually all, rival keyboard manufacturers eventually adopted it. The VHS standard, on the other hand, still was owned when the format became dominant and the market large and mature.

22. For example, Shapiro and Varian present the QWERTY example on page 185 and 186. After presenting Paul David's strong lock-in story as if it were true, they mention in the last sentence or two that something appears wrong with the story because computer keyboards are so easily reprogrammed that strong form lock-in would seem impossible. Yet on page 233 they are back to stating that QWERTY is an inferior design. They do cite (but in a footnote) the Liebowitz and Margolis 1990 presentation of the typewriter history, but it appears to be more an example of covering themselves against claims that they missed a relevant article than attempting to present full information for their readers. For readers interested in other fables that economists and others like to claim are true see Spulber (2002).

23. For the original academic claim to economists see David (1985). For the refutation of David's story see Liebowitz and Margolis (1990).

24. David admitted, to a *Wall Street Journal* reporter, that he had never read the Navy study that he talked about in his article (see Gomes (1998)).

25. This is also discussed in Liebowitz and Margolis (1990).

26. See 'US plans to test new typewriter', *New York Times*, 1 November 1955; 'Revolution in the office', *New York Times*, 30 November 1955; 'Key changes debated', *New York Times*, 18 June 1956; 'US balks at teaching old typists new keys', *New York Times*, 2 July 1956; and Peter White, 'Pyfgcrt vs. Qwertyuiop', *New York Times*, 22 January 1956, at 18.

27. See for example: Yamada (1980). Yamada has claimed that Strong was biased against Dvorak, a claim that is repeated by current advocates for the Dvorak keyboard.

28. Paul David has been promising a rejoinder since the early 1990s. Instead of just admitting that his original 1985 paper had grievous historical inaccuracies, he has tried to muddy the waters by writing papers on related but different topics. See, for example, David (1997) in which he states: 'Consequently, it is proper for me at the outset to caution those readers who are hopeful of finding herein some further technical details and narrative material on the evolution of typewriter keyboard layouts. Although they are going to be disappointed on that account, there will be another, more suitable place in which to consider my detailed rejoinders to the dubious factual allegations that have circulated concerning the "true story" of QWERTY.' He also states: 'The historical arguments and evidence offered to support that critique are re-examined in my forthcoming paper: "Neoclassical economists at the keyboard: Is there a cure for 'repetitive thought injuries'?"' This paper has yet to see the light of day, although David was apparently so proud of having thought up the title that he couldn't keep from referencing it as an upcoming paper.

29. See Liebowitz and Margolis, 1995a in note 17 above for a more detailed version of this history (itself based on the book *Fast Forward* by James Lardner (1987)). For a view that states that VHS won mainly because it had a superior coalition of firms, see Cusumano, Mylonadis and Rosenbloom (1992). There are several problems with their story, however. First, the number of firms likely to join a coalition is itself a function of the perceived likelihood of success of a product in the market. Second, Cusumano et al. pay too little attention to the inherent advantage in having a larger tape in allowing longer playing times and reasonable picture qualities. Analog recording of all types benefit from having more tape pass the head in a given amount of time, a feature that benefited VHS and that was crucial in having RCA, the largest American seller of televisions, join the VHS camp. Third, in order for the number of producers to matter, it is either their additional brand names or their additional capacity that must help. Their own evidence indicates that the brand names of the various camps was fairly evenly split in the market shares for televisions. Sony had a strong brand name (and Zenith, the number two television producer in the US put its name on the Betamax, as well as Sanyo and Toshiba). Cusumano et al., provide no evidence that there was a shortage of capacity in the Beta camp, even if their productive capacity was less than the VHS camp.

30. In fact, there were many previous videorecorder formats, all failures.

31. See Kirsch (2000). I should note that Stanford is the home of Paul David, of QWERTY fame (who was on the dissertation committee) and also was the home to Brian Arthur when he was writing on these topics.

32. On this there is a dissertation and paper by VanVleck that demonstrates that British railroad gauges were not a major mistake. See VanVleck (1997).

33. See David's paper 'At last, a Remedy for Chronic QWERTY-skepticism!' (1999). This paper can be found at. http://www.eh.net/Publications/remedy.shtml, especially the section titled: ' "Oompha-metrics" and the burden of proof'.

34. Here is the quote from the interview Arthur had with *Pretext Magazine*: 'As for the QWERTY keyboard, if Margolis and Liebowitz can prove it's the best, my hat is off to them.' The interview can be found at: http://www.pretext.com/may98/columns/intview.htm. He actually says much more, mainly in a rather *ad hominem* fashion. Here are a few nuggets: 'As far as I can see, the Liebowitz and Margolis arguments are ideological arguments for the far right . . . I find I'm puzzled by all of this because it's a bit like debating evolution with creationists . . . Well, again, you only get excited about that if you belong to the right wing of American ideology.' This probably is a nastier debate than most, but all the *ad hominem* attacks come from their ranks. Readers can determine for themselves why that might be.

35. For a discussion of these claims see Lewin (2001).

36. These results are taken from data reported in *PC Magazine*. For full information see Liebowitz (1999).

REFERENCES

Arthur, W. Brian (1990), 'Positive feedbacks in the economy', *Scientific American*, **262**, 92–9.

Arthur, W.B. (1996), 'Increasing returns and the new world of business', *Harvard Business Review*, **74** (4), 100, http://www.santafe.edu/arthur/Papers/Pdf_files/HBR.doc.

Arthur, Brian (1989), 'Competing technologies, increasing returns, and lock-in by historical events', *Economic Journal*, **99**, 116–31.

Carlton, J. (2000), 'Dot-com boom gives builder Bechtel a lift', *Wall Street Journal*, 1 March, p. B1.

Cusumano, M.A., Y. Mylonadis and R.S. Rosenbloom (1992), 'Strategic maneuvering and mass-market dynamics – the triumph of VHS over Beta,' *Business History Review*, **66** (1), 51–94.

David, P.A. (1985), 'Clio and the economics of QWERTY', *American Economic Review*, **75**, 332–37.

David, Paul A. (1997), 'Path dependence and the quest for historical economics: one more chorus of the ballad of QWERTY', http://www/eh.net/Clio/Publications/pathnotes.html.

David, Paul A. (1999), 'At last a remedy for chronic QWERTY-skepticism!', paper prepared for the European Summer School in Industrial Dynamics (ESSID), held at l'Institute d'Etudes Scientifique de Cargese (Corse), France, 5–12 September.

Farrell J. and G. Saloner (1985), 'Standardization, compatibility, and innovation', *Rand Journal*, **16**, 70–83.

Freedman, David (2001), 'Last guys finish first', Business 2.0, http://www.business 2.com/b2/web/articles/0,17863,513392,00.html, May 30.

Gomes, Lee (1998), 'Economists decide to challenge facts of the QWERTY story', *Wall Street Journal*, 25 February, B1.

Kapadia, Reshma (2001), 'AOL-Lotus deal doesn't satisfy rivals: critics say tests do little to move toward IM interoperatibility', Reuters, 15 August.

Katz, Michael L. and Carl Shapiro (1985), 'Network externalities, competition, and compatibility', *American Economic Review*, **75** (3), 424–40.

Katz, M.L. and C. Shapiro (1986), '1986 and Technology adoption in the presence of network externalities', *Journal of Political Economy*, **94**, 822–41.

Kelly, Kevin (1998), *New Rules for the New Economy*, New York: Viking.

Kirsch, David A. (2000), 'The electric vehicle and the burden of history', Rutgers: Rutgers.

Krugman, Paul (1988), 'The legend of Arthur: a tale of gullibility at the *New Yorker'*, *Slate Magazine*, 14 January, http://slate.msn.com.Dismal/98-01-14/Dismal.asp.

Lardner, James (1987), *Fast Forward: Hollywood, the Japanese, and the Onslaught of the VCR*, New York: W.W. Norton.

Leibenstein, Harvey (1950), 'Bandwagon, snob, and Veblen effects in the theory of consumer's demand', *Quarterly Journal of Economics*, **64**, 183–207.

Lewin, Peter (2001), 'The market process and the economics of QWERTY: two views', *Review of Austrian Economics*, **14** (1), 65–96, available at http://www.utdallas.edu/~plewin/QWERTY%20condensed.pdf.

Liebowitz, Stan (1999), 'Product quality and the economic performance of firms', report prepared for McKinsey and Company, 15 October 1999, available at http://www.pub.utdallas.edu/~liebowit/mckinsey.pdf.

Liebowitz, S.J. and S.E. Margolis (1990), 'The fable of the keys', *Journal of Law and Economics*, **33**, 1–26, http://www.pub.utdallas.edu/~liebowit/keys1.html.

Liebowitz, Stan and Stephen E. Margolis (1994), 'Network externality: an uncommon tragedy', *Journal of Economic Perspectives*, **8** (2), 133–50.

Liebowitz, Stan and Stephen E. Margolis (1995a), 'Path dependence, lock-in and history', *Journal of Law, Economics and Organization*, 205–26.

Liebowitz, S., and S.E. Margolis (1995b), 'Are network externalities a new source of market failure?', *Research in Law and Economics*, **17**, 1–22.

Liebowitz, Stan and Stephen E. Margolis (1998), 'Network effects and externalities', *The New Palgrave Dictionary of Economics and the Law*, New York: Macmillan, 2, pp. 671–5.

Liebowitz, Stan and Stephen E. Margolis (2002), 'Network effects', in *Handbook of Telecommunications Economics*, vol 1, Amsterdam: Elsevier, pp. 76–97.

Manns, George (1999), 'First-mover advantage: what's it really worth?', The Street.com, accessed 26 January 1999, http:www.thestreet.com/tech/internet/682198.html.

Petzinger, Jr., Thomas (2000), 'So long, supply and demand: there's a new economy out there – and it looks nothing like the old one', *Wall Street Journal*, 30 January, p. S1.

Shapiro, Carl and Hal R. Varian (1998), *Information Rules: A Strategic Guide to the Network Economy*, Cambridge, MA: Harvard Business School Press.

Spulber, Daniel (2002), *Famous Fables of Economics*, New York: Basil Blackwell.

VanVleck, V.N.L. (1997), 'Delivering coal by road and rail in Britain: the efficiency of the "silly little bobtailed" coal wagons', *Journal of Economic History*, **57** (1), 139–60.

Yamada, H. (1980), 'A historical study of typewriters and typing methods: from the position of planning Japanese parallels', *Journal of Information Processing*, **2**, 175–202.

8. Should we teach an old economy dog New Economy tricks? The role of a postal service in the New Economy

Michael D. Bradley and Dennis W. Jansen

INTRODUCTION

It has generally been recognized that government policy must change in response to the changing character of the economy: 'The appropriate role of government in the economy is not a static concept: It must evolve as the economy and technology do. As economic activity shifts toward information-intensive goods and services, public policy is being presented with a series of challenges' (Stiglitz et al. 2000).

An excellent way to investigate how public policy might change in response to the 'new economy' is to examine the effects of the New Economy on a quintessential old economy institution and then investigate the possible roles of policy in dealing with those effects. An economic institution commonly associated with the old economy is the United States Postal Service. The term 'snail mail' itself reflects the association of the Postal Service with the old economy and is used to contrast the speed of email with the slow old-fashioned surface mail handled by the Postal Service. In this chapter we examine the impact of the New Economy on postal services, and then discuss public policy options associated with that impact.

Despite the fact that they are old economy institutions, postal services remain large industries, which are critical for the smooth functioning of the economy. The timely, secure and reliable delivery of personal and especially bulk mail communications remains a vital element of the economy's infrastructure. Thus, there is an important public policy issue associated with assessing the effect of the New Economy on postal services.[1]

That the US Postal Service is a large, important economic institution is undeniable. In 2001 it delivered over 207 billion pieces of mail, which is about 680 million pieces each delivery day to 138 million households and firms. It earned revenue of $65.8 billion, making it the eleventh largest company in the United States, in terms of revenue. It employed nearly 800 000 people, making it the second largest employer in the country. Many households and businesses critically depend upon physical mail for delivery of bills, documents, payments, and merchandise.

Given the size and importance of postal services, and their central role in providing informational transmittal services, it is of value to examine how the New Economy will affect them. One immediate reaction of those contemplating the effect of the New Economy on postal services is a knee-jerk feeling that the effect must be negative, because of the growth in email. Further investigation shows that while email is important, things are not that simple. In fact, there are some effects that are positive. For example, the growth in Internet shopping has spurred positive growth in both the package bulk mail and the expedited parcel bulk mail. As these markets have grown, Postal Service volumes in these areas have grown. In addition, advances in computing power have dramatically increased the sophistication of direct mailing in targeting selected audiences and reducing the cost of preparing such mailings. This has boosted growth in advertising mail. Finally, computerization of mail processing through advance barcode technology has dramatically increased the productivity of mail processing. A good letter clerk may be able to sort 500 letters in an hour but an advance barcode sorter can sort over 7000 pieces in an hour.

These positive events notwithstanding, the major anticipated effect of the New Economy on postal services is negative and revolves around the diversion of volume from the postal mail stream to the electronic message stream.[2] However, this diversion does not come from email in the usual sense. Most email is either household-to-household communication or personal communications among individuals within businesses. But this communications stream has not been the source of a large amount of physical mail for quite some time. If email has replaced any form of communications it is telephone calls, not letters. The household-to-household mail stream has evolved into the sending of 'sentimental' items like photographs, birthday cards, and letters of condolence. Thus far, this communications stream has been barely penetrated by email.[3]

Other types of communications are vulnerable to diversion however. These include bill presentment (from bulk mailers to household), bulk mail reply mail (from households to bulk mailers) and bulk mail documents (from bulk mail to bulk mail). It has been estimated that about one-third of the US Postal Service's First Class mail stream is made up of bills and statements, a portion of the mail stream that appears to be particularly vulnerable to electronic diversion (PricewaterhouseCoopers 2000). While it is uncertain how fast this diversion is going to take place there is general agreement that it will happen. Even the most optimistic view recognizes the electronic diversion will eventually take place. This view as articulated by the Postmaster General of the United States:

> So I think this whole technology thing is very very interesting. . . . You know, when it's all netted out, the Internet is going to help us. It doesn't – it's going to net positive because there's not going to be, you know, a rush to an epiphany of bills and presentment of payment. It's just not going to happen. It's going to be a slow, progressive thing. (Potter 2002)

The key question is what impact this diversion will have on the future of postal services, what role postal services will play in the economy and what response, if any, should be put in place to ensure the best social outcome in light of this change. We take a two-step approach in our analysis. First we construct a model of a postal service, embodying on the key aspects of its economic structure that relate to the effects of the New Economy on its performance. We then solve the model and produce a baseline scenario for estimating the effects of electronic diversion from the physical mail stream. In our second step, we use this baseline to examine the implications of a policy reaction that has been taking place in posts around the world. Posts have been actively entering the electronic services market and we examine the implications of this policy for reacting to electronic diversion.

MODELING THE EFFECTS ON THE NEW ECONOMY ON POSTAL SERVICES

In building our model of the effect of electronic diversion on postal services, we focus on aspects of the mail industry that are relevant for that analysis. The postal mail stream is made up of four parts, communication, publications, parcels and packages, and expedited. Communications includes personal messages, bill presentment, bulk mail documents, direct advertising, non-profit solicitations, bulk mail reply mail, catalogs, and similar messages. Publications includes newspapers and magazines. Parcels and packages includes shipments of merchandise and oversized documents. Expedited includes messages, merchandise and documents that must be delivered in a rapid fashion.

We will model only the communications mail stream and do so for two reasons. First, this is the part of the mail stream subject to electronic diversion. As mentioned above, both the package and the expedited mail streams are enhanced by Internet commerce and have been growing rapidly. They are expected to grow into the future (Morlock et al. 2000). In addition, the publications, parcels and packages, and expedited segments of the mail stream are all competitive; none are subject to the Private Express Statutes that provide the Postal Service with a legal monopoly on delivery. The public policy issues facing postal services do not relate to these products.

The second reason that we focus on the communications mail stream is because of its size. In the United States, the communications mail stream represents about 93 per cent of the Postal Service's piece volume (United States Postal Service 2001). Focusing on this important mail stream allows us to represent the lion's share of postal volumes while significantly reducing the complexity of the model.

We construct the demand side of the model by focusing on the demand for services by senders of mail. In the current structure of postal systems around the world, senders initiate the service and pay for it. It is certainly true that recipients also receive utility from the delivery of mail, but because they pay nothing for that benefit, we ignore it in the formal model.

We divide senders into bulk mailers and single piece mailers. Bulk mailers send substantially larger mailings than single piece mailers. Their mail is cheaper to process and deliver because it is prebarcoded and presorted.[4] This means the cost to the postal service of handling a piece of bulk mail is substantially lower than the cost of handling a piece of single piece mail. It also means the bulk mailers must incur some additional costs to prepare the mail. When a postal service provides discounts (lower rates) for bulk mail, it does so in recognition that the total demand for its product will depend upon the total cost to the mailer, including the mailer's own preparation costs.

In building the model, we first consider the bulk mail sector. We will model the fact that it sends both physical messages and electronic messages, and the model includes a demand curve for each. We view the two types of messaging as being imperfect substitutes. Electronic mail has the advantage of being fast and cheap, but physical mail has the advantage of permanence and flexibility, in the sense of being able to include a variety of messages in one mailing. For example, bill presentment is a type of bulk mail. However, this type of bulk mailer likes being able to include advertising inserts along with the bill.

For the reasons explained above, along the physical mail demand curve the 'price' a bulk mail customer faces includes both the postal rate and its own cost of preparing the mailing. The 'preparation' involves things like presorting or prebarcoding the mail. For convenience it is assumed that there is no firm-specific cost for preparing the electronic messages.[5] The demand for electronic messages is limited by the proportion of the bulk mail sector's target population that is prepared to receive electronic messaging. Note that the 'ability to receive electronic messaging' may be a greater requirement than simply access to email capabilities. For example, electronic bill presentment is a potential electronic message that firms would be interested in sending. However, many households are not yet ready to participate in electronic bill paying. It has been estimated that only 6 per cent of US households participate in electronic bill presentment and payment, although this proportion is expected to rise rapidly in the near future (PricewaterhouseCoopers 2000).

The following two equations are the assumed demands for physical and electronic messages by firms:

$$v_p^b = \chi_p^b - \lambda_1 (R_p^b + \mu) + \lambda_2 P_e^b \qquad (8.1)$$

$$v_e^b = \theta^b \chi_e^b + \lambda_3 (R_p^b + \mu) - \lambda_4 P_e^b \qquad (8.2)$$

Where:

v_p^b is the volume of bulk physical mail

v_e^b is the volume of bulk electronic mail

R_p^b is the postal rate for bulk physical mail

P_e^b is the price of bulk electronic mail

μ is the cost the bulk mailer incurs in preparing physical mail

θ^b is the proportion of bulk mail message customers that can receive electronic messages.

χ_e^b is the inherent demand for bulk electronic mail

χ_p^b is the inherent demand for bulk physical mail

Similarly, the single-piece sector has two demand functions, one for physical mail, and one for electronic messages. Here, however, we are not assuming any additional preparation costs on the part of the single-piece mailers. The single-piece demand functions are given by:

$$v_p^h = \chi_p^h - \lambda_5 R_p^h + \lambda_6 P_e^h \qquad (8.3)$$

$$v_e^h = \theta^h \chi_e^h + \lambda_7 R_p^h - \lambda_8 P_e^h \qquad (8.4)$$

where the variables have similar interpretations.

We now specify the cost side of the model. Our specified postal service cost function captures the three essential characteristics of postal production: (1) large 'quasi-fixed' costs; (2) returns to scale in the provision of any individual product; and (3) economies of scope between products.

In the following cost function, the first term, F_p, capture the fact that a postal service, as a labor-intensive network industry, has a large amount of cost that does not vary with variations in the level of volume. (Labor costs are about 80 per cent of total United States Postal Service costs, but only about 65 per cent of total costs are considered 'volume variable.'). These non-variable costs are primarily labor costs, but due to the public nature of postal organizations and their corresponding labor agreements it is difficult for postal services to vary their workforces. It is also difficult for the postal services to close facilities and these facilities (including the workers assigned to them) represent a fixed cost of mail provision. Finally, most postal services (including the US Postal Service) have a universal service requirement that compels them to go to every address in the country. Because of this requirement, a postal service cannot easily shrink its service network in the face of declining volume. In fact in 2001, the United States Postal Service's network was growing (by adding 1.7 million delivery points) while volume was declining. There is an irreducible cost of serving this network even at low volumes and this cost is also part of a postal service's large quasi-fixed cost.

Our model's cost equation also incorporates returns to scale and scope through its quadratic terms. It is true that scale and scope economies can be imparted with just fixed cost, but we make our model quadratic to reflect the fact that the marginal cost of mail provision falls with increase in volume.[6]

The postal cost function is given by:

$$C_p = F_p + \alpha_1 v_p^b - \alpha_2 (v_p^b)^2 + \alpha_3 v_p^h - \alpha_4 (v_p^h)^2 - \alpha_5 v_p^b v_p^h \qquad (8.5)$$

Based upon the preparation that mailers do, we expect that the marginal cost of bulk mail will be less than the marginal cost of single piece mail:

$$a_1 - 2\alpha_2 v_p^b - \alpha_5 v_p^h < (a_2 - 2\alpha_4 v_p^h - \alpha_5 v_p^b).$$

Production of electronic services is assumed to have a large fixed cost and small but constant marginal cost. This means that electronic services cannot be perfectly competitive and will have to recover their fixed costs through a markup. Electronic message costs are given by:

$$C_e = F_e + \beta_1 V_e^b + \beta_2 V_e^h \qquad (8.6)$$

We expect $\beta_1 > \beta_2$ as bulk mail services are more complete and sophisticated (security, verification. etc.) than single-piece services.

We complete our model building by specifying the objective functions for the two sectors. We treat the electronic mail sector as a profit maximizing monopolist with sufficient market power to discriminate between bulk mail and single piece customers. While the electronic bill paying, email, etc. section is not a monopoly, it is not perfectly competitive either. Because it plays a subsidiary role to the postal sector in our analysis, we simplify and abstract. Due to the large fixed cost, setting price equal to marginal cost does not provide sufficient funds to keep firms in bulk mail and a markup is required. The simplest way to do this is with a monopoly sector. Including a more sophisticated model of imperfect competition is an important part of future work.

The profit function for the provider of electronic services is given by:

$$\Pi_e = P_e^b v_e^b + P_e^h v_e^h - F_e - \beta_1 v_e^b - \beta_2 v_e^h \tag{8.7}$$

Solving for the profit maximizing prices yields the following pricing rules for the electronic messaging sector:

$$P_e^b = \frac{\theta^b \chi_e^b + \lambda_3 (R_p^b + \mu) + \beta_1 \lambda_4}{2\lambda_4} \tag{8.8}$$

$$P_e^h = \frac{\theta^h \chi_e^h + \lambda_7 R_p^h + \beta_2 \lambda_8}{2\lambda_8} \tag{8.9}$$

The postal service, in our model, is a public sector entity and is not a profit maximizer. In developing its objective function, we mimic the regulatory structure of the US Postal Service. Specifically, the Postal Service must provide 'universal service at a reasonable uniform price'. In addition, prices are set in a regulatory structure, so as to have the Postal Service break even in an expected value sense. Because of the large quasi-fixed costs and increasing returns to scale, the Postal Service must set its prices above marginal cost. Setting prices is equivalent to setting markups, the ratio of rate to marginal cost:

$$R_p^b = \rho^b MC^b \tag{8.10}$$

$$R_p^h = \rho^h MC^h \tag{8.11}$$

To understand the markup process, consider the simplest case in which the single-piece and bulk mail markups are the same. The breakeven constraint requires total revenue to equal total cost. With a common markup, ρ, this can be expressed in terms of the overall markup over marginal cost:

$$\rho MC_p^b v_p^b + \rho MC_p^h v_p^h - TC = 0. \tag{8.12}$$

In other words, the markup consists of the ratio of total cost to what is known as 'volume variable cost'. This latter cost measure is the total cost of production under the counterfactual assumption that all units were produced at the marginal cost of the last unit. The formula for the common markup is:

$$\rho = \frac{C_p}{\left(\frac{\partial C_p}{\partial v_p^b}\right) v_p^b + \left(\frac{\partial C_p}{\partial v_h^b}\right) v_p^h} \tag{8.13}$$

Of course, it is atypical for different products to have the same markups. As soon as we allow for different markups, a host of factors come into play in determining the individual markups. For example, one could derive the markups consistent with Ramsey prices. The net contribution from all products must be sufficient to cover the gap between total cost and total volume variable cost, but the relative markups could be set entirely on the basis of relative demands. In the actual US regulatory structure, the Postal Rate Commission sets the relative markups in response to a variety of economic and political forces. We again mimic this actual institutional structure and attempt to replicate the relative pattern of markups between bulk mail and single piece products. The postal rate for single piece mail exceeds that for bulk mail for a piece of equal size and weight, but because the marginal cost for bulk mail is well below that for single piece mail, the markup on bulk mail actually exceeds that on single piece mail. Thus, we will impose the following pattern of markups:[7]

$$r = \frac{\rho^h}{\rho^b} < 1. \tag{8.14}$$

In our model, the relative markup, r, will be set exogenously to the model's postal service reflecting the institutional constraint that it is set externally to the United States Postal Service by the Postal Rate Commission. With this additional constraint we can precisely pin down the two markups and thus postal rates. For example the markup on bulk mail is given by:

$$\rho^b = \frac{C_p}{MC^b v_p^b + r\, MC^h v_p^h}. \tag{8.15}$$

To solve the model, we must find the vector of postal rates and electronic mail prices that will bring both the postal market and the electronic mail markets to equilibrium. To find useful expressions for the markups, we must substitute for cost function, the marginal costs and the demand curves into equation (8.15). Doing so yields the following expression for the bulk mail markup in terms of postal rates and electronic messaging prices:

$$
p^b = \begin{bmatrix} F_p + \alpha_1(\chi_p^b - \lambda_1(R_p^b + \mu) + \lambda_2 P_e^b) - \alpha_2(\chi_p^b - \lambda_1(R_p^b + \mu) + \lambda_2 P_e^b)^2 \\ + \alpha_3(\chi_p^h - \lambda_5 R_p^h + \lambda_6 P_e^h) - \alpha_4(\chi_p^h - \lambda_5 R_p^h + \lambda_6 P_e^h)^2 \\ - \alpha_5(\chi_p^h - \lambda_5 R_p^h + \lambda_6 P_e^h)(\chi_p^b - \lambda_1(R_p^b + \mu) + \lambda_2 P_e^b) \end{bmatrix}
$$

$$
* \begin{bmatrix} \alpha_1(\chi_p^b - \lambda_1(R_p^b + \mu) + \lambda_2 P_e^b) - 2\alpha_2(\chi_p^b - \lambda_1(R_p^b + \mu) + \lambda_2 P_e^b)^2 \\ + r[\alpha_3(\chi_p^h - \lambda_5 R_p^h + \lambda_6 P_e^h) - 2\alpha_4(\chi_p^h - \lambda_5 R_p^h + \lambda_6 P_e^h)^2] \\ - (1 + r)[\alpha_5(\chi_p^h - \lambda_5 R_p^h + \lambda_6 P_e^h)(\chi_p^b - \lambda_1(R_p^b + \mu) + \lambda_2 P_e^b)] \end{bmatrix}^{-1}
$$

$$(8.16)$$

An expression for the single piece mail markup can then be derived from the expression for the bulk mail markup by recognizing that $\rho^h = r * \rho^b$

We have four markets that have to clear: bulk mail physical mail and electronic messages and single-piece mail and electronic messages. Because of the cross-price effects, we solve simultaneously equations 8.1, 8.2, 8.3, 8.4, 8.8, 8.9, 8.10, 8.11, 8.14 and 8.16 for the following ten variables: P_e^b, P_e^h, R_p^b, R_p^h, v_e^b, v_e^h, v_p^b, v_p^h, ρ^b, ρ^h. Inspection of equation 8.16 shows the solution to be highly nonlinear and seemingly intractable. We thus solve the model numerically. Not only does this provide us with a benchmark but it also allows us to extract dynamic paths in prices and quantities as diversion proceeds.

To numerically solve the model, we must first calibrate it. We do so based upon the prices and costs for the US Postal Service.[8] To determine the accuracy of that calibration, we compare the values for key endogenous variables from the model with their corresponding actual values for the Postal Service in fiscal year 2000. Table 8.1 presents that comparison. While such a comparison does not lend itself to the calculation of a single value of goodness of fit, a review of the values in the table suggests that the model does a good job of replicating the current postal environment.

Once the model is calibrated, we can use it to investigate the impact of the New Economy on the Postal Service. In this chapter, we are focusing on the effect electronic diversion will have on the Postal Service and do not allow for growth-enhancing effects of other impacts. Because the electronic diversion effect is likely to be the largest, by far, we feel comfortable focusing on this particular effect.

As the New Economy evolves, more physical messages should become electronic messages. Connection to the Internet will increase through time, as will households' familiarity with and confidence in electronic communications. This suggests that there will be a migration of demand away from

Table 8.1   Calibrating the baseline model

	Actual postal service values	Calculated model values
Bulk mail volume (units)	138.5 billion	138.7 billion
Single piece mail volume (units)	55.1 billion	54.6 billion
Bulk mail MC (dollars)	$0.104	$0.102
Single piece mail MC (dollars)	$0.236	$0.237
Bulk mail rate (dollars)	$0.204	$0.207
Single piece mail rate (dollars)	$0.406	$0.407
Bulk mail markup (ratio)	2.01	2.03
Single piece mail markup (ratio)	1.71	1.72
Total revenue (dollars)	$50.6 billion	$50.9 billion

physical messaging to electronic messaging. It is very difficult to anticipate how large and how rapid the diversion will be. Obviously, the smaller and the slower the diversion, the less pressing the policy questions are. To gain insight into the implications of the diversion rather than the diversion itself, we specify a simple constant linear diversion. We assume that single piece market experiences exogenously determined erosion from physical to electronic messaging of 3 billion messages a year and bulk mail market experiences a diversion of 6 billion messages per year. At current volume levels this amount of diversion represents about 5 per cent for single piece mailers and 3 per cent for bulk mailers.

As volumes are diverted, the postal service must raise its rates to offset the lost revenue associated with lost volume. Because both of the demands for postal products are inelastic at current prices, this strategy works, at least initially. Moreover, the volume declines have several effects. First, marginal costs start to rise as economies of scale are reversed. Second, falling volumes imply higher markups as fewer pieces of mail are available to markup and recover the quasi-fixed costs. These two effects mean the rates must continually be increasing for breakeven to occur. But as rates rise, elasticity rises. As Figures 8.1 and 8.2 show, at some point this response becomes unsustainable. Those figures show that as diversion proceeds, rates start rising at an accelerating rate. On our simulation, after 11 periods, there were no postal rates that allowed the postal service to break even. At this point further increases in rates reduced volumes so much that revenues sufficient to cover fixed and variable costs could not be obtained. At this point the postal service would no longer be self-sustaining and some policy action would have to be taken.

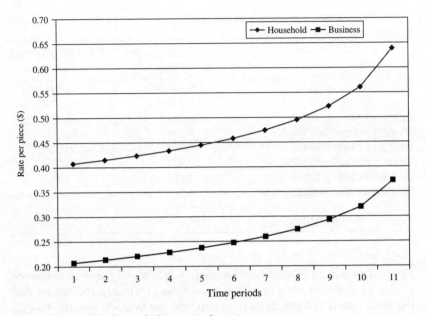

Figure 8.1   The effect of electronic diversion on rates

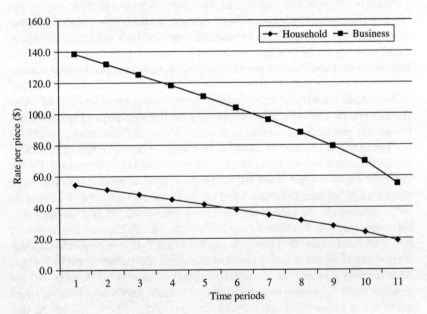

Figure 8.2   The effect of electronic diversion on volumes

It is important to note that the model's postal service has not withered away when it becomes unsustainable at any rates. It is still a sizable institution. In the last sustainable period the model's postal service delivered 55 billion pieces of bulk mail, 18 billion pieces of single-piece mail and earned revenue of over $32 billion.

A POSSIBLE POLICY RESPONSE TO AN UNSUSTAINABLE POSTAL SERVICE

Given the possibility that electronic diversion could lead the Postal Service into a 'death spiral' in which it could not raise rates enough to break even, we now investigate a policy action which has been growing among the posts of the world. This approach to dealing with electronic diversion is to hit the problem head on by allowing or encouraging the postal service to enter the electronic market. While this has not been a major thrust in the United States (although the US Postal Service has launched an electronic bill-paying service call eBillPay), in Europe and Canada, postal services have been actively entering the electronic communications sector.

Canada Post provides an array of electronic services including, electronic postmarks, electronic bill paying, electronic banking, electronic shopping, electronic bills and electronic advertising. Similarly, Deutsche Post provides a broad spectrum of Internet services to both single piece mailers and bulk mailers. For example, Deutsche Post provides an electronic security service called SignTrust. This service includes digital certificates, electronic signature, and encryption. Digital certificates are used to authorize entry into secure websites where electronic signatures are used to authenticate the source of messages.

Denmark Post entered a joint venture called Gatetrade.net, which is an electronic platform for business and government enterprises in northern Europe. Gatetrade.net is an electronic market designed to reduce search time and facilitate exchanges. Demark Post has also announced plans to enter additional electronic services such as supply chain management, financial services, and logistics.

Royal Mail (UK, previously Consignia) provides an electronic billing service called Bills On-Line. It also has a fulfillment management service, an integrated ecommerce infrastructure service, and electronic and hybrid mail services. It has started a joint venture called Opetcon, that is a transactional billing service throughout the UK and Europe. In this hybrid service Opetcon receives electronic billings and forwards the hardcopy to the consumer without electronic bill paying ability.

LaPoste has extended Internet access throughout France in a project called 'Cyberpost'. It has installed over 1000 terminals in rural and small post offices throughout the country. Through this project, LaPoste offers a free web address and permanent electronic mailbox to each French citizen (McGrath 2001).

These examples highlight the active entry into electronic communications by post. In this section we analytically model this approach to dealing with electronic diversion and examine its potential effects on the death spiral dynamics presented in a prior section.

If the postal service is permitted and/or encouraged to enter the electronic message market we must change the structure of the model to capture this entry. The first set of changes is to add demand curves for the postal service's electronic product in the bulk mail and single piece markets. In addition, the postal service's electronic products are now imperfect substitutes to both the private sector's electronic products and its own physical products. Appropriate cross-price effects must now be included in all demand equations. With these changes, the demand equations describing communications originating in the bulk mail sector are given by the following three equations:

$$v_p^b = \chi_p^b - \lambda_1 (R_p^b + \mu) + \lambda_2 P_e^b + \delta_1 R_e^b \tag{8.17}$$

$$\hat{v}_e^b = \theta^b \hat{\chi}_e^b + \hat{\lambda}_3 (R_p^b + \mu) + \hat{\lambda}_4 P_e^b - \hat{\delta}_2 R_e^b \tag{8.18}$$

$$\tilde{v}_e^b = \theta^b \tilde{\chi}_e^b + \tilde{\lambda}_3 (R_p^b + \mu) - \tilde{\lambda}_4 P_e^b + \tilde{\delta}_2 R_e^b \tag{8.19}$$

The first equation describes the demand for physical messages by the bulk mail sector and it is altered only by the inclusion of the postal rate for electronic messages originating at bulk mails (R_e^b). Electronic bulk mail messages can be sent either through the postal service or the private sector provider. The second demand curve, with the 'hat' notation represents the demand for electronic messages through the postal service. The third equation, with the 'tilde' is the corresponding demand curve for service through the private sector. These two equations can be combined to model the total demand for electronic messaging:

$$v_e^b = \theta^b(\chi_e^b) + (\hat{\lambda}_3 + \tilde{\lambda}_3)(R_p^b + \mu) + (\hat{\lambda}_4 - \tilde{\lambda}_4) P_e^b + (\tilde{\delta}_2 - \hat{\delta}_2) R_e^b \tag{8.20}$$

We expect that direct effects of a price change will dominate cross-effects and thus expect that $\hat{\delta}_2 > \tilde{\delta}_2$ and $\hat{\lambda}_4 < \tilde{\lambda}_4$. Under these restrictions, we have a well-behaved market demand curve.

A similar set of equations captures the single piece sector:

$$v_p^h = \chi_p^h - \lambda_5 R_p^h + \lambda_6 P_e^b + \delta_3 R_e^h \qquad (8.21)$$

$$\hat{v}_e^h = \theta^h \hat{\chi}_e^h + \hat{\lambda}_7 R_p^h + \hat{\lambda}_8 P_e^h - \hat{\delta}_4 R_e^h \qquad (8.22)$$

$$\tilde{v}_e^h = \theta^h \tilde{\chi}_e^h + \tilde{\lambda}_7 R_p^h - \tilde{\lambda}_8 P_e^h + \tilde{\delta}_4 R_e^h \qquad (8.23)$$

Equations 8.22 and 8.23 can be combined to express the total single piece demand for electronic messages:

$$v_e^h = \theta^h \chi_e^h + (\hat{\lambda}_7 + \tilde{\lambda}_7) R_p^h + (\hat{\lambda}_8 - \tilde{\lambda}_8) P_e^h + (\tilde{\delta}_4 - \hat{\delta}_4) R_e^h \qquad (8.24)$$

with $\hat{\delta}_4 > \tilde{\delta}_4$ and $\hat{\lambda}_8 < \tilde{\lambda}_8$.

The cost function for the private sector provider of electronic services is not changed, but the postal service cost function must be modified to include the cost of providing electronic products. We assume that there will be some product-specific fixed costs associated with electronic products, as in the private sector, but electronic products will be provided at constant marginal cost. We also allow for the possibility that there are scope economies in the provision of both electronic and physical messages. For example, the postal service might be able to provide a 'hybrid' mail service in which it receives a set of electronic messages from a single mailer and forwards the message in electronic form to those who are connected to the Internet and delivers the message in physical form to those who are not. This construct provides for scope economies to being able to provide both types of messages.

$$C_{pe} = F + \alpha_1 v_p^b - \alpha_2 (v_p^b)^2 + \alpha_3 v_p^h - \alpha_4 (v_p^h)^2 - \alpha_5 v_p^b v_p^h$$
$$+ F_e + \alpha_6 v_e^b + \alpha_7 v_e^h - \alpha_8 v_p^b v_e^b - \alpha_9 v_p^h v_e^h \qquad (8.25)$$

There is no change in the cost function or the profit function for the private sector provider of electronic messages. However, the pricing rules have changed to allow for competition from the postal service in the electronic messaging sector:

$$P_e^b = \frac{\theta^b \tilde{\chi}_e^b + \tilde{\lambda}_3 (R_p^b + \mu) + \beta_1 \tilde{\lambda}_4 + \tilde{\delta}_2 R_e^b}{2 \tilde{\lambda}_4} \qquad (8.26)$$

$$P_e^h = \frac{\theta^h \tilde{\chi}_e^h + \tilde{\lambda}_7 R_p^h + \beta_2 \tilde{\lambda}_8 + \tilde{\delta}_4^h R_e^h}{2 \tilde{\lambda}_8} \qquad (8.27)$$

In this policy approach, the postal service is still a break even public sector firm with an exclusive privilege for the delivery of physical mail. However, it is allowed to enter the electronic message market with the goal of maximizing profits in that sector to help maintain its overall break even status. In the absence of scope economies, the optimization process for the postal service could proceed recursively, first finding the profit maximizing prices for electronic offerings and then finding the break even prices for physical mail. With scope economies, the price of electronic products will depend, in part, on the price of physical mail products and vice versa. The four prices must be set simultaneously, so we solve the equilibrium prices by solving four pricing conditions in a simultaneous structure.

To derive the four pricing rules, we break the problem into its two parts. We solve for the profit maximizing electronic prices contingent on the vector of physical mail prices and then derive the breakeven pricing (markup) rules for the physical products given the vector of electronic product prices.

The profit-maximizing electronic rates are obtained from optimizing that portion of the overall postal service profit function that is associated with electronic products. For convenience the electronic products profit function is provided below:

$$\hat{\Pi}_e = R_e^b \hat{v}_e^b + R_e^h \hat{v}_e^h - \hat{F}_e - \alpha_6 \hat{v}_e^b - \alpha_7 \hat{v}_e^h + \alpha_8 \hat{v}_e^b v_p^b + \alpha_9 \hat{v}_e^h v_p^h \qquad (8.28)$$

Optimization yields the relatively complicated pricing rules for electronic products. The complications arise because of the potential scope economies between physical and electronic products. The pricing rules must account for the feedback from setting electronic prices, which influence the demand for physical products and affects their equilibrium volumes. This, in turn, affects the marginal costs of the electronic products and their profitability. The bulk mail and single piece pricing rules are given by:

$$R_e^b = \left[\frac{(1 + \alpha_8 \delta_1)[\theta^b \hat{\chi}_e^b + \hat{\lambda}_3 (R_p^b + \mu) + \hat{\lambda}_4 P_e^b] + \hat{\delta}_2 \alpha_6}{2\hat{\delta}_2(1 - \alpha_8\hat{\delta}_1)} + \frac{- \hat{\delta}_2 \alpha_8 [\chi_p^b - \lambda_1 (R_p^b + \mu) + \lambda_2 P_e^b]}{2\hat{\delta}_2(1 - \alpha_8\hat{\delta}_1)} \right] \qquad (8.29)$$

$$R_e^h = \left[\frac{(1 + \alpha_9 \delta_3)[\theta^h \hat{\chi}_e^h + \hat{\lambda}_7 R_p^h + \hat{\lambda}_8 P_e^h] + \hat{\delta}_4 \alpha_7}{2\hat{\delta}_4(1 + \alpha_9\hat{\delta}_3)} - \frac{\hat{\delta}_4 \hat{\delta}_9 [\chi_p^h - \lambda_5 R_p^h + \lambda_6 P_e^h]}{2\hat{\delta}_4(1 + \alpha_9\hat{\delta}_3)} \right] \qquad (8.30)$$

Our last equations are for the breakeven postal rates on physical products. The revised breakeven constraint requires the revenue from physical postal products plus the profit on electronic postal products to cover the cost of producing the physical postal products. In addition, the revenue on postal products depends upon the postal rates, which are based upon markups over marginal cost. The break even condition in this circumstance is given by:

$$\rho^b MC_p^b v_p^b + \rho^h MC_p^h v_p^h + \hat{\Pi}_e - C_p = 0 \qquad (8.31)$$

Derivation of the breakeven markups requires use of the profit maximizing price rules for electronic products. Inserting them into equation 8.31 leads to relatively complex markup rules shown in equations 8.32 and 8.33.

$$
p^b = \left\{
\begin{array}{l}
F + \alpha_1 v_p^b - \alpha_2 (v_p^b)^2 + \alpha_3 v_p^h - \alpha_4 (v_p^h)^2 - \alpha_5 v_p^b v_p^h \\[4pt]
+ F_{e+} \alpha_6 v_e^b + \alpha_7 v_e^h - \alpha_8 v_p^b v_e^b - \alpha_9 v_p^h v_e^h \\[8pt]
- \left[\dfrac{(1+\alpha_8\delta_1)[\theta^b \hat{\chi}_e^b + \hat{\lambda}_3 (R_p^b + \mu) + \hat{\lambda}_4 P_e^b] + \hat{\delta}_2 \alpha_6}{2\hat{\delta}_2 (1-\alpha_8\hat{\delta}_1)} \right. \\[6pt]
\left. + \dfrac{-\hat{\delta}_2 \hat{\delta}_8 [\chi_p^b - \lambda_1 (R_p^b + \mu) + \lambda_2 P_e^b]}{2\hat{\delta}_2 (1-\alpha_8\hat{\delta}_1)} \right] \hat{v}_e^b \\[10pt]
- \left[\dfrac{(1+\alpha_9\delta_4)[\theta^h \hat{\chi}_e^h + \hat{\lambda}_7 R_p^h + \hat{\lambda}_8 P_e^h] + \hat{\delta}_4 \alpha_7}{2\hat{\delta}_4 (1-\alpha_9\hat{\delta}_3)} \right. \\[6pt]
\left. + \dfrac{-\hat{\delta}_4 \hat{\delta}_9 [\chi_p^h - \lambda_5 R_p^h) + \lambda_6 P_e^h]}{2\hat{\delta}_4 (1-\alpha_9\hat{\delta}_3)} \right] \hat{v}_e^h
\end{array}
\right\}
$$

$$
* \left\{
\begin{array}{l}
(\alpha_1 (\chi_p^b - \lambda_1 (R_p^b + \mu) + \lambda_2 P_e^b) - 2\alpha_2 (\theta^b \chi_p^b - \lambda_1 (R_p^b + \mu) + \lambda_2 P_e^b)^2 \\[4pt]
-\alpha_8 (\theta^b \chi_e^b + \hat{\lambda}_3 (R_p^b + \mu) + \hat{\lambda}_4 P_e^b - \hat{\delta}_2 R_e^b) \\[4pt]
+ r [\alpha_3 (\theta^h \chi_p^h - \lambda_5 R_p^h + \lambda_6 P_e^h) - 2\alpha_4 (\theta^h \chi_p^h - \lambda_5 R_p^h + \lambda_6 P_e^h)^2] \\[4pt]
- r\alpha_9 (\theta^h \chi_e^h + \hat{\lambda}_7 R_p^h + \hat{\lambda}_8 P_e^h - \hat{\delta}_4 R_e^h) \\[4pt]
- (1+r)[\alpha_5 (\theta^h \chi_p^h - \lambda_5 R_p^h + \lambda_6 P_e^h) (\theta^b \chi_p^b - \lambda_1 (R_p^b + \mu) + \lambda_2 P_e^b)]
\end{array}
\right\}^{-1}
$$

$$ (8.32) $$

$$ \rho^h = r^* \rho b \qquad (8.33) $$

Determination of the equilibrium prices for physical and electronic products requires simultaneous equilibrium in the markets for single piece-originated physical mail (equations 8.21 and 8.33), bulk mail-originated physical mail (equations 8.17 and 8.32), single piece-originated, electronic mail (equations 8.24, 8.27 and 8.30) and bulk mail-originated electronic mail (equations 8.20, 8.26 and 8.29). This highly nonlinear system is even more complex than the previous one, so again we solve it by numerical methods. We again calibrate the model to current Postal Service parameters and Table 8.2 presents the results of the calibration of this version of the model.

The calculated model values line up quite well with the actual Postal Service values, although the total revenue on physical mail is a little high. This comes in part due to the overall breakeven constraint. Because of the very small initial market penetration and the requirement for fixed costs, the modeled postal service actually earns losses on electronic products in the baseline year. The total cost of providing electronic products, including the fixed cost in the base year is $1.03 billion but the associated revenue is only $409 million.

After the model is calibrated, we simulate electronic diversion at the same rate as in the death spiral case but allow the model postal service to react by entering the electronic messaging market. In our parameterization of the model, this policy response allows the modeled postal service to avoid the death spiral over the model's horizon. By entering the growing electronic message market, the postal service can avoid increasing its rate on physical mail to the unstable region. This is shown in Figures 8.3 and 8.4 which show the postal rates for physical mail under diversion with and without entry into the electronic market. Although postal rates for physical mail increase,

Table 8.2   Calibrating the electronic penetration model

	Actual postal service values	Calculated model values
Bulk mail volume (units)	138.5 billion	138.5 billion
Single piece mail volume (units)	55.1 billion	55.1 billion
Bulk mail MC (dollars)	$0.104	$0.102
Single piece mail MC (dollars)	$0.236	$0.236
Bulk mail rate (dollars)	$0.204	$0.209
Single piece mail rate (dollars)	$0.406	$0.411
Bulk mail markup (ratio)	2.01	2.05
Single piece mail markup (ratio)	1.71	1.74
Total revenue on physical mail (dollars)	$50.6 billion	$51.1 billion

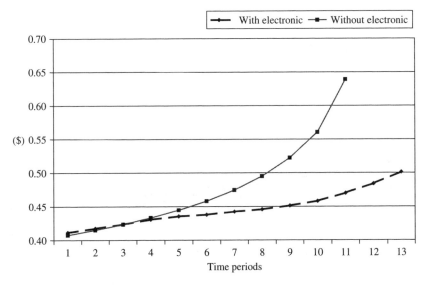

Figure 8.3   Household mail rates by scenario

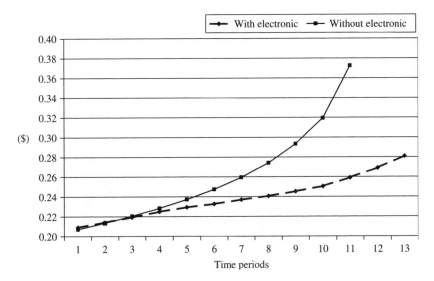

Figure 8.4   Business mail rates by scenario

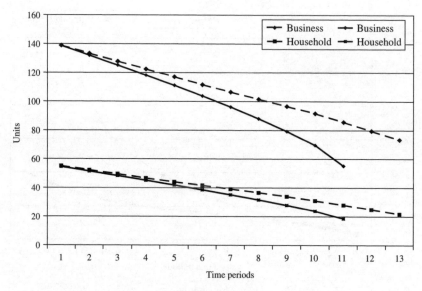

Figure 8.5   Effects of diversion on volume

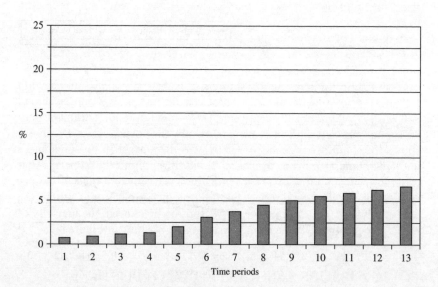

Figure 8.6   Postal share of electronic mail revenues

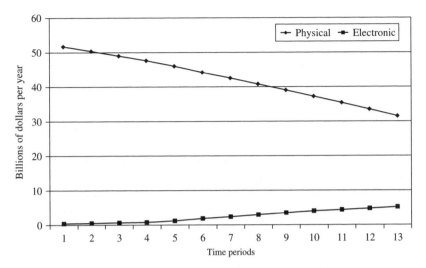

Figure 8.7   Revenues from physical and electronic products

the contribution from electronic products keeps them from becoming unstable.

Avoidance of the death spiral occurs despite significant loss in volumes. As Figure 8.5 shows, bulk mail volumes have fallen by over a third at the point at which the postal service was no longer self-sustaining in the previous simulation. In addition, the figure shows that bulk mail volume could fall as much as 50 per cent and a set of equilibrium rates on physical mail still exist. Avoidance of the death spiral also does not require dramatic penetration of the electronic messaging market by the postal service. Figure 8.6 shows the share of revenue from the electronic market (both single piece and bulk mailers) going to the postal service throughout the scenario. That ratio varies from a low of seven-tenths of 1 per cent to a high of 6.6 per cent. Similarly, the postal service has not become an 'electronic' firm by the end of the scenario. Despite the restrictions of breakeven, the majority of revenues continue to come from physical mail, as show in Figure 8.7.

POLICY ISSUES ASSOCIATED WITH POSTS OFFERING ELECTRONIC SERVICES

The above analysis suggests that entry into electronic messaging by posts may preclude or at least significantly defer the 'death spiral'. That, in and of itself, is not enough to recommend it as a policy. There are a number of other issues that must be considered before such a recommendation could be made.

One concern is that the 'death spiral' comes from inefficient public sector provision of postal services and not electronic diversion. In this view, the inability of postal services to deal with declining volume comes not from inherent scale and scope economies but from excess wages, union work rules, and poor incentives. If the ultimate outcome of a public postal service is unsustainability, then this view would suggest that it might make sense to pursue privatization of the postal service before the death spiral occurs. To the extent privatization induces efficiency and flexibility in providing postal services, the death spiral may be avoided. This is the approach that has been followed in Sweden and New Zealand and is underway in Holland and Germany. Standing in the way is the fact that the path to a privatized or commercialized postal service is multifaceted with difficult questions relating to issues like the exclusive privilege and universal service obligations. In addition, the anthrax attacks of 2001 raised new questions about whether there is an inherently public nature to a secure mail stream.

Our simulations indicated that even modest contributions earned in the electronic messaging field could defer the onset of the death spiral scenario without requiring a general subsidy from taxpayers. Yet this approach raises certain questions. The first is the general advisability of having a government agency compete with private sector firms. The possibility of 'unfair' competition from the US Postal Service in the area of electronic messages was raised by a *Wall Street Journal* editorial (2002) which suggested that the Postal Service might use its monopoly on letter mail to cross-subsidize a foray into electronic services:

> If the Postal Service were truly private and competing on the same footing with everyone else, that would be one thing. But it now enjoys a number of plum advantages, including its exemption from taxes, antitrust suits and much labor law. Not to mention the huge cash flow that its monopoly on letters provides, which could allow it to undercut private competitors on price.

The concern is partially mitigated by recognizing that the 'huge cash flow' disappears in the face of material electronic diversion and the postal service would be attempting to offset losses in its physical mail stream. In the electronic diversion scenario, the postal service ultimately does not have profits on the physical mail stream that it could use to subsidize electronic products. But, as our simulations show, it is quite likely that the postal service would initially incur losses on its electronic services, which does raise a legitimate cross-subsidy issue.

Even if one does grant that there is some rule for public postal service in the electronic services industry, there remains the question as to where that entry is appropriate:

'The central question needs to be whether the proper role for a 21st century postal authority is to compete with private businesses or to merely provide only the kinds of services that a central, nationally trusted entity can provide' said Eric Arnum, editor of Messaging Online, an information service devoted to electronic messaging issues.

There are beneficial roles for a postal authority to play in an information society, said Arnum, citing digital signatures, e-mail directories, e-mail time-stamping and change-of-address services as places where post offices can do the most good for society. (McGrath 2001)

Finally, this policy approach also assumes that the postal service will be successful in offering electronic services. If it is not, and earns ongoing losses on electronic services, this policy approach will hasten, not defer, the death spiral.

Like many complex public policy issues, there is no simple answer. Moreover, it bears emphasis that the alternative policy approaches presented in this chapter are not mutually exclusive. In Germany, Deutsche Post is being privatized as it aggressively enters the electronic services field. Although finding the right answer is not simple, it is important, because postal services will continue to play a critical role even in the New Economy.

NOTES

1. In a recent survey by Pitney Bowes, respondents were asked which medium was most private and secure. While 67 per cent said mail was most secure and 20 per cent said telephone, only 5 per cent identified email.
2. For a discussion of these issues see Jackson (2001).
3. A recent study of mailing habits found that 'Regular mail' is overwhelmingly preferred as the method for sending sentimental items and sensitive materials. Pitney Bowes (2000).
4. This work might be done by the mailing firm, it could be done by a specialized firm known as a 'presort bureau'.
5. Alternatively, the cost of preparing physical mail could be thought of as the relative cost for physical mail compared to electronic mail.
6. Evidence on declining marginal costs is provided in Bradley and Colvin (1999) and Bradley and Colvin (1995).
7. For the US Postal Service, this ratio is 85 per cent.
8. Household mail is defined as first class single-piece mail. Business mail is defined as presorted mail including both first class presort and standard presort. This latter category includes both regular and non-profit presort mail. The household and business mail streams include letters, flats, and cards. All data are taken from Cost and Revenue Analysis, Fiscal Year 2000, United States Postal Service.

REFERENCES

Andersson, Peter (2001), 'Deregulation and Internet: new challenges to postal services in Sweden', working paper, Linkoping Studies in Arts and Sciences, Linkoping, Sweden.

Bradley, Michael D. and Jeff Colvin (1995), 'An econometric model of postal delivery', in *Commercialization of Postal and Delivery Services*, Dordrecht: Kluwer Academic Publishers, pp. 137–54.

Bradley, Michael D. and Jeff Colvin (1999), 'Productivity and technical change in a public service enterprise', in Michael A. Crew and Paul R. Kleindorfe (eds), *Emerging Competition in Postal and Delivery Services*, Dordrecht: Kluwer Academic Publishers, pp. 75–88.

Bradley, Michael D., Jeff Colvin and John S. Panzar (1999), 'On setting prices and testing cross-subsidy with accounting data', *Journal of Regulatory Economics*, **16**, 83–100.

Bradley, Michael D., Jeff Colvin and Mary Perkins (2002), 'Assessing liberalization in context: the importance of pre-liberalization structures', in Michael A. Crew and Paul R. Kleindorfe (eds), *Postal and Delivery Services: Pricing Productivity, Regulation and Strategy*, Dordrecht: Kluwer Academic Publishers, pp. 53–74.

Jackson, Jonathan (2001), 'Whither snail mail?' eMarketer, www.emarketer.com, 19 March.

McGrath, Dermot (2001), 'LaPoste downplays escargot mail', *Wired News*, 15 January 2001, available at www.wired.com/news/technology/0,1282,4127,00.html.

Morlock, Edward, Bradley Nitzberg and Karthik Balasubramaniam (2000), 'The parcel service industry in the US: its size and role in commerce', working paper, Department of Systems Engineering, University of Pennsylvania,.

Pitney Bowes (2000), 'Americans' feelings about mail, a research study', available at http://www.postinsight.com/files/feelings.pdf.

Potter, Jack (2002), 'Testimony before the U.S. Senate', posted on www.postalfacts.com/epay.htm at page 1.

PricewaterhouseCoopers (2000), 'Projecting electronic diversion for first class mail in the H.R. 22 simulation model', manuscript.

Stiglitz, Joseph E., Peter R. Orszag and Jonathan Orszag (2000), 'The role of government in a digital age', manuscript.

United States Postal Service (2001), 'Cost and revenue analysis, fiscal year 2000', available at http://www.usps.com/financials/_pdf/cra_/fyoo.pdf.

United States Postal Service (2002) *Annual Report 2001*, available at http://www.usps.com/history/anrpt01/.

Wall Street Journal (2002), 'Please mister postman', 10 April, p. A18.

World Bank (2000), *The Postal Industry in an Internet Age: Case Studies of Postal Reform*, Washington, DC: World Bank.

Subject Index

AT&T 110
  Bell system 111
  competition in local markets 111
  foreclosure of independents 111, 113
  monopoly in long distance 111
accounting 13, 19, 28–9, 35, 48, 53, 58,
  65, 80–81, 112, 140
Adobe Acrobat Reader 103
adjustment costs 29
Amazon 109, 154
antitrust 1, 5–7, 11, 97, 107, 114, 166,
  194
  Schumpeterian competition 116
Arthur Anderson 147
August Dvorak 164–5
automatic teller machines 148
automobile 8, 75, 79, 115, 144–5,
  150–52, 160
Average Labor Productivity 15, 19
  growth 15, 19–21

B2B (business to business) exchanges
  96, 100, 115
B2C (business to consumer) exchanges
  96
barriers to entry 107–8, 155
Baumol's Disease 3–4, 34, 59
Bills On-Line 185
bottleneck
  'access organization' 111, 112
  'access termination' 111, 112
  anti-competitive consequences 111
  one-sided 110
  one-way 111
  regulation 112
  telecommunications 111
  two-sided 110, 112, 113
broadcasting 96, 145
Brookings Institution 2, 38, 41, 58, 59
bulk mail 174–86, 188, 190, 193
  bill presentment 9, 177
  cost function 181

electronic messages 178, 182
  marginal cost 179, 181
  markup 181, 182
  physical mail 178, 182
  postal rate 181
  volumes 193
Bureau of Economic Analysis (BEA)
  13, 16–17, 20–21, 24, 37–40, 42,
  55, 57–8, 64–5, 81–2
  capital flow table 58
  GDP by industry accounts 58
Bureau of Labor Statistics (BLS) 12,
  16, 35, 39–40, 55–9, 64–5
  Producer Price Index (PPI) 59
Bush administration 86
business 1, 5, 8–9, 12, 16–17, 20–23,
  25–6, 29–30, 35, 48, 50, 58, 64–5,
  74–5, 79, 81, 88, 100–101, 109,
  115, 119, 127, 185
  brick-and-mortar 168
  Internet 168
business cycle 1, 5, 21–2, 25–6, 75
business nonfarm output 79
business sector 12, 20–21
  hours growth 21
  non-farm 17, 23, 29–30, 35, 88

Canada Post 185
capital 3, 5, 22, 74, 79–80, 86–7, 109,
  147–9
  contributions of 19, 36, 57
  deepening 2, 13, 15, 19–20, 27
  income 39–40, 57, 65
  IT 2, 15, 30, 35–7, 40–41, 48, 50, 52,
    54, 57–8
  non-IT 35–6, 40, 48, 53–4
  quality 17, 19, 22, 25–6, 28
  service flows 14, 16–17
capital share 15, 22, 24, 26, 39–40, 57,
  65
capital service 2, 14–16, 35–6, 40–41,
  48, 52, 54, 56, 58, 64

capital stock 16–17, 19, 25–6, 40
    aggregate 17, 21
    effective 16–17, 26
    growth 19, 26
    reproducible 16, 21–2, 26
    total 16, 22
cash 74, 91, 109, 194
    demand for 74, 91
Census Bureau 22–3, 57, 59
central bank 5, 73–4, 85, 87, 90–93
    liabilities 74, 90–93
    reserves 91
commodity exchanges 115
communication 4, 7, 9, 32, 92–3,
        144–5, 174–7, 182, 185–6
    information 4, 40, 92–3, 145
    mail 9, 144, 174, 177
    one-way 145
    technology 4, 40, 92–3
    two-way 145
competition 5–8, 11, 24, 29, 117, 152,
        156, 180, 187, 194
complementary good(s) 100, 101, 104,
        110
computer 6, 28, 30, 37, 40, 72–3, 75,
        81–2, 96–7, 145, 152, 161
    hardware 6, 13–14, 16, 24, 40, 81, 96
    software 6, 13–14, 16, 82, 96
Congressional Budget Office (CBO)
        23–4, 28–30
constant returns to scale 14
consumer(s) 5–7, 16, 74, 79, 82–3, 88,
        122–8, 132, 135, 140, 145–6,
        150–54, 158–62, 185
    informed 126
    price-sensitive 122
    uninformed 126
consumer durables 16
consumer electronics 7
    peripherals 126, 135
    software 126, 135
    variable MSRP 135
consumer price index 82–3, 88
    for medical care commodities and
        services 83
consumption 14, 86, 98, 126
    cost function 124, 178–9, 181, 187
    postal service 187
Council of Economic Advisors (CEA)
        15, 19, 36–7

currency 90–91, 155
Current Population Surveys (CPS) 17,
    21

Denmark Post
    Gatetrade.net 185
Deutsche Post
    Internet services 185
    privatized 195
    Sign Trust 185
duopoly 107
dynamic efficiency 115
dynamics 22, 104
    death spiral 186

Ebay 109, 154
e-commerce 185
    business models 150
    winner-takes-all 154
e-money 91
economic growth 14, 17, 22, 29, 58, 86,
    148
Economides-Flyer model 107
economies of scale 8–9, 100, 149, 151,
        153, 161, 167, 183
    automobile companies 151
    similar to networks effects 151
education 17, 23–4, 47
efficiency 10, 116, 194
    allocative 97
    dynamic 97, 115
    productive 97
Efficient Components Pricing Rule
        (ECPR) 112
elasticity 9, 183
electronic bill paying 178–79, 185
Emerson 158, 162
employment 17, 42, 57, 75, 77
    temporary 77–9, 86, 92
Enron 115, 147
equilibrium 6–7, 11, 25, 101, 104,
        107–8, 116–17, 181, 188, 190, 193
    symmetric 124
equipment 3, 13, 40, 78, 81–2, 145,
        153
    communications 14, 16, 40
    telecommunications 13, 24, 73
externalities 82, 92
    direct 100
    financial 101

indirect 100
B2B exchanges 101

factor utilization 28–9
fax machine 82, 150, 160
Federal Communications Act 111
Federal Communications Commission
(FCC) 112, 118
finance 5, 74, 92, 101
innovations in 5, 74
financial exchanges 96, 115
financial institutions 39, 48
depository 39
nondepository 39
financial intermediaries 79, 90, 92
financial markets 73, 77, 85
firm heterogeneities 140
first-mover advantage 156
in information industries 156
Internet retailing 155
first-mover-wins 159
central to the information economy
163
lock-in 162, 163
VHS/Beta 165
fiscal policy 4, 72, 85, 87, 92
FOMC 88, 90
free entry 107–8, 124

GDP 13, 16, 20, 37, 39, 58, 64–5, 73,
77, 80–82, 88–9
by industry 39, 58, 64
nominal 16, 89
potential 3, 73
real 73, 76, 88–9
GLS
coefficient estimates 135
heteroskedasticity 135, 137
General Services Administration
(GSA) 164–5
government 1, 9–10, 31, 59, 72, 78, 82,
85–6, 91, 118, 174, 185, 194
growth accounting 13, 19, 28–9, 35, 48,
65, 80

health 23, 59, 60
hours 17, 19–24, 26, 35, 75
growth 19, 22–4, 26–7, 30
worked 3, 13, 15, 17, 19–23
hybrid mail service 185, 187

ICOT (information, communication
and other information
technology) 40, 48, 50, 52
hotel industry 50
imperfect competition 29, 180
income tax 85–7
increasing returns 98, 152, 154,
180
cell-phone systems 148
incremental cost 98
incumbent(s) 109, 112–14, 116–17
dominant technology 161
efficient 162
Industrial Revolution 72
industry 5–6, 8, 15, 21, 24–5, 27, 29,
34, 37–42, 45–8, 50, 52–60, 64, 96,
101, 108, 113–14, 116–18, 145,
147, 153, 157, 176, 178, 195
IT-intensive 41, 55
technically based 157
inflation 3, 5, 12, 72–5, 81–4, 87–91,
93
medical 83
target levels 87
variability 87
Volcker-Greenspan period 90
Information Economy 1, 12, 144, 146,
150, 156, 162–3
information technology (IT) 2–5,
13–17, 19–20, 22, 24–8, 30–31,
34–8, 40–41, 48, 50, 52–5, 57–8,
60, 74–5, 80–81, 83, 91
capital 80
equipment 3, 13, 41, 81–2
deflator for 81
output shares 22, 27
IT capital 2, 15, 30, 35–7, 40–41, 48,
50, 52, 54, 57–8, 60
deepening 2, 48, 60
services 15, 41, 52, 54, 57–8
IT intensity 41, 58
as a proportion of total capital
services 41
as a proportion of total cost 41
IT investment 14–17, 19, 26, 31, 37–8,
50, 52, 80
IT-producing industries 15, 36–7
IT-using industries 37–8, 41
IT contributions 37
MFP contributions 37

innovations 5, 10, 29, 38, 74, 114
  discrete 29
  technological 1, 11
instant scalability 152–3
intellectual property 108
interest rate 5, 72–4, 85, 90, 93
  effect on growth 93
intermediate inputs 35–6, 39–40, 48,
    50, 52, 57–8, 60, 64–5
Internet 5–9, 11, 72, 75, 81, 83, 96,
    111, 122, 124–5, 128, 138, 140,
    144–50, 152–5, 167–8, 175–6,
    182, 185–7
  broadband 111, 145
  commerce 176
  computers 72, 145
  economics of the 149
  firms 128, 149, 152, 154
  infrastructure 8, 145
  meltdown 147
  price comparison sites 7, 122, 125,
    140
  price spreads 146
  pricing mechanisms 168
  products 7, 149
  profits 168
  spider 125
  two-way transmission mechanism
    145
inventories 5, 7, 16–17, 74, 92, 123, 147
  fluctuations 76
  just-in-time 76
  recessions 147
investment 4, 13–14, 21, 26, 30, 40, 65,
    80–82, 86–7, 115–16, 144–5, 150,
    157
  boom 26, 30
  goods 14–7, 19, 31
  IT 14–17, 26, 37–8, 50, 52, 80

keyboard
  Dvorak's design 164
  Navy Study 164
  QWERTY machine 164, 166
  strong-form lock-in 166
knowledge 117, 119
  economic growth 148
Kodak
  aftermarket for repair services 115
  anti-competitive 115

labor 3, 12, 22, 38–9, 57, 65, 73, 77, 85,
    92, 178–9, 194
  costs 178–9
  compensation 39, 57, 65
  quality 2, 15, 17, 19–24, 26, 30
  self-employed 17, 39–40, 65

labor force 13, 19, 21–3, 30, 77, 92
labor productivity 2–4, 12–15, 19, 22,
    26–9, 34–8, 42, 46–8, 50, 52–5, 57,
    59–60, 80
  acceleration 4, 35–7, 42, 45–8, 50,
      52–4, 59–60
    intermediate deepening
        contributions 53
    IT contributions 48, 52
    MFP contributions 4, 52–4, 60
  decelerations of 47–8
    economy-wide 37, 42, 48, 55, 60
  growth 2–4, 12–13, 20, 26–30, 34, 36,
      42–3, 46, 48–52, 54, 57, 60, 80
    business services 48, 50
    capital's contribution to 36
    intermediate inputs contributions
      35, 48
    IT capital contributions 36, 50,
      52, 60
    IT capital services contributions
      52
    MFP contributions 36, 48, 50,
      54
    services industries 34, 42, 46,
      48–51, 53–4, 60
    transportation services 48, 50
    wholesale trade 48, 50
  medical care 59
LaPoste
  Cyberpost 186
law of one price 5, 7, 11
  convergence to 7, 123
  retail markets 122
lock-in 7–8, 116, 168
  markets 156, 157
  network effects 8, 158
  weak and strong forms 159

machinery 37, 153
  industrial and commercial 24
macroeconomic policy 1, 4–5, 72, 85
manufacturing 4, 29, 46, 151

marginal cost 9, 103, 179–81, 183, 187–9
  constant 103, 179, 187
marginal product 17, 19, 26
market(s) 1, 5–8, 10–11, 14, 24, 26, 73–4, 77, 79, 83, 85–6, 92, 122–4, 126–8, 130, 140, 146, 148, 150, 152–3, 155–65, 167–8, 175–6, 179, 181–3, 185–6, 188, 190, 193
market power 6, 8, 179
market shares 7, 150, 152–3, 157, 159–62, 167
  inequality 104,107, 108, 117
  influencing expectations 161
market structure 6
  with network externalities 119
marketable debt 77, 79
McKinsey 37, 167
McKinsey Global Institute (MGI) 37–8, 42, 50, 52
Microsoft 11, 82, 118–19, 166
monetary base 10, 87
monetary policy 3–5, 10, 72–4, 85, 87, 89–93
monetary transmission mechanism 72, 74
monopolization 6, 96
monopoly(ies) 6, 92, 146, 177, 179–80, 194
  innovation in 116
  local exchange carrier 110
  locational 146
MFP 3–4, 34–8, 48, 50, 52–3, 55, 57–60, 80
  growth 37, 54, 80
  mismeasurement 57
  performance 50

NASDAQ 81, 100, 155
  bubble 24, 26
NYSE 100
national accounts 38–40, 42, 58–9
National Income and Product Accounts (NIPA) 16–17, 20–21, 81
natural oligopoly 117
network(s) 5–8, 10–11, 16, 82, 92, 98, 113, 115, 144, 148–55, 158–62, 167, 178–9
  antitrust issues 119

bundling 114
cell-phone system 148
complementaries in 111
complementarity of components 100
complementary goods 114
financial 100, 148
incumbent 114, 159
market coverage 104
non-price discrimination strategies 114
positive critical mass 103
pricing strategies 114
social 148
technical standards 6, 114
telecommunications 110, 111
telephone 6, 96, 100, 150
transportation 110
value to subscribers 113
VHS vs. Beta 158, 160
WordPerfect users 150
network effect(s) 5–6, 8, 10–11, 98, 100, 102, 104, 107, 110, 117, 148–51, 153–5, 158–9, 161–2, 167
  AOL Instant Messenger 155
  Internet companies 154
  oligopoly 116
  path-dependence 109, 110
  perfect competition 116
  self-reinforcing nature 104
network expansion 104
network externalities 82, 92, 98, 100–101, 103, 105–7, 109, 119
  one-way networks 101
  two-way networks 101
  vertically-related markets 100, 101
network goods 102
  law of demand 100
  pure 105
network industry(ies) 5–7, 11, 96–7, 108–9, 119, 178
  anti-competitive actions 6, 116
  antitrust 5–7, 11, 116
  competition policy issues 6, 110, 118
  computer software and hardware 6, 96
  financial 96, 97
  fundamental properties of 103
  importance of dominance 116
  increasing returns to scale in consumption 98

inequality of market shares 113
inequality of prices 113
installed base 7, 113, 116
market structure of 107
path dependence 7, 116
price discrimination 104
regulation 118
retail 96
technical standards 6, 115
technological change 118
telecommunications 6, 96–8, 118
transportation 96, 97
network meltdown 8, 144
network size 103
New Economy 1–6, 8–11, 34, 38, 72–3,
    75, 82, 84–5, 87, 89, 92–3, 119,
    144, 148, 157, 174–6, 182, 195
Nike 148
Nintendo
    antitrust challenge 113
    dominance of the game market 113
non-network industries 6, 98, 104, 107,
    109
nonfarm business sector 76, 88
nonprofit organizations 39

output 4, 5, 12, 14–16, 21–2, 24–6, 28,
    30, 36, 38–9, 42, 47, 55, 57–60, 65,
    73–5, 79, 84, 87–90, 105, 108, 112,
    151

participation rates 23
    female 23–4
perfect competition 103, 107
PERL programming language 125
perpetual inventory method 16
physical mail 9, 10, 175–6, 178, 182,
    188
pipelines 41, 43, 47–50, 67
population 23, 177
postal production
    economies of scope 178
    quasi-fixed costs 178
    returns to scale 178
postal service(s) 8–11, 96, 183, 185, 187
    cost function 178, 187
    death spiral 195
    diversion of volume 175
    electronic message market 9, 10, 188,
        193

equilibrium prices 188
impact on the New Economy 174,
    175
labor agreements 179
marginal costs 183, 189
markups 183, 189
privatization 194
public nature of 179
quasi-fixed cost 179, 183
rates 181, 183, 190
revenue 185, 193
scale 194
scope economies 194
universal service requirement 179
volumes 175
Postmaster General of the United
    States 176
price 5, 7, 11, 15–17, 19, 24, 28, 30–31,
    73, 81–4, 87–8, 91, 101, 103–9,
    111–4, 118, 122–41, 146, 154–5,
    158, 163, 177–8, 180–83, 186,
    188–90, 194
price comparison 7
    Shopper.com 126
price dispersion 7, 11, 122, 128, 132
    across products 7, 123
    across time 7, 123
    branding, reputation, and trust 138
    coefficient of variation 130, 135
    consumer electronics products 7, 122
    cost heterogeneities 138
    equilibrium models of 122, 141
    firm heterogeneities 128, 136, 138,
        141
    Internet markets 122
    persistence of 122, 130, 132, 135,
        140–41
    prescription drug markets 123,
        130
    retailer heterogeneities 124
    shipping and handling charges 132,
        136
    temporal 140
    unexplained 7, 123, 140–41
    volatility 132
price index 82–3, 88
    quality-adjusted 16
PricewaterhouseCoopers 175, 178
pricing strategies 7, 103, 109, 122, 126
    randomized 7, 122

product cycle 25, 27, 30–31
  semiconductors 13, 24–5, 27–8, 30
production 3, 5, 13–16, 20, 24–5, 28–30,
    35–40, 42, 44–5, 50, 54, 57, 64, 72,
    74–5, 81, 92, 98, 105, 107–8, 110,
    117, 148, 151, 153–4, 178–80
  capital's contribution to 57
production function 37, 54
  Cobb-Douglas 29–30
production possibility frontier 14
productivity 1–5, 9–10, 12–16, 19–20,
    24–31, 34, 37–40, 47–8, 50, 52, 55,
    58–60, 73, 80–82, 87–90, 93, 175
  accelerations 37, 45–8, 50, 52–4, 82,
    88
  business sector 12
  growth 2–4, 12–13, 15–16, 20–22,
    24–30, 34–6, 38, 42–3, 46–52,
    54, 56–7, 60, 73, 80–82, 87–8,
    90, 93
  multifactor 3–4, 34, 38, 80
    contributions of 3, 34–6, 52
    in the IT-producing industries 36
  non-manufacturing 46
  performance 50, 60
  revival 13, 20–21, 28, 30
  trend 4, 55, 60, 89
profits 6, 86, 152, 167–8, 179–80,
    187–9, 194
  antitrust law 108
  monopolist's 112
purchased intermediate inputs 39, 48,
    50

quality improvement 15, 30
QWERTY 165

race 13, 23
Ramsey prices 181
random walk 29
recession 1, 12, 76–7, 85–6, 147
  post-WWII 85
reservation value(s) 124
  effect on equilibrium number of
    firms 124, 135
  effect on overall market surplus 124
  effect on price range 125, 135
  variation in 123
retailers 7, 122, 124, 138, 140
  reliability ratings 146

returns to scale 14, 98, 178–80
returns to scope 179
Royal Mail
  electronic and hybrid mail service
    185
  electronic billing 185
  Opetcon 185

sales 75, 77, 79, 98, 100–102, 105–6,
    113, 126, 150, 154, 161
scale economy(ies) 29, 151, 154, 156
securities 5, 74, 77–9, 86, 92
  asset-backed 5, 74, 78–9, 86, 92
  mortgage-backed 77
self-employed 17, 39–40, 57, 65
semiconductors 24, 27, 37, 75
  prices 24
  technological progress 25
services industries 3–4, 34, 38–42,
    45–8, 50, 52, 54, 58–60
  capital service flow estimates 40
  diversity in performance 52
  labor productivity 42–3, 45–52, 54,
    60
  measurement problems 38, 59
  MFP 4, 34, 38, 50, 54, 60
  productivity 45–6, 52
    acceleration 45–6, 52
    growth 3–4, 34, 42–3, 46, 48–52,
      54, 60
Shopper.com 125, 135, 140
  Bizrate.com 127, 128
  branding, reputation and trust 127
  Cnet Certified Store status 127, 128,
    138
  cost structure 126
  delivery options 127
  disclosure policies 128
  discriminatory pricing 126
  exchange policies 138
  Gomez merchant rating 127
  price dispersion 138
  product availability 127
  restocking policies 138
  return policies 127
  shipping cost 127, 138
SIC 37, 39, 42, 55, 65
single piece mail 185
  cost 177
  electronic messages 182, 190

marginal cost 179, 181
markup on 181, 182
postal rate for 181
physical mail 190
software 6, 13–14, 16, 18, 40–41, 80,
    82, 96, 98, 103–4, 113, 116–17,
    126, 128, 135–7, 151, 153, 164,
    167
  investment 16, 18, 40
  markets 103, 164, 167
  natural oligopoly 117
Sony 165
  Beta format 109–10
strong lock-in 159, 160, 161, 163
  antitrust prosecutions 166
  business strategy 166
  costs of switching 162
  electrical generation 166
  inefficiency 162
  internal combustion engine 166
  keyboard story 164
  operating system 166
  self-compatibility 162
supply 23, 75, 83, 87, 146–8, 150,
    167–8, 185
supply and demand 147, 167
surplus 81, 124
  consumers' 105, 106, 107, 108
  producers' 105, 106

taxes 7, 17, 64–5, 85–6, 91, 194
  corporate 86
  individual 86
technological change 13, 15, 40,
    117–18
technological progress 25, 27, 90
technology 1–5, 13–14, 25, 27–8, 34,
    40–41, 52, 72, 74–5, 80–81, 83,
    91–3, 97, 103, 116–17, 127, 147,
    157–9, 161, 165, 167, 174, 175–6
Telecommunications Act of (1996)
    111–13
total cost 41, 151, 177–8, 180–81,
    190
total factor productivity (TFP) 2,
    13–16, 19–20, 25–7, 29
  contribution 21
  growth 16, 19–20, 22, 25, 27–30
  non-IT sources 21
transitional dynamics 22

transportation 8, 47–8, 50, 57, 65,
    96–7, 110
  costs of 8, 144

unbundled network elements (UNE)
    112
unemployment 3, 19, 22, 80
United States Department of Defense
    75
United States (US) Postal Service 8, 9,
    174–5, 177, 179, 185
  impact of the New Economy 182
  increasing returns to scale 180
  labor costs 178
  monopoly on letter mail 194
  quasi-fixed costs 180
  reasonable uniform price 180
  regulatory structure 180
  revenue 174
  universal service 180
United States vs. Microsoft 118
US economy 2–3, 12, 16, 24–5, 30, 34,
    37–8, 41, 58, 76–7, 79–80, 83

VHS 109, 152, 158–60, 165
value added 39–42, 45–6, 55, 57–8, 64,
    148
Varian's model 138
  informed consumers 124, 125
  number of firms 123, 137
  range of prices 123, 137
  reservation value 123
  uninformed consumers 124, 125
vertically integrated firm
  discrimination in prices 114
  discrimination in quality 114
vertically-related industries 103
virtual network 6, 96, 113, 150
  externalities 98

Wall Street 109, 146, 156, 194
Wall Street Journal 146, 156, 194
weak lock-in 163
  business strategies 161
  consumers' switching costs 162
  distinct from the strong form of
      lock-in 161
  protection to incumbents 161
wealth 16, 40, 147
West Texas Intermediate 83–4

Windows (95) 6, 96, 148
winner-take-all 149, 152, 153, 154, 156, 158
winner-take-most 104, 108, 152
World Wide Web (WWW) 6, 96

Yellow Pages 6, 96
Yahoo/Google 6, 96, 109

Zellner's Seemingly Unrelated Regressions 137, 138

Author index

Aizcorbe, Ana 31
Arthur, W. Brian 148–9, 157–8, 162–3, 166, 169–71
Aylor, Tim 58

Baily, Martin N. 12, 30, 55, 58
Bakos, Yannis 141
Basu, Susanto 28–9
Baumol, William J. 3, 4, 34
Baye, Michael R. 7, 122, 123, 141, 142
Berndt, Ernst R. 59
Bonds, Belinda 58
Bosworth, Barry P. 3, 4, 34, 38, 46, 53, 57, 58
Bradley, Michael D. 5, 8, 9, 10, 174, 195
Bryan, Michael F. 94
Brynjolfsson, Erik 122, 138, 141
Burdett, Kenneth 123–4

Carlson, John A. 141
Cecchetti, Stephen G. 72, 94
Colvin, Jeff 195
Corrado, Carol 62
Cusumano, M.A. 171

David, Paul A. 163–6, 169–71
DeLong, J. Bradford 12, 31, 93
Domar, Evsey D. 61

Economides, Nicholas 5, 6, 7, 96, 102, 104, 106–7, 112–13, 115, 120
Ellison, Glen 141
Ellison, Sara Fisher 141
Estrella, Arturo 94

Farrell, J. 170
Flyer, Fredrick 104, 106–7
Freedman, Charles 93
Freedman, David 169
French, Mark W. 28–9, 31

Friedman, Benjamin M. 93
Fuchs, Victor R. 58

Gali, Jordi 89
Gomes, Lee 170
Goodhart, Charles A.E. 93
Gordon, Robert J. 16, 28, 30, 36–7, 55, 57–8, 61, 94
Griliches, Zvi 17, 35, 38, 52, 58–60, 61
Gunter, David 58

Hansen, Bruce E. 29
Herman, Shelby W. 16, 40
Himmelberg, Charles 102, 120
Ho, Mun S. 2, 12, 16, 23
Hobijn, Bart 31

Jackson, Jonathan 195
Jansen, Dennis W. 1, 8, 174
Janssen, Maarten 141
Jorgenson, Dale W. 2, 3, 12–17, 19–20, 23–4, 31, 35–6, 38, 50, 60, 61
Judd, Kenneth L. 123–4

Katz, Arnold J. 40
Katz, Michael L. 149, 169, 170
Kelly, Kevin 157
Kirsch, David A. 171

Leibenstein, Harvey 169
Lewin, Peter 167, 171
Liebowitz, Stan 144, 149, 166, 168–71
Lum, Sherlene K.S. 39

Margolis, Stephen E. 149, 164, 166–71
McCarthy, Jonathan 31
McConnell, Margaret Mary 75
McGrath, Dermot 186, 195
McGuckin, Robert 58
Moraga, Jose Luis 141
Morgan, John 5, 7, 122–3, 141
Mylonadis, Y. 171

Narasimhan, Chakravarthi 141
Nordhaus, William D. 38

Oliner, Stephen D. 15–16, 19–20, 28,
　36, 60, 80
Orphanides, Athanasios 89

Parham, Dean 61
Pescatrice, Donn R. 141
Petzinger Jr., Thomas 146–8, 157
Potter, Jack 93, 176
Pratt, John W. 141

Quiros, Gabriel Perez 75

Reinganum, Jennifer F. 123, 141
Roberts, John M. 28, 31
Rosenbloom, R.S. 171
Rosenthal, Robert W. 141

Saloner, G. 170
Salop, Steven C. 141
Scholten, Patrick 122, 141
Schreyer, Paul 61
Shaked, Avner 120
Shapiro, Carl 141, 149, 156, 164–5,
　169, 170
Sharpe, Andrew 46, 52
Shilony, Yuval 141
Sichel, Daniel E. 15–16, 19–20, 28, 36,
　60, 80

Siow, Aloysius 120
Slifman, Lawrence 62
Smith, Adam 141
Smith, Michael D. 122, 141, 138
Solow, Robert M. 35
Sorensen, Alan 123, 130, 142
Spulber, Daniel F. 141, 170
Stahl II, Dale O. 141
Stigler, George 7, 122, 140
Stiglitz, Joseph E. 141, 174
Stiroh, Kevin J. 2, 12–16, 19–20, 31,
　36–8, 47, 58, 60, 61
Stock, James H. 31
Summers, Lawrence M. 12, 31,
　93
Sutton, John 120

Triplett, Jack E. 2–4, 34, 38, 46, 52,
　58–9, 61

VanVleck, V.N.L. 171
Varian, Hal R. 7, 122–5, 137–8,
　140–41, 156, 164–5, 170
Villas-Boas, M. 141

Watson, Mark W. 31
White, Lawrence J. 112
Woodford, Michael 93

Yamada, H. 170
Yuskavage, Robert E. 39, 57–8